LUMIANA

ALEX BENKAST

www.alexbenkast.com

ISBN: 9781521010723

Editing (2020 Edition): S.W.C.
Editing (2017 Edition): Lynn Turner
Developmental edit: Nancy Doherty
Cover design: Alex Benkast
Cover photograph: Blake Cheek | Unsplash

For Marisa & Manuel

To Mateo
I wish you could grow up in a world where
people celebrate their differences.

"Music was my refuge.
I could crawl into the space between the notes
and curl my back to loneliness."

—MAYA ANGELOU

PART 1

1

WRONG SIDE OF A LOVE SONG

"Where words fail, music speaks."

—HANS CHRISTIAN ANDERSEN

THE WILTERN, LOS ANGELES, CALIFORNIA

THREE WEEKS PRIOR...

Andie arrived at the crowded theater half an hour into Johnny's concert. The sound of thumping bass and screaming fans filtered out into the cool evening air, raising the hair on her skin. She patted the back pocket of her skinny jeans, thinking she could use a cigarette but remembered her promise to her dad that she would quit.

Magnum, Johnny's intimidatingly large bodyguard and personal trainer, opened the heavy stage door with a look that made her feel like a scolded child.

"I know. I'm late again," she said to the gentle giant who was sporting his trademark red Hawaiian shirt and matching fedora. "How mad is he?"

"I doubt he'll be singing a love song for you tonight," Mag quipped as he led her around a corner and onto a platform just off stage.

Andie joined the group of people sitting on the stage's left wing, where they could see the band up close and had a partial view of the ecstatic audience.

Andie's best friend Claudia got up and took her aside. "Johnny's pissed," Claudia said while the rest of Johnny's entourage eyed Andie with the same accusatory look Magnum wore earlier. Among them were Ben Richstone, Johnny's uptight manager; Juliana Porter, his spunky publicist; and Johnny's brother Jason, a hotshot attorney who could moonlight as a fashion model. She gave them all a rueful smile before she and Claudia sat on the upholstered beech wood chairs five feet away from the rest of the group.

Andie trained her gaze on Johnny and his band. The four men were performing Lenny Kravitz's cover of "American Woman." Johnny's bluesy vocals put him somewhere between James Morrison and Jonny Lang, but Andie knew that Kravitz's retro style was one of Johnny's greatest inspirations.

When Johnny shrugged out of his distressed leather jacket, showing off his toned, tanned body in a snug white t-shirt, the audience screamed.

Andie smiled to herself. *Sex on fire, that one.*

"You're one lucky bitch," said Claudia, her pale cheeks flushed almost the color of her crimson hair.

It was the man's face that did it though. The defined jawline, the long straight nose, his sinful mouth. A mouth that Andie couldn't wait to feel all over her again.

She pursed her lips. No matter how much others wanted him, she was the one who got to take him home at the end of the night. Or so she hoped.

Forty-five minutes and two encores later, Johnny sauntered off the stage to deafening applause without so much as a single glance at her. After a quick chat with Claudia, Andie went to the dressing room, where the guys were changing into fresh street clothes. Johnny still wouldn't look at her.

"Can we talk, please?" Andie murmured into his ear, but he shook his head sharply without a word.

"Ready?" Magnum asked, casting a compassionate glance at Andie before he opened the door.

She'd always liked the man. Kind and solid, Mag seemed to care more about Johnny than

Johnny's own father did.

Johnny waved goodbye to the room and followed his bodyguard out the back entrance. In her suede Louboutin pumps, Andie barely managed to keep up.

Outside the theater, cheering fans pushed against the steel barricade. Johnny made his way to the front of the crowd, signing a few autographs and posing for pictures before Magnum signaled them to head toward the black limo at the curb. As they did, a young woman clambered over the railing and dashed toward them.

Johnny grabbed Andie's hand. Together they ran the short distance to the limo while his bodyguard held the girl back. This wasn't the first time a fan had tried to get a one-on-one encounter with Johnny. Andie knew from interactions with her own fans that there was always a moment of dread when a stranger started to rush toward you or crowded you without your consent.

The limo driver hurriedly opened the door as Mag escorted the fan back behind the barrier.

"Damn, boy, your fans are getting more intense every year," Magnum said as he climbed in front next to the driver.

Johnny shrugged.

Andie closed the privacy screen between them and the front seat, but Johnny turned to stare out the window. She watched him brood. "Great show tonight."

"Thanks."

One word. From a man known for his chatty personality.

"I'm sorry I didn't make it on time. My shoot ran later than I thought."

He grimaced. "It's always like this, Andie. We're hardly ever in the same place."

"You can't fault me for having a career."

"I'm not. But work seems more important than our relationship."

"What are you saying?" Andie searched his hazel eyes. There was no fire in them, no fight.

"We've spent so much time apart the past two months. We lead completely separate lives."

"Is this because I'm more famous than you? Because I make more money?" That had been the problem with her previous boyfriend.

"That's not the reason, Andie." He cursed at the car roof. "Don't you think we both deserve a partner who's there for us on a day-to-day basis, which our schedules apparently make impossible?"

"I can try to cut down on the jobs I take."

"That's what you said the last three times we've had this conversation." Johnny dragged a hand through his short, tousled hair. "I can't do this anymore."

She reached for his hands. "I love you, Johnny. Please, let me prove I want this, that I can be there for you."

He shook his head. "I don't want to ask you to spend less time doing what you love. You'll resent me for it."

She would've argued if she thought he'd change his mind, but she couldn't remember the last time Johnny's eyes lit up when he looked at her. If work were the real problem, they would've found a way to be together more. Maybe it was time to accept that for him the thrill was gone. "I'm sorry."

Pulling her close, Johnny kissed the top of her head. "I know. Me too."

***

PRESENT DAY...

Three weeks after his breakup with Andie, Johnny sat in the lounge of his Los Angeles recording studio, staring at the issue of *A Bene Placito*, which had just come in the mail. Landing an interview with the magazine had been the fourth thing on his bucket list, and something he could now happily cross off.

Ignoring the flutter in his chest, he reached for the magazine. No matter what he said or how careful he was, those sly reporters managed to spin his words to suit their own purposes. The media had called him a lot of things over the years—Virtuoso, Playboy, Douchebag Extraordinaire. Who cared whether any of it was true? Everyone wanted a piece of him as long as he kept selling. But no one wanted all of him. Especially not the broken parts.

Johnny heard a grunt and glimpsed Adam Tsukino's back as the man stalked past to get his caffeine fix from the kitchenette. The band's drummer didn't speak until he had coffee in his system.

Johnny kept leafing through the glossy pages.

There it is, he thought as he recognized his own words on the page. *"Music is what feelings sound like, a language everyone understands."* As if on cue, music started blasting through the studio speakers. *"A song can be a rescue vessel, a seductive lover, or sentimental treasure..."* he trailed off as the singer's hauntingly beautiful voice enveloped him. *Warm and colorful with a smoky midrange.* The song itself resembled Etta James's "At Last."

Johnny was so immersed in the music he didn't notice Adam had joined him until his best friend kicked him in the shin. "So? What do you think?"

"Um... about what?" Johnny tossed the magazine onto the coffee table.

"The singer." Adam handed him a mug and pointed with his chin at the speaker on the wall. "She's pretty good, huh?"

Johnny took a sip of coffee and closed his eyes to focus on the voice.

'Pretty good' didn't do the woman's talent justice. She had an unmistakable strength in her voice that gave him goosebumps, and then, a twist in the gut.

'Get a real job,' his family had told him a hundred times since he started his career. Two platinum records later and those words still haunted him whenever he had too much free time. Everyone expected him to be happy now that he was at the height of his career. But they didn't understand what it was like to live with the pressure of producing another successful album—waking up in cold sweat, the restlessness, the self-doubt. What he needed was inspiration. Or maybe—this fascinating voice?

Johnny propped his burnished Tom Ford leather sneakers on the coffee table. "Who is she, and why haven't I heard of her before?"

Adam's grin turned complacent. The two of them were always trying to outdo each other in their pursuit of exceptional musicians. A contest that had started back when they were pimply kids hanging out at the vintage record and tattoo shop that Adam's Japanese grandmother owned. Johnny B. Goode was to this day one of their favorite hangout spots, and they had both the ink and the musical prowess to show for it.

Adam settled into the overstuffed armchair. "Do you remember my friend Shawn?"

Johnny ran a hand over his stubble. "You told me about him, but I don't think I've met the guy."

"You'd remember him if you met him." Adam smiled into his coffee. "I recorded this song at Shawn's birthday party over the weekend. It's his sister Lumiana. The girl's got some major pipes."

"Man, I'd love to work with her," Johnny decided after the singer effortlessly hit a high note. "Could you ask your pal to arrange a meeting?" He felt a jolt of inspiration. He could feature this sultry voice on his third album—the one he hadn't started yet and which according to his fans, and more critically, his label, was long overdue.

***

Adam knew Johnny Graham was a man used to getting what he wanted. When he told Johnny two days later during band practice that Shawn's sister 'politely' declined his offer, he almost laughed at Johnny's look of surprise.

Johnny tipped his head to the side. "She said no?"

Adam also knew his friend's smugness was mostly an act. Johnny wasn't so entitled that he'd never heard the word 'no' before. He just didn't let a 'no' stop him. Which was why he was so successful. That, and his indisputable talent.

"She doesn't even want to meet me for a chat? Did you tell her who I am?"

'No' wasn't all Lumiana had to say about Johnny's invitation, but Adam chose to paraphrase his way out of telling the whole truth. "Who you are might be part of the problem." *The* problem, really.

Johnny paced the room. "I don't get it. I'm an award-winning musician. Shouldn't she be ecstatic that I'm considering a collaboration with her?"

"I know, right?" Adam did his best impression of outrage. "She has a full-time job though. Singing is her hobby."

Johnny plopped down on the worn leather sofa and frowned at the coffee mug on the messy glass table. "Do you have another recording of her?"

Adam grinned. A voice as forceful and well-rounded as Lumiana's was a rare find. "I have a video of her singing an upbeat version of 'Stand By Me.'"

"Who are you talking about?" their bassist Toni Giacomo asked when he and keyboarder Earl Jones joined Johnny on the couch.

"Lumiana Harding. My friend Shawn's sister." Adam squeezed in between Johnny and Earl so everyone could see the screen of his smartphone. The video showed a group of young people sitting around a bonfire. Some of them were singing along with Lumiana while others were bopping to the rhythm set by a guy playing a Peruvian drum.

"Reminds me of those happy-go-lucky beer commercials," said Johnny, tapping out the beat on his thigh.

Lumiana sounded as spectacular on the video as she did on the audio recording. She had something about her that conveyed free spirit—the way she moved, the fervor in her voice. Her style was eclectic too. She wore a bright yellow sweat-shirt, beaded hibiscus earrings, and a cobalt scarf tied on top of her head like one of those late 1940s propeller beanies—only cuter.

Earl stroked his goatee. "How old is she?"

"Why?" grumbled Adam.

Earl was a womanizer with an impressive success rate, despite the fuzzy beard and the pretentious horn-rimmed glasses.

"Just checking if she's legal before I ask her out."

"She's in her late twenties, I think."

Earl rubbed his hands together eagerly.

"She looks young enough to be my daughter," said Toni. At thirty-eight, he was by far the oldest band member.

The camera zoomed in on Lumiana's face. "I don't know what it is about this girl," Johnny said, "but check out her eyes…"

Adam tapped the screen. "It's heterochromia iridum."

"What is?" Johnny asked without looking up.

"Her eyes. Her irises are different colors." While this defect enchanted most people, it raised the hair on Adam's neck whenever he met Lumiana's gaze.

He noticed the expression on Johnny's face—as if he'd unwrapped a sparkly new toy. Adam knew this look well. His friend was hooked and wasn't going to stop until he got to play with it.

Three hours later, after they finished practicing for an upcoming charity event, Johnny asked Adam to replay the recording. The singer's sense of pitch and melody were highly sophisticated for an amateur. Vocally they'd be a match.

"There must be something I can do to change her mind." His determination was both a blessing and a curse.

"She said no," Adam reminded him. "Let's leave it at that."

"Come on, Adam, there's always a way."

After a moment's thought, Adam said, "There's one thing I suppose you could try, but it wouldn't be easy."

As if that would deter him. He needed this— something to kick his ass and inspire him, so he could get past this episode of creative constipation.

"She's an anthropology professor at the California Institute of Natural and Social Sciences in Las Espitas, up in Ventura County. The spring semester is about to start. You could try signing up for one of her courses," Adam suggested. "Who knows, you might learn something."

Probably. But anthropology? He was more of a poet than a scientist.

"Her courses are in high demand. Shawn said students have to submit an essay to be considered for admission, and she only takes sixteen students per class."

Johnny thought about it. Now might be the time to capitalize on his fame, but he needed to be discreet. Paparazzi had been watching him more closely ever since he started dating high-profile women.

He glanced at the magazines on the coffee table. Most of the tabloids had either his or Andie's face on their covers wearing expressions of anger and sadness, emotions which in reality had nothing to do with their breakup. After years in the business, nothing the media did or said surprised him.

One cover showed his ex's glowing face above the caption *Andie Woodhull—Strong, Sexy, Single--How She's Doing Now*. That was fast. Last week's headline read *PREGNANT & DUMPED—Johnny chooses partying over family*. Or their personal favorite: *I Will Destroy You! Andie is threatening to air their dirty laundry—and it's Johnny's worst nightmare*.

A couple of days ago, Andie had texted him a picture of herself looking smugly into the camera, the magazine cover in one hand and a lacy stocking dangling from the other. They'd had a good laugh about it. Whoever said 'exes can't be friends' hadn't met Andie Woodhull.

Right then, his phone buzzed. Johnny checked the caller ID—Juliana Porter—and picked it up. "Can you tell me who comes up with this shit?" he asked his publicist.

"I take it you saw the latest round of tabloid reports." When he responded with a growl, Juliana said, "Why do you even read them?"

"The guys lined the studio with tabloids as a practical joke." He pushed the magazines out of sight. "What's up?"

"You got another letter from your super-fan. Some nude pics and ramblings about how now that slutty Andie is gone, you two can ride into the sunset together."

"And I should care about this why?" He got over-the-top fan mail all the time.

"She's getting more aggressive. I talked to Ben, and we agree we shouldn't take this lightly. He told Mag to be on high alert. You have to take him with you whenever you leave the house."

Johnny sighed. "I appreciate your concern, Jules, but I don't need a babysitter."

"Better safe than sorry, Johnny. Just be extra careful for now."

***

Friday afternoon, Johnny took the hour-long drive up to the California Institute of Natural and Social Sciences. He'd never been to Las Espitas, didn't even know this tiny college town existed.

He knocked on the half-open door of the dean's office, and Dr. Wheeler asked him to come in.

"May I help you?" The dean, a striking Haitian woman in her fifties, gestured for him to sit.

"We spoke on the phone last week. Johnny Graham." He shook her hand, then sat across from her. "I'm here for Dr. Harding's class."

"Ah, yes, Mr. Graham. We appreciate your generous donation to the institute." Dr. Wheeler's long red nails made a clicking sound as she typed on her laptop. "Did you bring the non-disclosure agreement you wanted us to sign?"

Johnny handed her the paperwork his brother Jason had drawn up. The last thing he needed was for the press to find out he was going back to school, or link him to yet another woman. "What is she like?" he ventured to ask because Adam hadn't said much about her.

Leafing through the NDA, the dean hesitated. "Well, Dr. Harding is... special."

"Special?" Johnny scratched at his temple.

"Yes. Her unusual background inspired her unique approach to her subject matter. I'm sure you'll enjoy her class. According to the faculty's quarterly evaluations, her students consistently describe her as brilliant."

The next two hours might not be so boring after all.

The dean handed him a printout with directions and told him to hurry because the lecture was about to start.

2

NICE TO MEET YOU ANYWAY

*"Important encounters are planned by the souls,
long before the bodies see each other."*

—PAULO COELHO

Johnny arrived at the classroom fashionably late,
surprised to find that Dr. Harding was running
even later than he was. Sixteen curious faces
stared at him when he paused in the doorway for
dramatic effect.

Johnny gave a nonchalant nod and strolled toward the back of the room, which looked more
like an antique office than a lecture hall. A solid
mahogany desk, Turkish rugs, and floor-to-ceiling bookcases furnished the room.

Leaning against the paneled wall, he took

out his iPhone and pretended not to notice the young women ogling him.

A few minutes later, voices faded and eyes turned to the entrance as the esteemed professor swept into the room, her pace assertive, like the second hand of an analog clock. She strode up to the board to write her name in the upper left corner.

He couldn't wait to hear her voice.

Lumiana stepped around to the front of the desk and leaned against it.

She sure didn't look like any of his former professors. The short white dress she was wearing gave a beautiful contrast against her brown skin. Her legs were long and shapely but not skinny, and the multicolored strings from her cork-soled sandals wrapped around her ankles like silk thread bangles.

Her lush black hair was much longer than in Adam's video, cascading over her shoulders and down her back in soft waves.

When their gazes met, his pulse quickened. In this light he couldn't make out the color of her eyes, but one eye was noticeably darker than the other.

Her face showed no signs of surprise, or any other emotion for that matter. She treated him like she did everyone else.

With a warm, infectious smile, the professor introduced herself—as Lumiana, not Dr. Harding. Then she began her lecture, casting the kind of spell Dr. Wheeler had hinted at.

"I remember when I was little, my father used to tell me about the Savage of Aveyron—a wild boy who survived for many years alone in the wilderness before he was captured in southern France in 1800." Lumiana had a faint, indeterminable accent, a few words now and then pronounced a bit unusually. "Never did I imagine that with an ill turn of fate I would find myself in a similar situation two centuries later."

Lumiana went on to tell the rapt class that she grew up in remote areas without much contact to others. She was an orphan by age six, lost in an unmarked part of Las Madres forest until an old woman from South America rescued her, who then kept her from the outside world for a decade.

"Growing up isolated and surrounded by nature allowed me to study societies and their cultures with fresh eyes, but also left me utterly unprepared for life in civilized society."

Johnny studied her closely. Lumiana had something almost otherworldly about her. The way her body moved as she spoke, the way her voice ebbed and flowed like a lovely melody. She told her story so lively it felt like they were there with her, watching it all unfold. She was a tremendous storyteller. *A strong but bruised soul.*

Takes one to know one, he thought, noticing how Lumiana clasped her locket whenever she mentioned her parents. She'd told them her dad had died of hypothermia after saving a tourist girl from the rapid river that ran by their house. And six months later, she lost her mom during a camping trip.

After the lecture, some students stayed to ask follow-up questions. Wanting to speak with her in private, Johnny decided to grab a quick latte from the artisan coffee stand outside the building.

By the time he returned to the classroom, Lumiana was gone.

**

Thanks to the dean's directions, it didn't take Johnny long to find Lumiana's office. The door was open, and she stood on tiptoes in front of a towering bookcase. In one hand she held a printout while with the other she reached for a book on an upper shelf.

"Let me help you," Johnny said as he entered the room. He took down the book she'd been trying to grasp and handed it to her.

The woman had scars on her hand. Small ones, as though she gardened.

He caught a whiff of something flowery when Lumiana stepped away without looking at him.

After a long, awkward silence she mumbled "thank you," still focused on the article in her hand.

Johnny got a closer look at her golden heart-shaped locket and the dark buttons running down the left side of her long-sleeved dress. The way it hugged her curves, the pencil dress appeared custom-made.

"The Link Between Creativity and Eccentricity," Johnny read, tapping the book cover, his interest piqued. Was it a dig at him? Maybe she'd recognized him after all.

Lumiana looked up now, her gaze boring into him with such angry intensity he felt the urge to close his eyes.

"Why are you here?" Her words cracked like a whip. "I thought I made myself clear to Adam. I wish for you to leave. Now."

So she did know who he was.

Johnny rolled his shoulders. "I need to know why you didn't want to meet me."

She pushed her hands through her hair, held it back, and released it. "I'm grateful for your invitation and flattered by your interest, but I am not, nor will I ever be, interested in collaborating with you."

Johnny held her gaze, annoyed that his stomach fluttered. "Come on, Doc. Tell me why you don't want to work with me."

She gestured toward the door. "Just leave."

"Why are you so—" he wanted to say 'angry and uncooperative' but it didn't quite fit her refined speech, so he went with "cantankerous."

"Cantankerous?" Her gaze fierce, she straightened to try to match his stature. Her eyes level with his mouth, she said, "What will it take to make you drop out of my course and never come to see me again?"

Crossing his arms, he resisted taking a step back.

Lumiana stalked over to her desk. Johnny followed but stopped abruptly when she turned around and extended her arm. "Don't," she said.

He stood still, feeling her hand firmly pressed against his chest.

"Your heart is thumping," Lumiana murmured as she stepped closer, awe in her voice. But her eyes... they had taken on a faraway look, like she was someplace else. Like she was seeing someone else.

When she put her ear to his chest, her hand placed next to it, Johnny held his breath, stunned by the intimate gesture. He didn't know whether to hold her or push her away.

Cautiously, as if she were as fragile as gold leaf, he covered her hand with his.

Peering up at him, Lumiana appeared disoriented for a moment, then grabbed her coat and fled the room.

Maybe it was out of curiosity, or to make sure she was okay, but something pushed him to run after her.

"Wait!"

She didn't.

Fast like a damn cheetah.

It dented his ego a little that he hardly managed to keep up with her. He followed her through the deserted hallway, down a dimly lit staircase, and out the front entrance.

She paused on the flagstone walkway, but Johnny was still too far behind to talk to her without shouting. He'd almost caught up to her when she dashed across the lawn and into the forest bordering the institute's grounds.

What the hell?

Now that no one could hear them, Johnny shouted after her. "Hey, stop!"

Lumiana didn't respond and instead led him through a rocky woodland that seemed never-ending.

Johnny kept pleading with her as he followed behind, but to no avail.

Is that woman out of her mind? And what was he doing, chasing her like some psychopath?

He considered letting her be, but what if something was wrong with her? He couldn't let her wander off into the woods never to be seen again—Juliana would kill him for that PR nightmare.

After they'd been running, then jogging, then walking for what must've been two or three miles, Lumiana finally came to a halt.

"Why?" She turned to face him, raising her hands before letting them fall to her sides. "Why can't you leave me alone?" she yelled, tears swimming in her eyes.

The desperation in her voice made him cringe. He didn't mean to upset her, or even worse, hurt her. He had no idea what was happening, but he'd probably triggered her somehow. Didn't the dean say she was special? Maybe she suffered from PTSD or some other mental disorder. Growing up the way she had must've been traumatizing.

"Why are you following me, here of all places?" Lumiana swiveled around, arms spread wide, indicating their surroundings. Nothing but rocks, shrubs, and trees.

"You're the one who led me here!" he panted. "I didn't realize we were running away from civilization."

"I prefer to be away from civilization."

Johnny bent over, propping his hands on his knees to catch his breath. Lumiana came up to him and lightly squeezed his shoulder.

"I'm sorry," he uttered.

Lumiana placed a hand on his cheek, her touch so gentle it raised the hair on his skin. She helped him straighten up. "You will be fine."

"I don't know what I was thinking. I didn't mean to upset you, especially not so much you'd feel the need to run out—"

"Shh," Lumiana whispered.

"I'm trying to apolo—"

"Quiet. Now," she hissed, coming to stand right in front of him. "Look to your right. But do not move."

He glanced to the right and recoiled. A black bear stood a few yards away, scratching his back on the trunk of a tree. Johnny's instinct was to run, but Lumiana grabbed his hand and clasped it, holding him in place.

"Don't run," she said in a low and resonant voice, "She will think you're prey. She hasn't seen us yet. If we stay still, she will leave on her own."

Nodding, he took her other hand in his, nearly crushing it. He didn't do bears. He'd grown up in the city—the opossum he'd spotted once was as wild as it got. Johnny shuddered at the memory. Those things were like genetically modified rats, but at least they were small.

"No need to be frightened," Lumiana said, still resonant. "Black bears are an important part of California's ecosystems. They are the gentlest and least aggressive of the species. If she were to attack she would paw at the ground and grunt while swishing her head back and forth. But even then you don't run. You make yourself as tall as you can and back away slowly." They stood in silence for a moment. "She's beautiful, isn't she?"

Johnny admired her calmness. There was something enchanting about people who connect with nature and its magnificent creatures.

After the bear lumbered away, Lumiana let go of his hands and took a few steps back. She did smell of flowers, a strong yet sweet scent of jasmine that took him back to the memory of his childhood home.

For a moment he could hear his parents argue as vividly as if it were yesterday, their shouts turning into whispers as he closed the attic's heavy mahogany door. Among boxes of mementos, seasonal decorations, and jasmine-scented candles, he'd discovered his grandfather's dusty phonograph. When Etta James's "At Last" soared through the brass horn, her powerful voice filled him with wonder, spurring his dream of becoming a musician.

"You smell nice," he said without thinking.

Lumiana regarded him skeptically. She didn't need to speak to tell him what she thought. He'd never met anyone with a face as expressive as hers.

It was getting chilly beneath the tree's canopy as they stood there staring at each other. Then Johnny noticed a subtle change in her expression. "What is it?"

"It will rain soon."

Seriously? They were in sunny California. The state was facing one of its worst droughts on record. Yet he chose to believe the woman who'd lived in a forest for half of her life. Besides, storms weren't unheard-of during this time of year, and he vaguely remembered Adam babbling about canceling his weekend getaway because of weather conditions.

Fishing for a cell phone signal, Johnny asked, "Do you have any idea where we are or how to get back?"

"We are close to my house," she mumbled.

"What's that?"

"I said we are relatively close to my house. I didn't plan on having you as a guest, but we won't make it back to campus before the storm, and I cannot leave you here by yourself." Although she looked like she'd considered doing just that. "With this drought, if there's lightning, it can start a wildfire."

That was the downside of living in the Golden State. Those wildfires got more destructive every year. He knew people who'd lost their homes to the fires.

"Thank you, Dr. Harding, you're far too kind," he said, mocking her, because half the time the woman sounded like she'd swallowed a British aristocrat. "You speak so properly."

Her eyes narrowed. "I'm sorry, we can't all be Neanderthals."

"Don't get me wrong," he said with a chuckle. "It's hot that you're so highly refined."

She angled her head as if she was trying to figure out if he was joking. After a moment, she shrugged. "English isn't my native tongue. I learned most of it from historical books and scientific papers."

"Well, your English is definitely better than mine. I bet you even curse elegantly."

A small smile flitted across her lips. "We need to go."

"After you, Doc." He gestured for her to take the lead.

Leaving the shelter of the woods, they walked

along chaparral-clad hills until they came to a gorgeous plain carpeted in grass and wildflowers. Since they weren't talking, Johnny had time to take in the mesmerizing beauty around him. He tried to remember the last time he'd gone for a walk that didn't involve getting a latte macchiato.

Just as the sun was setting they reached the peak of a hill, where they paused to marvel at the rich colors in front of them: the mountains were tinged with pink, a stark contrast to the deep greens of the surrounding vegetation.

Behind them, Johnny could see dark clouds looming, ready to burst. The wind picked up and Lumiana pulled on her red trench coat while he fastened his leather jacket.

Soon they reached a narrow path. Lumiana led them through a broken chain-link fence, the first indicator of a return to civilization.

A few minutes later, the rain hit with such force it felt like needles piercing their skin.

"I know this is unfortunate," she shouted over the raging wind, "but let's just run! We're almost there."

Johnny dragged a hand through his sopping hair.

Great, more running.

Bracing himself, he followed after her.

As the rain grew heavier and bored holes in the ground it was getting harder to move forward. In a moment of inattention, Lumiana stepped in a hole and stumbled to the ground.

Johnny pulled her up. Seeing the anguish in her face, he instinctively drew her into his arms. She resembled a helpless child now, not the strong woman who held his hand when they were facing a wild animal, or the distinguished professor who inspired students with her vivid storytelling.

"Could you help me get over there to that big oak tree, please?"

"Are you asking me to carry you, Dr. Harding?" He wouldn't mind doing it, but thoroughly enjoyed teasing her. Lumiana seemed prickly and fidgety, but he'd glimpsed a fire in her that he couldn't help but stoke.

"I'd rather crawl on all fours," she said with a huff.

Before Lumiana had the chance to protest, Johnny scooped her over his shoulder and carried her to the tree. The oak's canopy rustled violently but blocked at least some rain.

Lumiana wiped the hair off her face. "Thank you. But if you ever try that again I will rip your arm off and beat you with the bloody end."

He gave her points for imagery.

When he grinned, she said, "I mean it. You have already stalked, chased, and manhandled me. I don't care for this."

He still wasn't sure why he'd run after her. And because she reminded him of Adam's grandmother, who wasn't a woman of empty threats either, he apologized.

Lumiana spread her mud-stained coat out on the grass, offering him a seat next to her.

He shook his head. His clothes were expensive. It irritated him that they were dripping wet, he didn't need to get them dirty too. "Do you think the rain's going to stop soon?" Because Lumiana was shivering, he asked, "You okay?" though she clearly wasn't.

She nodded.

"You need to work on your poker face, Doc." How could this woman have so much pride she'd rather suffer than accept his help? "Mind if I ask how old you are? You seem rather young to be a professor."

Lumiana knitted her brows. "Why does it matter how old I am?"

"You're awfully defensive about it."

"My entire life people have taken issue with my age. They fail to understand that it's not how old I am that determines my capabilities—my education and training do." She sighed. "If you must know, I'm twenty-seven."

According to Adam she wasn't an Assistant Professor, so she must be gifted to achieve tenure this young. "You look barely legal." Her responding scowl made him smile. "I meant it as a compliment."

"Thank you," she said, and left it at that.

After a few more minutes of watching her shiver, Johnny could no longer stand it. He took off his Margiela jacket and draped it over her shoulders.

"Thank you, but this is unnecessary." She handed his jacket back.

Shaking his head, he placed it over her shoulders again. "You're a real pain in the ass, you know that? Why are you giving me such a hard time?"

Lumiana stared at her feet. "Who is giving whom a hard time now?"

Johnny let it slide.

"How do you feel about a little singing?" he asked. "They say it's cathartic."

He'd expected her to shut him down, but instead she sang about the rain reminding her of tears she cried in bed, her soulful voice giving him goosebumps.

"Who would've thought that line would actually work on you. That was beautiful."

"The original is a reggae song by Martin Jondo called 'Raindrops.'" She rubbed her shins. "We should go before it gets too dark."

Johnny took three steps toward the washed-out path, intentionally ignoring her. "Are you coming?" he said over his shoulder, watching as she struggled to get up without putting pressure on her injured foot. "I'd be happy to help. All you have to do is ask," he teased because he couldn't help himself. Recklessness was ingrained in him. 'Don't do it, Johnny! You're gonna get hurt,' his little brother Jack had shouted when Johnny stood at the edge of the cliff near their vac-ation home, ready to dive into the cool water below. He'd jumped that day, and he'd jumped at chances ever since. It worked out in his favor most of the time.

Lumiana's nose crinkled as she considered her options. "Fine." She gave an exaggerated smile. "Could you please help me get home?"

Johnny strode over to her, reached for her hands, and pulled her up. "Was that so hard?"

She snarled, and part of him wanted to nip her full and inviting lips. Why the professor's de-fiance turned him on was a question for his ther-apist.

Holding on to him, Lumiana limped the rest of the way. When the trail morphed into a nar-row gravel road, Johnny belted out a few lines of "Singin' in the Rain." Lumiana surprised him by joining in. "You know about the additional verse. I'm impressed." He knew they were made to sing together. Now all he needed was to convince her to work with him on his new album. "It's amaz-ing how one little song can make a bad situation so much better."

Lumiana nodded absently, then pointed to their right. "I live over there. It's about a mile further."

In the growing darkness, Johnny could just make out a house and another to its left, and if he wasn't mistaken, a few more farther out. But other than that, they seemed to be in the middle of nowhere. Why would she, or anyone, choose to live out here?

***

Johnny watched as Lumiana turned on the outdoor lights and deactivated the alarm. The gate opened, and together they made their way down the long driveway toward a modern Japanese-style house. He admired the two river rock columns framing the entrance and wondered if it was possible to deduce what kind of person someone is by the way they lived.

Lumiana unlocked the front door and motioned him inside her unlit home. "Wait here. I'll get us dry clothes," she said, beginning to undress right there in the entrance hall. Her trench coat hit the hardwood floor like a wet rag. And then, with considerable effort, she pulled off her soaked dress.

Johnny pinched the bridge of his nose when she stood there, practically naked. "What are you doing?" he asked, not that he didn't appreciate the view. Her back and arms were strong like an athlete's, her hips curved and wide. He did his best not to let his gaze linger on her sexy backside.

Lumiana twisted her limp hair into a bun and wrapped it in a headscarf. "I can't stand being in these sticky clothes for one more second, and I won't move about the house dripping all over the floor."

Johnny shrugged. "Your house, your rules."

"Stay where you are. I'll be right back." Lumiana hobbled toward a stairway with floor-to-ceiling pillars and curving wooden treads that resembled the vertebrae in a spine. Below the half-landing, she'd planted a small indoor garden.

The house sure was as interesting as its owner.

As Johnny waited there, appreciating the staircase's unusual design, something nuzzled his leg.

"James Tiberius Kirk, get over here!" Lumiana ordered as she came down the stairs, wearing an oversized UCLA sweatshirt, her long legs as bare as her feet.

"You named your weird pet after a Star Trek character?"

Lumiana gave him a smile that upped his body temperature.

Christ. She looked young even with a serious face, but that smile—it gave her an almost child-like air, mischievous, like she'd be the first to climb over a fence or jump off a cliff.

The pig made its way toward her, tripping over its own feet, running into things along the way like a drunken toddler. "What's wrong with this thing?"

"He is not a thing, he is a piglet." She knelt. "Kirk is half blind, half deaf. Orientation isn't his strong suit." Lumiana cradled the pig like a loving mother would her baby. "His owner abandoned him when he outgrew the tea cup."

Johnny took off his jacket and started with his shirt when he caught her ogling him. He didn't mind her watching, but enjoyed her flustered expression as he told her to face the other way.

"Whose clothes are these?" He pulled on a pair of sweatpants, surprised they fit. At six-foot-three, chances were he'd end up looking like a pathetic Michael Jackson impersonator. Most people didn't stock up on pants fit for giants— so why had Lumiana? "Not your boyfriend's, are they?"

She tugged at the hem of her sweatshirt and with the other hand clasped her locket through the worn fabric. "They belong to one of my brothers. I can give you a towel if you prefer."

"These will do. Thanks."

"Would you care for a bite to eat?"

"Well thank you, ma'am. I'd very much care for a bite to eat," Johnny mocked her highfalutin word choice, but the mockery was lost on her.

Without another word, she limped over to the open-plan kitchen.

Johnny admired her spacious home. The modern bamboo furniture and sparse decor encouraged peace of mind. Flower petals, scattered about on little plates, scented the air.

It struck him as odd that she had no pictures of loved ones on display. He didn't think of himself as sentimental, but even at his house there were photos of his family and his band on display. Which reminded him he still had to take down the pictures of him and Andie.

Leaning against the kitchen counter, Johnny watched Lumiana as she took a food container from the fridge and placed it on the counter top. She pulled two spoons from a drawer, handed him one, and then hopped up on the counter.

Hesitantly, he sat next to her, the glass bowl between them. Given her polished communication style, he expected a more formal dining experience, but he liked that Lumiana was comfortable enough around him not to worry about making a good impression.

They dug in.

"This is delicious." He took another spoonful. "What's this dish called?"

"Milchreis—German rice pudding. My adoptive mom is a first-generation immigrant from Germany. This is one of my family's specialties."

"About that," Johnny gestured with his spoon, "Adam mentioned Shawn is your brother but you said in your lecture that your parents died when you were little. It kind of sounded like you were an only child."

Lumiana ate in silence for a moment before answering. "I was an only child until my first day of college when I met a young woman from Argentina. Her parents took me in. The Arendt-Garcías have adopted many children over the years. Shawn and Candela are just two of my brothers and sisters."

After they finished the rice pudding, Lumiana pushed the bowl aside and examined her ankle.

"How's your foot?" Johnny touched it. Despite various scars, her skin was supremely soft.

"Much better, thank you. Would you care for a cup of tea?"

Johnny nodded. He could still feel the chill that had seeped through his wet clothes and into his bones.

Lumiana opened a drawer that gave off a sweet herbal fragrance. It held small bamboo boxes filled with assorted herbs, leaves, and flowers. She chose a chamomile-lavender mix and then prepared the tea so mindfully he got the impression it was something of a ritual.

After placing the two steaming cups on a bamboo tray, she handed it to him carefully.

Balancing the tray in both hands, he followed her as she limped to the living room to a large sofa adorned with green and beige pillows. Johnny placed the tea on the table. Then he reclined on the sofa, letting his fingers glide over the smooth fabric.

Everything about this place—the scent, the clean lines, the colors—had a calming effect on his mind.

This was exactly what he needed after beating himself up over his lack of inspiration for the past few weeks. He'd been feeling a lot like that anxious, withdrawn kid again, but he was too old now to hide out in his parents' attic or at Johnny

B. Goode with Adam's grandmother. Besides, the tattoo shop wasn't a smart idea in his current state. He'd promised his mom he would leave one forearm free of ink, and he was dangerously close to breaking that promise.

As they settled on the sofa, Lumiana handed him a plush cotton blanket and covered herself with another. With her injured foot propped on a pillow, she warmed her hands on a mug emblazoned with Lionel Richie's face and the words *Hello... is it tea you're looking for?*

Johnny inhaled the steam rising from his own cup. "What a day, huh?"

"It's all your fault. You should have stayed away. Now I'm stuck with you for the night."

Johnny's sense of serenity shattered. "I can leave if you prefer."

"I'd very much prefer that." She carried on in the same matter-of-fact tone. "I tried to arrange for your departure earlier while I was upstairs getting dry clothes, but a rock slide is blocking the road. It won't be cleared away until tomorrow afternoon at the earliest."

Johnny could hear the wind and pelting rain washing over the patio. There was no way he'd set a foot outside. "Great," he muttered, burrowing further into the blanket.

She glared at him over the rim of her mug.

"What?" he barked.

"I'm very cross with you."

His irritation melted. "Yes, I got that," he said,

trying not to smile. She was adorable when she talked like that. It made him want to scoop her into his arms and kiss the crinkled space between her brows. Which was weird. He didn't usually like his women aloof. "Do you think you're ever going to tell me why you didn't want to meet me?" Feeling more at ease now, he couldn't resist putting the topic back on the table.

Lumiana released a sigh that ended in a yawn. Her face softened when he smiled at her.

"Tomorrow. I promise." She got up, waiting for him to follow. "We should go to bed. Let me show you to the guest room."

He drew her back to the sofa. "I'd like to sit here with you a little longer."

She hesitated before replying, "A few more minutes. It's late."

"You sound like a mom." Johnny offered her a seat under the blanket.

She returned to where she sat but inched closer to him. "Please keep your hands to yourself."

He wondered if she could read his mind. "Are you sure you're okay having a stranger spend the night?"

She gave him the side-eye. "I can handle myself. And you look rather harmless with your manicured fingernails and beauteous face."

"I'm taller and stronger than you." Johnny flexed his arm to showcase his chiseled biceps.

"Touch it."

She shook her head, but when he kept his arm on display in front of her, she gave in and squeezed. "Satisfactory, but insufficient to prove your hypothesis."

"Do you want to wrestle me to see who's stronger?"

"I'd rather go to bed."

"Come on, Doc. Show me what you got." He poked her in the side, but she merely frowned.

"Why is it important to you to prove your strength?" she asked, her eyes drifting shut.

"You sound like my shrink." Johnny folded his hands behind his head. "It's not about strength. I could be an ax murderer and you don't seem all that concerned about your safety."

"And what about your safety? How do you know that I don't eat pretty men like you for breakfast?" Yawning, she patted his cheek.

"I deserved that," he said, noting that for a woman who spoke to him like he was a nuisance she couldn't wait to get rid of, she was touching him a lot.

They sat quietly for a while.

Johnny felt Lumiana's hand next to his and grappled with the urge to hold it because, just like that delicious tea, she had a calming effect on him.

He brushed against her hand and smiled when she linked her fingers with his, her head settling on his shoulder. There it was, that sweet tingling sensation.

He didn't breathe for a moment, worried that any sudden movement would make her retreat. She wasn't unlike that wild animal they'd encountered in the woods: beautiful to look at, but one wrong move and it would either run away, or worse, attack—and he'd seen her do both.

After a few minutes, he realized she'd fallen asleep, and gently placed a pillow under her head. Lumiana seemed so young and innocent, it was hard to see her for what she was: a grumpy professor with a powerful voice that reminded him of Soul Queens past and present.

***

That night, Lumiana was dreaming of the first time she met Jayjay.

She was standing still in the midst of hundreds of people roaming the busy UCLA campus, as if caught in the eye of a storm. A knot formed in her throat. She felt light-headed and unable to breathe. Shivering, she ran to the nearest tree and hugged it.

When a hand touched her shoulder, she jumped.

"You okay?" asked a kind, masculine voice from behind her.

She turned around and looked up into a young man's face. Fascinated by his beauty, she reached out to touch him, but he took a step back.

"Do you want me to call someone for you?"

Lumiana waved the information sheet in front of him. "Sir," she took a deep breath and pointed at a name on the sheet, "could you please help me find Professor Aurelia Kindley?"

"Sir?" He raised his eyebrows. "How old do you think I am?"

"Twenty, sir. My name is Lumiana Harding. I have a meeting with Professor Kindley."

"All right, Miss Harding," he said, grinning, "let's get you to the dear professor." He led her toward the entrance of a building with an ornate terracotta brick facade. "You guessed my age right, by the way."

They walked side by side while Lumiana focused on her breathing. The swarming students reminded her of the time she'd mistakenly poked a beehive.

"Lumiana was it? What kind of name is that?"

"*Lou-me-ana* as in *Ghana*." She corrected his pronunciation. "I'm from Finland. 'Lumi' is one of the words that describe snow in Finnish. It comes from Latin *lumen*, which means light."

When he said she didn't look Finnish, she told him her mother was Pardo Brazilian and her father South African of Zulu and Dutch ancestry.

"I'm Jordan Jackson, but everyone calls me Jayjay. My father was South African too," he said. "Xhosa, to be precise." He made a clicking sound when he said Xhosa—a distinctive feature of the Bantu language. "My mother was Japanese." He went on: "You aren't a student here, are you? Or let me put it this way, you seem way too young to be a student here."

Insulted by the inquiry, she snapped, "People have a tendency to underestimate me, but I am in fact here to obtain my anthropology degree."

"I'm sorry, I was just stating the obvious. I mean, you have to admit, you look no older than, I don't know, twelve maybe."

"Looks can be deceiving," she lectured him. "I turn sixteen in two weeks."

"Sixteen? That's still rather young to start college. Are you a genius?"

"People say I'm quite brilliant."

He couldn't have smiled any wider.

They stopped in front of the professor's office. Jayjay knocked on the door and a friendly voice told them to come in.

Lumiana turned to the handsome stranger, and with a simple "thank you" followed by an awkward bow, she said goodbye.

When Lumiana woke from the dream, she felt warm and safe until she remembered that the arm protectively wrapped around her wasn't Jayjay's but Johnny's. She touched her locket to calm her racing heart.

It was still dark outside, but the rain had stopped.

Careful not to wake him, Lumiana slid out of Johnny's embrace and hurried upstairs to take a shower. As the cool water poured down on her, she allowed herself to cry.

3

BLACK HORSE & THE CHERRY TREE

"How wild it was, to let it be."

—CHERYL STRAYED

In the morning, Johnny woke to the melody of "Burning Love." Rubbing his eyes, he looked around until he remembered where he was. *The magnificent abode of Professor Grumps-a-lot.* Lumiana was quite the character, he thought, smiling to himself. *Where is she anyway?*

Yawning, he got up from the couch and headed for the kitchen, where he tripped over a cantaloupe-sized turtle.

What the hell?

He rubbed his eyes again.

There was no sign of Lumiana, but in the corner he saw the piglet sharing a meal with a dog, a cat, and a goose. When Johnny crouched down, the dog came over to be petted.

"I like your little zoo of misfits," he said to Lumiana, who joined him in the kitchen a few minutes later.

"I see you have met my Australian shepherd, Monroe, my calico Persian cat, Marilyn, who thinks she is a puppy—"

"Looks more like a tumble-dried guinea pig," he scoffed.

With a frown on her face, she continued, "This is my Pomeranian goose, Doggie, who limps from an old injury, in case you would like to make fun of her too." She pointed at the turtle. "This is Walter." Then she cuddled the pig. "And you remember Kirk from yesterday."

"At least you're not some weird cat lady." She was still plenty weird though. Who domesticated geese?

Ignoring his comment, Lumiana poured them each a glass of water that had a slight citrus taste to it. "Would you care for some breakfast?" she said without looking at him.

"Sure, thanks." He bit his lip. She didn't look the way she talked, and to him that was as peculiar as it was riveting. "How's your ankle?" he asked after noticing that she was walking with more ease.

"Better, thank you." She put some fruit on a

tray and handed it to him. "We'll eat outside."

Johnny sat on a sofa in the outdoor lounge, which was roofed and therefore dry, while Lumiana cleared some stray branches the storm had blown down. Part of the stunning backyard resembled a Japanese tea garden, with a temple-like lodge and a steeply arched, red wooden bridge over a pond. Farther out lay a vegetable garden and a small lake framed by majestic trees. The view beyond her property was spectacular: wildflowers dotted a blanket of lush meadow grass, and rocky hills stretched toward the distant horizon.

Johnny savored the crisp, clean air. He could understand why she'd want to live out here.

They ate in silence until Lumiana caught him eyeing the moon bridge. "You wish to climb it, don't you?"

"I know it's weird, but do you mind if I do?"

"Go ahead. Anyone who visits asks me that."

They strolled over and Johnny climbed to the top of the bridge, then gave Lumiana a hand up the last step.

"I can't get over how beautiful this view is." Johnny inhaled deeply. The air still smelled of wet grass and flowers. He wondered if there was even the slightest chance he could stay here for a while, rent out the guest room until he finished the album.

Goosebumps spread across Lumiana's legs. Johnny thought about putting an arm around

her but hesitated. "Remember what you promised me last night?" he said instead.

"I do, but I'd rather we didn't talk about it."
She scrubbed her hands over her face.

He touched her arm. "Please. I know how I am
—not knowing, it's going to drive me crazy."

Her face hardened. "I'm freezing. I want to go
inside."

"Fine, let's go inside, but don't think you're
off the hook. I still want to know why you didn't
want to meet me."

After they cleared the dishes, Johnny leaned
against the counter. Lumiana was standing in
the middle of her kitchen but her mind appeared
to be somewhere else. He'd noticed it before. It
was as if she routinely escaped into a world of
her own. "Well, are we going to have that talk?"

She seemed to consider his question for a moment, then grabbed his hand and led him to the
living room couch. They sat facing each other,
but Lumiana kept quiet and toyed with one of
the throw pillows.

"You're making me nervous," he said, putting
a hand over hers.

"Let me get us a cup of tea." She got up, but he
pulled her right back down.

"No more excuses, Doc. Give your ankle a
break and give me a break, and let's get it over
with." He took her hands. "Come on, you can tell
me." Watching her squirm did strange things to
his insides.

Lumiana cleared her throat. "I feel silly telling you this, especially now, here, like this." She paused when the cat hopped onto the sofa. "I can't understand why you came to see me."

Johnny saw the flicker of anger in her eyes. "I'm sorry I forced the meeting, but what I don't regret is meeting you and getting to experience this beautiful place." The combination of being surrounded by undisturbed nature and spending time with someone as odd and interesting as her was creative gold. He could already feel the buzz of an idea coming on.

Marilyn, who looked like a fluffier, more colorful version of Garfield, nudged his leg. When he stroked his hand over her fuzzy fur, the cat purred with delight, which made Lumiana smile. But the light in her eyes dimmed instantly when he said, "I didn't take no for an answer because the truth is, people don't tell me no very often. But it wasn't just that. You have an amazing voice that goes well with mine. It would be fun to collaborate."

Flattery didn't seem to work; her facial expression stayed the same. Perhaps he could appeal to her altruism. "I'm having a hard time getting started on my new album. I need inspiration."

Nothing. She didn't even blink.

"And there's something in it for you too. I can introduce you to the right people, give you an audience, you know, vouch for you. Most people would be thrilled about an opportunity like that. Why aren't you?"

"Because it's not what I want," Lumiana insisted. "I don't want to be a famous musician. I don't see myself as a musician at all. It's a hobby. What I am is a teacher and a researcher, and I love my work. Look where we are." She gestured around the room.

"There is a reason why I live out here, in seclusion. I am uncomfortable around people who aren't part of my family. I don't care for noise or crowds. Nor do I want people following me or taking my picture. And I certainly don't want to be judged by the way I look or have people dissect my every word, every action. None of that is appealing to me."

"Makes sense. I have to say though, it's a pity no one's going to hear your beautiful voice." When she covered her face with her hands, he touched her knee. "What I can't understand is why you didn't just say that from the beginning?"

"I did! To my brother and Adam when they told me you wanted to meet me."

That part seemed to have gotten lost in translation. He eyed her sharply. "You couldn't tell me this yourself, over coffee or something?"

"Maybe under different circumstances, but I didn't want to meet you, as a person. When Shawn and Adam told me you wished to arrange a meeting, I didn't know who you were. I love making music by myself or with my family, but I rarely listen to the music that is popular these days. I don't have a television, or radio, or the Internet. And you might not be aware of this, but your reputation precedes you, and not always in the best way—"

"I'm curious," he ground out, "What exactly have you heard about me?"

"Does it matter?"

He huffed. "It matters to me. I have masochistic tendencies, so please, let me have it."

Lumiana shook her head. Her silence only worsened the pressure in his chest.

"Let me guess. Something along the lines of 'he's an eccentric, self-involved douche, a womanizer.' Sexist? Oh no wait, probably a racist, huh? Which is it? All of it? And of course you believed that shit because—"

"Stop it!" Lumiana raised her voice. "You are blowing this out of proportion. I declined your invitation not because I thought you were any of those things, but because you attract too much attention and I can't have that."

She sat up straight now. "I based my decision on what is best for the people close to me. You have no idea to what lengths my family, our friends, and the people around us have been going over the years to shield us from unwanted attention. My family isn't your typical American family. You already know part of my story, but my siblings—they have their own tragic stories.

If I get seen with you and it ends up in the papers they will dig until they find something. And believe me, there is a lot to find."

Lumiana took his hands. Her grip was strong but her eyes were soft. "I can't go into more detail, but I have to do what is best for my family. Please, you need to understand..."

He stared at their linked hands, fascinated that neither of them was letting go. "We don't need to go anywhere together, we can work here. I can bring my guitar and whatever else we need. I promise I won't tell anyone."

"I cannot see you again." She released his hands as she got up. "It would be best if you were to leave now. I'll call and check if they have dealt with the rock slide."

Five minutes later, Lumiana returned. Her frowny face broadcasted 'I have bad news' even before she told him they were still working on clearing the road. "It may take all day because it's the weekend, and we aren't a priority out here."

"So what you're saying is, I'm stuck here." He stretched out his legs, smiling.

"You aren't upset."

"Why would I be? I wanted to spend more time with you, and now I can. Makes me pretty happy, actually." He stood. "I'm good company. I promise," he said when she sighed. "Let me make a few calls. That is, if I can get reception out here." Johnny realized he hadn't even thought of his phone since the night before and tried to remember where he'd left it.

"The signal is a bit weak but it should work. If you're looking for your phone, it's in the laundry room with your clothes. They should be dry by now."

When Johnny strolled down the hallway, he spotted himself in a mirror and did a double take. He looked younger, as if he'd been on vacation. Probably because he hadn't slept this well in a long time.

Then he went and grabbed his phone to clear his weekend schedule. Maybe that collaboration was happening after all.

Johnny returned to the living room half an hour later.

Lumiana was on the couch, leafing through a pile of student essays. It was mesmerizing to see her immersed in a task—the way her brows creased in concentration, the fluidity of her movements, the obliviousness to the world around her. There was something almost magical about her that made it hard to look away.

When she caught him watching her, he asked, "What do you do for fun around here since you don't have a TV, radio, or Internet?"

"When my family visits we have barbecues and karaoke nights, or we go for a hike or swim in the lake." She piled the student essays on the coffee table and got up. "Sometimes we invent our own games and activities."

"Your own games and activities? Can you give me an example?"

"How about I show you instead?"

"Color me intrigued." He saw her flash a smile before she crouched in front of a credenza and retrieved some kind of folded fabric. "What is it?"

"Your choice of words," she said, leading him through the patio doors.

Outside, Lumiana handed Johnny the large white sheet and instructed him to spread it across the lawn.

She returned with containers filled with a rainbow of colors. "This is homemade Holi powder," she explained. "It is used in the Hindu custom to celebrate the end of winter and the arrival of spring."

Lumiana took off her UCLA shirt and draped it over a chair a safe distance away, which left her in a sports bra and skimpy shorts. He was fantasizing about all those nice games you could play half-naked when Lumiana hit him in the face with a handful of red powder.

"Oh no you don't," he warned, grateful he was still wearing her brother's clothes and not his own.

She responded with a blast of blue powder.

Johnny dashed over to the containers, hurling a fistful of yellow powder at her, but she narrowly escaped.

"Step up your game, Graham!" she called, smiling triumphantly.

He tried again with more success.

Once all bins were empty, and they were both covered in powder head to toe, they strolled over to the moon bridge. Johnny admired Lumiana's colorful behind as they climbed to the top.

"It's beautiful, isn't it?" she said, nodding toward the multicolored sheet.

"It's pretty cool," Johnny agreed. "And a lot of fun too." He put an arm around her. "Thank you for doing this."

"Sometimes it's good to be a bit silly. You shouldn't tame your infinite imagination just because you're a grown-up." She gave him a smile that warmed him inside.

They sat quietly for a while. Johnny tried to imagine what life would be like living the way Lumiana did, isolated from prying eyes and the bustle of daily life in a big city. Maybe that's what he needed, to get away from it all for a while. "Are you happy?" The words just fell out of his mouth.

"Are you?"

Johnny took a moment to take stock, unsure how to answer. He felt her thumb stroking his hand.

"Right now, being here with you, I'm happy. It feels almost surreal. You have a very calming effect on me, even more so when you touch me." Johnny smiled at the sky when she let go of his hand. "I hear less mental chatter, which makes for a welcome change from my otherwise constant rumination." He probably shouldn't mention that he'd spent the better part of this week drunk or high—or both. At least he'd managed to stick with whiskey and weed, though he kept fantasizing about the bottle of Vicodin he'd buried in his backyard. Fuck. He needed to get out of this creative slump.

Without thinking, Johnny reached out and gently rubbed his thumb over a smudge of yellow powder on Lumiana's cheek. To his surprise, she leaned into his touch and closed her eyes, relishing the contact. Maybe she hasn't been touched like this before, he thought, or the last time had been a long time ago. Because he felt tempted to trace the curve of her lips, he asked, "How about you?"

Her hands were a little unsteady when she pushed them into her hair. "I choose to be happy, and therefore I am. That is the simple, straightforward answer." She stared at her powder-covered forearms. "I learned early in life that unfortunate things happen, and that no matter how much I wanted them to be different or go back to the way they were before, that was never going to happen."

Johnny could only imagine what it must've been like to lose both parents the same year and then grow up isolated and trapped in a foreign country.

"I had to make a choice," she said. "Do I give up? Or do I attempt to see the best of my situation?"

So strong and so damn beautiful, he thought, inching closer, his gaze dropping to her mouth when she swiped the tip of her tongue over her bottom lip. Just then, a tinny "La Vie En Rose" melody brought the moment to an end.

"Is that your phone?" his voice came out gravelly. Of course it was her phone—who else would choose a song from the 1940s as her ringtone.

"Normally I keep it mute or on vibrate, but I'm expecting a call. Excuse me." Lumiana climbed down the bridge and hurried over to the chair where she'd left her phone and sweatshirt.

"Hi, *angelito*, how is it going?" Johnny heard her say as he climbed down.

He didn't expect her to have someone special. It didn't fit. And why did he care? He'd just met her, and she wasn't even his type.

"I love you too," she chirped when Johnny entered the dining room where she was finishing up her call.

Lumiana left the phone on the table and came over to him, putting her hand on his cheek. "You look different. Are you not feeling well?"

He ordered himself to relax his jaw. "It's nothing." Was he really just imagining the pull between them? "I didn't mean to eavesdrop, but do you have a boyfriend or a husband?"

She stared at him for a long time, and then, honest to God, said, "Would you care for a cup of tea?"

He gave a dry laugh at the absurdity of her deflection. "No. I'd like you to answer my question."

She crossed her arms. "I do not wish to discuss my personal life with you."

"And why is that?"

"Why are you so nosy? I told you my privacy is important to me."

"Friends trust each other."

"I have no desire to be your friend."

She might as well have doused him with cold water.

***

Social cues had never been Lumiana's strong suit, but as soon as she said she didn't want to be Johnny's friend, she could see the look in his eyes change and his body collapse like a deflated balloon.

You hurt his feelings, Lumi.

"I am... I... I was with someone," she admitted as they sat cross-legged on the bamboo floor between the kitchen island and the dining table, so it would be easier to clean up any residual powder later.

She wished she hadn't said anything, because her chest always ached when she had to use the past tense. She never talked about Jayjay, and definitely not with strangers. Yet here she was, telling Johnny the one thing that hurt her more than anything else ever had.

"Jayjay was the first and only man I ever loved." Noticing her trembling hands, she hid them behind her back. "He died five years ago." Almost to the day. Late Monday afternoon she would meet her family at Casa de Esperanza to turn the backyard of the home they shared into an ocean of candlelight in his memory.

"He was on his way to work when a woman crashed her car into his. She was texting while driving—*B there in 5*—" a strangled laugh escaped her as she recited the woman's text message. "Can you believe it? *B there in 5*, that's all it took to end two lives." Her vision blurred. She reached for the wooden leg of one of the bar stools to ground herself but was drawn into Johnny's arms instead.

He was strong—something she wouldn't admit to his face. Nor would she acknowledge that his tight embrace made her light-headed, or that her lips quivered when his hard muscles pressed against her chest. But she could still take him down if she wanted, she thought. She'd been fantasizing about wrestling him ever since she spotted him in her classroom. The audacity of that man!

The moment she became aware that her fingers were digging into his back, she pulled away, forcing a smile. "I apologize. I didn't mean to burden you with this." Pushing to her feet, she reached for the uncapped Mason jar on the counter and took a sip of the tepid water.

"Don't say that. It's not a burden."

He was so gentle. His voice, his eyes, his

touch. She considered letting him hold her until the soreness in her throat subsided.

"It happened years ago," she repeated, her voice almost a whimper.

"Have you been with anyone since he died?"

She lowered her gaze to her bare feet.

"I know you said you don't want us to be friends," he said, putting a hand on her upper arm, "but there's something here." He motioned between them. "Maybe you miss being close to someone."

As much as she had intended to keep Johnny at a distance, she liked spending time with him. And even though she was mad at him for ambushing her at work, she hadn't been this comfortable with anyone outside her family since Jayjay.

But she couldn't possibly be attracted to Johnny, she reasoned. So whatever she was feeling must be the result of proximity.

He needed to leave. Perhaps he could sit with Linus in the little office by the community gate until they finished clearing the road.

"I apologize. You are right. I shouldn't be using you as a substitute."

Johnny's mouth formed a grim line. "It doesn't feel like you're using me," he assured her. "Am I anything like him?"

"No, you could hardly be more different."

"So wouldn't that mean that you truly like me for me? Wanting to be close to someone you like, it's normal. That's how I feel about you too." He took her hand, but she pulled it away. "Please, don't overthink this. We're having a good time, and I don't want it to be over just yet."

She needed space to breathe. Without a word, she stormed out of the house.

She barely made it to the patch of lawn by the lake before the memories of everything she'd lost swamped her. Breathing heavily, she lay down, savoring the cool grass against her hands and feet.

***

When Johnny came outside, Lumiana was on the grass, stomping and screaming. She really was a force of nature, he thought, a wild child who hadn't been socialized into suppressing her inner urges. Fascinated by her raw emotions, and sure he shouldn't interfere, he sat on the patio steps to jot a few lines on a recycled paper napkin.

After ten minutes, Lumiana seemed to have calmed down, and he cautiously approached. But as soon as she spotted him, she begged, "Please, just leave me alone."

He took a few more steps toward her.

She held up a warning hand. "Who do you think you are to force yourself into my life and make me feel and remember things I don't want to feel or remember?" She didn't wait for his answer. "Go away!"

The knot in his throat tightened. "I don't want

it to end like this, and I don't think you do either."

He took another step forward, almost close enough to touch her, but she spun around, ran across the narrow pier, and dove into the lake. When Lumiana resurfaced, she was gasping for air.

"What the hell is your problem?" He was so confused he started laughing. And he'd been right about her too—she was the kid that went over the fence first, a rebel child. Despite himself, he jumped into the shockingly cold lake.

As soon as he reached her, he grabbed her, but she struggled against him like a slippery fish. Grateful his feet could reach the ground, Johnny held her tight until she stopped moving, then loosened his grip. His body felt as if it housed an ant colony. There was a fierce spark in her eyes, the water dripping from her long eyelashes like raindrops from reeds. "Seriously, what were you —"

Her mouth captured his, muffling his words.

For an instant everything fell away.

Her soft lips flitted against his in harmony with the motions of the water. It was beauty incarnate. Delicate, but with a bright fire simmering below the surface.

Slowly, his surroundings seeped back into his consciousness—the cool water lapping against his skin, the rustling trees, the rays of sunshine warming the back of his head.

Then she pulled back.

Johnny stared at her, bewildered. "What the...
Why did you do that?"

"I'm terribly sorry," she said, wavering. "This
is so unlike me."

"Maybe you like me more than you care to
admit."

"I don't know anything anymore." She swirled
around, and without giving him the chance to
say anything else, she swam toward the dock.

4

THE WATERS OF MARCH

*"True healing is not the fixing of the broken,
but the rediscovery of the unbroken..."*

—JEFF FOSTER

They didn't speak again until Lumiana tossed a denim waffle towel at Johnny, both of them avoiding eye contact as they stripped off their wet clothes. Once he'd wrapped the towel around his midriff, Johnny walked up to her. "If it makes you feel any better, I probably would've kissed you if you hadn't kissed me first."

"That doesn't make me feel any better at all." Her face, however, looked less tense.

Johnny nudged her toward the house.

"Promise me we'll never speak of this again,"

she said as they went inside. "It was a one-time thing, a momentary lapse of judgment."

Thanks, how flattering.

Johnny kept walking until she grabbed his arm.

He spun around, booming, "Stop saying never. There's always uncertainty, and as a woman of science you should know that."

She had one hell of a grip, he noted as he tried to shake her off. "And maybe I don't want this to be a one-time thing. We might feel the urge to do it again. Why shouldn't we act on it?"

She let go of his arm. "If you feel the 'urge,'" she air-quoted, "please don't act on it. In fact, from now on, let's keep an arm's length between us at all times."

"That's ridiculous!"

The glare Lumiana shot him could've restored melting ice caps.

"Fine," he muttered, "arm's length."

***

They ate dinner in silence while Lumiana kept obsessing about the thread count and manufacturing process of her cloth napkins. She didn't dare look at Johnny or his mouth. Her faulty brain wasn't allowed to analyze that one.

Once they cleared the dishes, Johnny suggested a jam session. The rational part of her knew it was a dangerous idea because his voice touched something deep inside her, and she had to keep her distance. But even his talking voice, low and raspy, sounded like music. She wished she could pick up her favorite books and have him read them to her.

"Come on, Doc, what better way is there to get your mind off things?"

Since Jayjay's sudden death, making music had been her favorite form of therapy, allowing her to transform her pain into something beautiful. Maybe she needed this more than she needed the distance.

Wanting to forget the past hour, Lumiana led Johnny downstairs to the basement, where she kept her instruments. Her Steinway grand piano took center stage in the room, which was decorated with framed vintage posters of Stevie Wonder, Elvis Presley, Aretha Franklin, and Michael Jackson.

"I have the perfect song for you," she said, leafing through a pile of sheet music. "Do you know Toby Lightman's 'Everyday?'"

Johnny shook his head.

"It's one of my favorites. What she sings about reminds me of you." She took a sheet and sat at the piano.

"Can we waive your arm's-length rule for a moment?" he asked, gesturing at the two-seater. "It's impossible with a bench of this size."

She patted the velvet seat cushion. "The rule only applies when we're facing each other."

Johnny sat next to her, puckering his lips as he

leaned closer. "Right, because it's so hard to kiss you when I sit next to you."

She saw the flaw in her logic but chose to ignore it. Instead, she hit the piano keys and sang about the struggle between wanting to speak honestly and not wanting to hurt the people around her. Johnny joined in after the chorus, and they finished the song with their voices combining so harmonically Lumiana couldn't deny how much joy she felt.

"Your voice is very beautiful," she told Johnny, glancing down at her fingers, then up at him when he gave her a gentle nudge.

"Thanks." He smiled at her.

Johnny was beautiful too, the kind of beauty depicted in western cultures' twenty-first century romance novels: tall, well-built and virile, with capable hands, big feet, and a face as striking as his abs.

"Can you keep still for a sec?" he asked, his arm grazing hers.

"Why?" But before she could protest, he kissed her on the cheek. "Stop being so nice to me," she ordered because he made her stomach flutter. She didn't want to have a physical reaction to him. She shouldn't be having a physical reaction to him in the first place.

"Another song?"

She nodded. "Do you have something in mind?"

"How about 'It Ain't Over 'Til It's Over?'"

Johnny did a remarkable Lenny Kravitz impression as he sang the first line of the chorus.

She frowned at the suggestive song title but knew her disapproving facial expressions didn't have the same effect on Johnny as they had on others. He liked them. There was clearly something wrong with him.

"Let me think..." His brow knitted in concentration.

Much to her dismay, it looked both cute and sexy on him, so she trained her gaze on the piano keys. Up until the 1950s, piano keys were made from elephant tusks. There, that disturbing fact sufficiently tampered her newly awakened libido.

"You like it old school, right?" He tapped her thigh because she refused to look at him. "So how about 'Ain't No Mountain High Enough?' It's a love song, but—"

Lumiana belted out the song's famous first lines. Because she took Marvin Gaye's part, Johnny was stuck with Tammi Terrell's and had a little fun with it. He made her laugh, and in that regard he was a lot like Jayjay.

***

"Would you like to go for a swim?" Lumiana suggested when they made their way back upstairs.

How long had they been down there, Johnny wondered because the rest of the house was plunged in darkness except for a dim light in the hallway.

Lumiana made no move to turn on the overhead lights. She just looked at him, apparently serious about her night swimming idea. He hadn't seen a pool, and if she thought he'd go swimming in that bone-chilling lake in the middle of the night, she was crazier than he thought—and possibly trying to dispose of his body.

"Are you seriously asking me to jump into that cold lake with you again?"

"No, not the lake." Taking his hand, she told him to close his eyes. "I want to show you something, but it's better if you don't see until we're there. You will like it, I promise."

Against his better judgment, Johnny closed his eyes and let her guide him outside. "If you throw me into the lake, I'll take you with me, just so you know."

The cool air sent shivers across his back, a stark contrast to the warmth of Lumiana's hand. Leaves rustled, and the ground felt springy under his shoes. He took a peek but in the dark he could only make out the outlines of shrubs and trees.

Once they arrived, Lumiana instructed him to face the trees and look straight ahead. His eyes adjusted. There was a bit more light now that they were standing on what appeared to be a meadow. "Take off your clothes," she said, undressing in front of him. He wondered if Lumiana was a traditional naturist, but how could he ask without sounding like a playboy or a prude.

"What are you waiting for?" she said, obviously thinking it was normal to undress here. Outdoors. On a field. With a stranger.

"Turn around." Better to sound like a prude than admit her lovely bottom made "Baby Got Back" run through his mind.

She rolled her eyes, but complied. "It's not like you have something I haven't seen before."

"Debatable." He took off his clothes. "Now what?"

"Close your eyes and turn around."

He sighed, turned, and heard the splash of water.

"Extend your foot." She linked her wet hand with his to keep him steady.

His foot slid over smooth stone and into surprisingly warm water.

"Put your hand on my shoulder and step down. It isn't deep."

Her skin was warm and soft, he noted as he splayed his fingers over her collarbone and lingered. His large hand covered a lot of skin.

"Ready?" she asked, her voice a little husky.

Johnny slipped in beside her. The water smelled of sulfur, but with its heat he felt like being swaddled in clouds. His stomach fluttered when Lumiana laid a hand on his cheek.

His lips parted.

"Open your eyes."

He gazed at her. With a delighted smile, she pointed at the sky. Johnny held his breath when he saw the sparkling sea of light hanging above them like a crystal-studded blanket.

"This is incredible," he murmured, grazing Lumiana's thigh in search of her hand.

They sat in silence for a while, entranced.

"You know what amazes me, other than this stunning view?" Johnny inched closer to her. "You're so comfortable in your own skin. That's rare these days." Lumiana was fit, but she wasn't slender. Yet she confidently bared it all: from her beautiful curves to the many scars that marked her limbs.

"I guess it's one of the advantages of growing up isolated. I wasn't exposed to all this nonsense about what is considered beautiful, or how obsessed people are with their appearance." She told him that Esperanza's cabin didn't have mirrors and that she wasn't even sure what she looked like until she moved in with Candela's family. "We all have different bone structure, and different hair and skin. 'One size fits all' doesn't exist. So why aspire to some abstract concept of beauty?"

Sitting up straight, she scooped her hair back, the swell of her breasts rising above the water. "I'm grateful I was taught to love and respect my body, including the parts that don't fit our society's beauty standard. But most people aren't as lucky. I remember Candela and I had a poster in our room that said, *You don't need bigger boobs. You need to read better books.*"

"You sure don't need bigger boobs," he pointed out and received a few splashes of hot spring water in the face.

After their bath in geothermal waters and a quick rinse under the outdoor shower, Lumiana led Johnny to the upstairs guest room. They paused at the door, glancing at each other without quite making eye contact.

What a day, he thought, sliding his hand along his jaw. He couldn't remember the last time he'd done so many strange and wonderful things. His new album was going to write itself. Adam had no idea what a favor he'd done for him.

"You're a remarkable person, Lumiana."

She leaned in to give him a kiss on the cheek. Her warm lips against his skin stirred something in him. He needed to get away from her, and fast, before he did something stupid. Like taking her up against the wall.

"I—goodnight."

Fleeing into the guest room, he shut the door and lay down on the bed.

He thought of their kiss, her body pressed to his, her curious eyes. When the sun had illuminated her face, he saw the lighter one was green, and the other a darker brown. Both had flecks of gold in them, and a dark border that brought out the striking colors.

And then there was this spark in them, angry and daring. He should've seen the kiss coming. She'd caught him off guard, or he would've tried to make it even more memorable.

He shook his head and groaned.

Get it together, man. She didn't want him in her life, and he needed to respect that.

***

Lumiana stared at the closed guest room door. Johnny had been calling her Doc or Dr. Harding all weekend, but the way he said Lumiana sent little shivers across her skin. She couldn't believe she kissed him, or that she'd almost kissed him again just now, because her lips hadn't aimed for his cheek.

Lumiana went to her bedroom and dove onto the bed. The moment she closed her eyes, she was jolted back to the lake. But this time, when her lips touched his, they lingered.

How did he do it? How did he make her so crazy? This wasn't her. He wasn't Jayjay.

Lumiana jumped to her feet and stormed out of the room, her nails digging into her palms. By the time she banged on the guest room door, her muscles were so tight, she felt like she was going to implode.

Johnny opened the door, and she strode past him into the room. "Why are you doing this to me?" She shoved him so hard he backed into the dresser. She wanted to hurt him, but when she was about to lunge, he grabbed her and held on.

Her arms rose and folded around his neck. *What am I doing here?*

He uttered "Lu—" before she pulled him into a kiss brimming with suppressed lust and frustration.

Why can't I stop?

He tasted so good—too good—his lips soft yet demanding, unyielding. Like they were fighting for the upper hand, in the most exquisite of ways.

Their breathing grew heavy as she pinned him with her hips, inadvertently increasing the pulsing pressure between her thighs.

"Johnny—" she panted, her heart racing.

His arm snaked around her waist as he drew her into another tango of lips and tongues so divinely executed part of her didn't want him to stop. His hand slid farther down, cupping her backside, increasing the pressure until she writhed with need.

She pushed against his chest. "Johnny, I can't." If they didn't stop grinding against each other, she'd come.

Kisses interspersed with moans. She was so close. His hands kneaded her bottom, his fingertips digging in at the juncture of her thighs. He was driving her out of her mind.

"Sorry," he rasped, loosening his grip the moment she came. "It's okay."

She burrowed her forehead into his chest, waiting for the last ripples of pleasure to fade, hoping he hadn't noticed how much he affected her. "Nothing is okay."

He caressed the side of her face. "I don't know what you want me to say."

Every cell in her body had conspired against her, trying to get closer to him. She forced herself to take a step back. "I hate what you are doing to me."

Extending his hand, he stroked along her shoulder and arm, making her skin bloom with goosebumps. "Your body doesn't seem to hate it."

"That's not what I meant." She ran her fingers over her mussed hair. "I mean—"

"I know what you mean, Lumiana."

She surprised herself when she admitted, "I don't want to sleep alone."

He huffed. "You're killing me, Doc."

She linked her hand with his and led him to her bedroom.

***

The next morning, Lumiana gave a sigh of relief when she remembered all she and Johnny had done in her bed the night before was hold hands and fall asleep.

Her head was on his shoulder, and because it was right there, she nuzzled his neck. She liked the feel of him, except it was a lot like lying on a heating blanket. Not only was he making her sweat, her fingers itched to touch him.

Carefully, she slid her hand under his shirt. His skin was smooth beneath her hand as she brushed over his abs and up to his chest. She lingered, feeling the hardening nub of his nipple under her fingertips. Until he stirred.

She tried to retrieve her hand, but Johnny swiftly covered it with his.

"It's okay," he said, tightening his grip around her waist.

She let him hold her a little longer. "This will never work."

"How do you know?" He trailed his fingers along her shoulder, kissed her forehead.

His gentleness was melting her defenses, and she couldn't have that. "Please, Johnny, let it go." With that, she got up and went to the bathroom.

***

How could someone so smart be so obtuse, Johnny thought as he lay there, staring at the ceiling.

Lumiana came back ten minutes later but paused in front of the bed.

He held her gaze for a few moments before he spoke. "Whether you admit it or not, whatever this thing is between us, it's not one-sided. You feel it too." He studied her face. "I could've explained it away—you kissing me when you get all riled up because it's been so long since you've been with someone. But the way you touched me earlier, that was different, that was deliberate."

She sat on the bed. She didn't speak but gave a small nod.

"Then why can't we act on our mutual attraction?"

She stared at her feet for a moment before she looked him in the eye. "Physical intimacy may be a recreational activity for you, but for me it's something I have only shared with the one man who meant everything to me."

He put his hand on her bare leg. "I can't change that I've slept with more than one woman. Not everyone is as lucky as you to find the one so early on in life."

She pushed his hand off her leg. "Yes, lucky me, losing the one person I loved most in the world before I even reached my thirties."

"Isn't it better to have loved and lost than never to have loved at all?"

"I'd like to slap the person who came up with that phrase."

"It's from Alfred, Lord Tennyson's poem 'In Memoriam A.H.H.' I'm afraid you missed your chance. He died in 1892."

Lumiana glared at him, but there had been a flash of surprise mixed in there too.

"I minored in English literature," he said, lifting his hands. "Sorry, go ahead."

She drew a deep breath. "You can't imagine how painful it is to lose the person you love, to never be able to speak to or touch them ever again. I can't survive another loss. So tell me, Johnny, how can I be with someone when the people I love keep dying and I'm always the one who is left behind?"

He reached for her, but she resisted.

"Tell me," she demanded, a tear rolling down her cheek. She quickly wiped it away.

"I don't know," he admitted, pulling at his ear. "But isolating yourself from the world and from people, not letting anyone in, can't be good for you either, at least not for the long term."

"And you know that how, Dr. Freud?"

"I know how often I've felt lonely... Come on, Doc, you know people get weird when they're alone—" He regretted those words as soon as they left his mouth.

Her eyes sparked with fury. "Are you saying that—"

"No. And you're not isolated in that sense. You have your family. Look, I'm not the right person to give you advice on how to open yourself up to love again after what you've been through. Hell, I suck at relationships. I'm not sure I've ever really loved someone. But you're going to miss out on so much joy and pleasure if you lock that part of your heart."

He took her hand, and this time she let him hold it. "I wish I could promise I'm never going to hurt you, or die on you, but that's not realistic— the people we love can hurt us the most." Wasn't he the prime example? "And what about your philosophy, 'I choose to be happy and therefore I am?'"

"I do, I just choose to be happy alone."

Was that even possible? Don't all people crave companionship? "You know what bothers me?" he said, tapping her knee. "You make it sound like it wouldn't mean anything to me if we slept together. Contrary to what most people believe, I don't have sex just to pass time, or to add another name to my list of 'conquests.' Not all rock stars fuck everything that moves—I don't anyway."

He was glad he made that clear because some of the tension left her body. "It's rare to feel a strong connection with someone within such a short time. I wish we could see where it leads. I feel different with you than I do with others, and I don't mean just other women. You're special to me, not an item on my 'to do' list."

Lumiana covered his hand with hers. "I appreciate what you are saying, but it doesn't feel right to be that intimate with you when it's something I associate with unconditional, 'I wish I could be with you forever' love."

"Right, and it can't be me because I attract too much attention." Obviously, she couldn't read his sarcasm because she nodded like it was fact. So he swallowed his disappointment—what else could he do? "I hope someday you find someone like that again."

Lumiana touched her lips to his.

So not fair. She tasted of coconut, or maybe it

was the scent of her skin.

"I could do this all day," he said as she released him. "Talking about it wasn't so hard now, was it?" He smoothed out the furrowed space between her brows.

She pinched him in the side, smiling.

As Johnny pulled off his shirt and headed for the shower, Lumiana caught him by the arm and hugged him tight. Her skin against his electrified him. He tried to move around her, but she held on, pressing her hips against his. "What's that for?"

"For being so understanding and sweet, and for being right. Talking about it made me feel better."

"Um, great, Lu. You need to move though, you're, you know—"

Biting her lip, she rubbed against his morning glory.

The good doctor had a naughty streak, who would've thought. He gave her a less than tender kiss. "Like I said, I could do this all day."

5

CURSE ME GOOD

*"Love your suffering.
Do not resist it, do not flee from it.
It is your aversion that hurts, nothing else."*

—HERMANN HESSE

Although Lumiana's ankle still bothered her, she couldn't sit around until they finished clearing the road. Being idle around Johnny led to kissing, and there had already been more kissing than she intended, so they had to stay in motion. Which was why, after breakfast, Lumiana packed her knapsack, and they set out on the short hike to the large rock at the east end of her property.

Even after five years of living here, the lush landscape never ceased to amaze her. The rolling coastal hills, the bigberry manzanita shrubs, the clean air. Her list of favorites was as abundant as the region's native plants.

Sticking with her ritual, Lumiana took a deep, deliberate breath. Usually it grounded her, but Johnny was walking so close to her their hands brushed. To resist temptation, she stretched her arms behind her back.

He chuckled.

"What?" She frowned at him.

"I could almost hear you arguing with yourself whether it would be a good idea to take my hand."

Coming to a halt, she propped her hands on her hips. "I certainly did not."

"You're a terrible liar, Doc. Either you lack practice or you have no clue how expressive your body language is."

Lumiana bit her tongue and walked ahead of him, but stopped shortly before they reached the rock when Johnny belted out the first few lines from Dion and the Belmonts' "A Teenager In Love."

"Interesting song choice."

"You must admit our encounter has a bit of a first crush quality." Johnny took her hands. "We're doing all these low-cost, old-school romantic activities, like singing in the rain, skinny-dipping, star-gazing, on what appears to be the longest first date in history. Then there's the seemingly unintentional touching, although you're secretly hoping for more. Holding hands, being all excited about getting to first base."

He kissed her to demonstrate his point, effectively weakening her knees. "The only thing missing is carving our initials into a tree with a little heart around it."

Grinning, she pointed at the coastal live oak behind him, which had names and dates engraved in the bark. "Most of them are from my family. Everyone who climbed the rock has carved something."

"Look, it has a—" Johnny pointed at the J + L inside a heart. "Jayjay and Lumiana, of course. I'm sorry. I didn't mean to taint your memories."

She gave him a hug. "It's not a memory. Jayjay passed away before I moved here. Someone else carved that into the tree for us." She opened her backpack and took out a pocket knife. "Here," she handed it to Johnny, "Carve your name and the date, so I have something to remember you by."

Johnny eternalized himself in the bark. It was fascinating to watch him as he did it with the enthusiasm of a Boy Scout and the precision of a surgeon.

"We need to climb up this tree to get to the top of the rock. Are you okay with that?"

"Hell yeah." He studied the tree. "You go first."

"Are you afraid?"

"No, but this way I can check out your butt."

She glowered at him, then climbed up first, convinced he was scared.

***

The view from the top of the rock was incredible, Johnny thought as he took it all in. Shrubs and trees, steep hills, plains covered in wildflowers and perennial grasses—like something out of a Kirichenko Gennadiy painting, but with the vibrancy of an Afremov.

Lumiana told him it was one of her favorite places and that she came up here whenever she needed to clear her mind. He could see why. Her land was serene, remote, and mostly undisturbed.

Johnny wrapped Lumiana in his arms.

Like she had done the afternoon they met, she put her ear to his chest.

"Are you listening to my heartbeat again?"

She tried moving away from him.

"It's okay. Go ahead," he said, holding on to her. "I was just wondering why you like doing this so much." She'd blindsided him when she did the same thing in her office, but he could tell even then that she did it because it had special meaning and not because she felt attracted to him.

Lumiana sighed. "Are you sure you wish to hear this? It will ruin the mood."

"I'll take my chances."

"When I was little my mother kept me close to her heart as often as possible. It was her way of showing me everything was going to be okay.

Esperanza, the old woman who found me in the woods, was the same. And later when I was with Jayjay, I listened to his heartbeat every night—it became my favorite lullaby. But when he died…" Lumiana pressed her fingers to her brow.

"You don't need to tell me if it's too painful."

She placed her hand over his heart. "When you confronted me in my office and I tried to push you away, your heart was beating so strongly, it jolted me back to the last time I felt Jayjay's heartbeat. I wasn't thinking. I just wanted to hold on to that memory."

Reaching for his hand, she brought it to his heart and covered it with hers. "I like listening to your heartbeat not only because it calms me, but also because it tells me how you feel. People lie and deceive all the time, but the heartbeat is pure. It's how I know you care about me, and why I trust you as much as I do."

He wanted to kiss her so bad. And not those sweet, innocent kisses either. He wanted the real deal—all that pent-up lust and passion he knew Lumiana had inside her. If only he could find the right thread to unravel it all.

"Now I want to try this myself," he said, eyeing her chest, wishing he could touch her there.

Following his gaze, she shook her head.

"Come on, Lu, that's not fair." He drew her closer.

She laughed, but took a step back. "I don't trust you that much." She gave him a bright smile. And because that sight aroused him even more, he put some distance between them. He didn't want to pressure her into something she wasn't ready for. But the more time he spent with her, the harder it was to ignore how much he wanted to get caught up in her.

Lumiana stepped closer. He stopped her and took another step back.

"Can you please go over there?" He pointed to the other side of the rock. "I need a moment to myself."

"Did I do something wrong?" she asked, looking genuinely clueless.

"Please, just go." Putting his hands on her shoulders, he turned her around.

"Fine, as you wish." She stalked over to the other side of the rock.

It wasn't just the physical attraction. He liked spending time with her and that was getting in the way of his actual goal. Time was running out, and he still didn't know how to convince her to help him with his album.

Johnny took a profound breath. Standing there talking to himself wasn't going to achieve anything.

"Are you feeling better?" she said as he approached her.

"No. You're driving me nuts!" Johnny strode past her and started to climb down the tree. In a moment of distraction, he slipped. He reached out to break his fall and his arm snagged on a branch, which prevented him from tumbling all the way down but cut deep into his skin.

As he half-fell the rest of the way, smaller branches ripped his clothes and slapped him across his cheek and forehead.

Back on the ground, he pounded his fist against the tree's trunk in agony and frustration.

"You're bleeding," Lumiana noted when she caught up with him. "Let me see."

He resisted, but she overpowered him easily, and then examined the gaping four-inch gash on his right forearm. "You need stitches."

"I thought you're a doctor of anthropology, not medicine."

"My brother is a surgeon. He taught me a few things. And even if he hadn't, have you seen how many scars I have?"

Lumiana helped him to his feet, took off her cotton scarf, and firmly wrapped it around his arm. Then she got her phone from her backpack and called someone.

"Are you home?" she said once the call connected. "I need you to come over. It's an emergency. Bring your gear." She hung up, taking him by the hand. "Come, you need an actual doctor."

They rushed back to her house, and when they came through the patio doors, there was a tall, sturdy guy in gym clothes sitting at the kitchen counter, a duffel bag propped on the stool next to him.

The man frowned at them. "What the hell,

Lumi? It's my day off."

Based on the man's slight accent, Johnny pegged him as Caribbean.

When the man noticed Johnny's bleeding arm, his annoyance turned into concern. "Shit." He pulled out a bar stool so Johnny could sit.

"Johnny Graham, meet Dr. Garon Arcus Young," Lumiana introduced them. "We call him Gus."

"Johnny Graham? Wait, isn't he the musician who—" Gus winced when Lumiana socked him in the arm. "Seriously, Lumi? How did that happen?"

"Some people don't take no for an answer." She chewed on the side of her bottom lip. "Can you help him or not?"

"Of course I can. Did you do that to him?"

"Gus, please, help him before he passes out."

"Thanks, Lu," Johnny muttered, because she might not be so far off. This was the most blood he'd ever seen, and it was oozing out of him.

"Lu, huh?" Gus grinned as he unwrapped the scarf. "You got a thing for my little sister?"

Her brother. Great. "Does my answer affect my treatment?"

Lumiana looked over her brother's shoulder. "Gus is among the country's most accomplished surgeons. He wouldn't do anything foolish."

Gus nodded. "She's right. I'm pretty exceptional."

"And oh so modest." Lumiana dropped a kiss

on the top of his perfectly shaved head. Seeing her interact with someone she loved was interesting. Somehow it made her less peculiar.

"First I need to clean the wound." After washing his hands, Gus put on a pair of latex gloves, and positioned Johnny's arm on a sterile pad.

"Can I do it?" Lumiana asked as she turned on the overhead light and washed her hands.

Gus handed her a set of gloves, and she put them on. Johnny cringed when she cleaned the gash.

"Argh, fuck. I really hate you right now," he gasped, clenching his fists.

Lumiana glared at him. "Sorry if that hurts—"

"If?" He bit his knuckle. He wasn't a violent man, but when she finished with his arm and moved on to dab his face with an alcohol-soaked cotton swab, he wanted to give her a hard shove.

"I can't imagine it's much worse than getting your tattoos," she said, turning to her brother who'd just finished setting up his tools. "Can I stitch him up?"

"Hell no." Johnny batted her away. His whole body hurt. It was nothing like getting his tattoos.

Gus pointed at a ragged scar on Lumiana's leg. "See this? She stitched this up herself."

"You're crazy," Johnny said to Lumiana before he turned to Gus, who was covering his right arm with a sterile drape. "I'll pay you a generous fee if you keep her away from me."

"Nah, it's fine. It's on the house." Gus numbed

the slash, took forceps from a tray, and threaded the curved needle, then inserted it into the skin, placing the first stitch in the center of the wound. Meticulously, he sewed suture after suture to close the wound edges. Once he finished, he wrapped Johnny's arm in a bandage.

Johnny thanked Gus, and declined the Percocet Gus offered, despite still being in severe pain.

Gus examined him from head to toe. "The rest looks like scrapes and bruises... Hey, is that my shirt?" If it was, there wasn't much left of it that wasn't torn or blood-soaked. He eyed Lumiana, who shrugged innocently. Gus extended him a hand. "Johnny, nice to meet you. Go see your doctor for a follow-up. Sis, I can't wait to hear the full story."

As soon as they were alone in the house, Lumiana brought him a glass of water and four ibuprofen.

He shook his head.

"If you don't want to take something for the pain because you think you have to prove that you are a tough guy, you're not as smart as I think you are."

Reluctantly, he took the pills. Easier than admitting his family staged an intervention a few years ago after he'd gotten a little too dependent on Vicodin and booze following an accident with his father's Porsche.

They headed over to the living room, but Lumiana stopped him before he could make himself comfortable. "Don't sit down yet. I'll get you clean clothes."

She came back a few minutes later and helped him change. He was grateful for the sweatpants but there was no way he'd put on another shirt before the painkillers kicked in.

"Gus just texted that they are almost done clearing the road. You can go home soon," Lumiana told him, and headed back to the kitchen.

Johnny didn't want their time together to end like this, but he was in too much pain to follow her. Instead, he lay down on the couch and closed his eyes.

***

Satisfied with the spiciness of her enchilada, Lumiana put the casserole in the oven and went upstairs to take a shower. She hadn't noticed the bloodstains on her own clothes until she saw herself in the full-length mirror.

What was she thinking, taking Johnny up that rock? He was a city boy who grew up in a Beverly Hills mansion, climbing that tree may have been a first for him. With all their differences, she thought as she undressed, it was surprising they understood each other at all.

After her shower, Lumiana checked on Johnny, who'd fallen asleep on the couch. She took a moment to appreciate his handsome face and athletic body, fighting the urge to touch him.

He looked peaceful but also rough enough with the scraped and unshaven skin to give her an unwelcome bout of primal lust.

When she sat next to him, he stirred and turned onto his side. She considered rereading Morrison's *Song of Solomon*, but felt too itchy to concentrate.

On her tenth glance at him, she noticed an error in the tattoo on his left shoulder blade.

Taking two steps over to one of the floor-to-ceiling shelves, she scanned the titles until she found the book on eighteenth-century Japanese art. And she was right, the *Tōji San Bijin*—Three Beauties of the Present Day—were missing their emblems.

Lumiana returned to the sofa and inspected his other tattoos. Johnny had more than she'd ever seen on one person, but they were aesthetically pleasing. And the artistry was impressive, all that detail!

His tattoos leaned heavily toward Japanese art. Probably Adam's influence, she mused, knowing Adam Tsukino was not only her brother's best friend since childhood but also Johnny's. Whoever designed these tattoos, knew what they were doing.

That moment, Johnny moved his arm and touched her face. She let out a squeal.

"Enjoying yourself?" He smirked. "What about the arm's-length rule?"

Lumiana tried to squirm away, but Johnny

grabbed her with his uninjured arm and pulled her onto him, trailing kisses along her neck and shoulder. Just as his hand slid up her thigh, the oven timer went off.

With a huff, Lumiana freed herself from his grip.

"Saved by the bell." Johnny sighed, resting his arm on his forehead.

Lumiana hurried to the kitchen. She wasn't sure whether she felt more relieved or disappointed about the interruption. And then it hit her. How could she betray Jayjay? He'd been her soulmate, and now she was tainting their sacred bond by offering herself to Johnny Graham, just like who knew how many women had done before her? Was that who she was?

As she tried to get the casserole out of the oven, she burned her hand and cursed out loud. *Wearing gloves might have been a sensible idea.*

A few moments later, Johnny joined her in the kitchen.

She was still holding her hand under cold water when he touched her arm.

"Are you all right?"

She flinched away. They needed to stop touching. It not only impaired her ability to think but also to follow her routines, and that was dangerous. Her brain didn't work the way most people's brains did.

Lumiana brought her hand to her forehead. Why did it have to feel so good to touch him, and to be touched by him?

She blew out a big breath, wishing she could just go to sleep.

He'll be gone soon, she reminded herself. Another hour, and she'd never have to see him again. But that thought didn't feel right either.

Leaning against the sink, she said, "I'm fine."

"Your hand doesn't look fine." When he tried to inspect her injury, she pulled her hand away. "Sorry. I just want to help."

"I don't need your help." She scooped an enchilada onto each plate and handed one to Johnny without looking at him.

They sat on the counter, eating another meal in silence.

Lumiana's behavior on the couch continued to gnaw at her conscience until Johnny reached for a glass on the shelf above her, displaying his chiseled muscles up close. She nearly choked on her enchilada.

"You okay?" he said with a grin as she coughed into the crook of her arm.

"Put on a shirt," she demanded, which seemed to amuse him more.

"You were the one telling me I have nothing you haven't seen before."

"Unfortunately, you have something I haven't seen in a long time. And stop laughing," she said as he came closer. She pushed him away. "Please don't tease me. I'm attempting to eat."

Taking a step back, he struck a pose. "Feel

free to touch me anywhere, anytime. I know you want to."

"I want you to put on a shirt!" Lumiana hopped off the counter.

Johnny followed her to the living room so closely he bumped into her when she stopped in front of the coffee table.

"Jesus, Lu." He rubbed the rib that had collided with her elbow. "I have enough bruises, don't you think?"

"Sorry," she murmured, giving him a peck on the cheek.

Tucking his arm around her waist, he kissed the top of her head.

"You need to go now, Johnny."

***

While Johnny changed into his jeans in the laundry room, Lumiana gathered his phone and jacket. Magnum would be waiting for him by the time they got to the community gate.

Crazy that it was Sunday already, he thought, trying to button his jeans with one hand. Even crazier that at the same time he felt like he'd known Lumiana for years. There was something that connected them, which made it even harder to comprehend that this was it, that he'd never see her again.

When Johnny came back to the living room, Lumiana was on the sofa cuddling with her pet pig Kirk. The dog, the cat, and the goose lay by her feet and her tortoise Walter crawled across the coffee table.

Without her noticing, Johnny took a picture of them with his phone. He wanted something to remember her by, and this weirdly wonderful picture captured her essence, her unusual beauty, and her childlike spirit.

"I'll miss you, and all of this," he said, struggling to put on his shirt.

Lumiana got up to help.

"Take a good look at what you'll be missing," he teased.

She took her sweet time pulling down his shirt, sliding her warm hands from his chest down to his abs, leaving goosebumps in their wake.

There was something about her touch, her gaze.

'Intense' would be the word he'd use to describe it. This whole experience had been intense, and exactly what he'd needed. He was sure it was one of those encounters in life that would shape his future, that he would still remember decades from now.

"Do you think you're going to miss me?" he asked as she helped him into his jacket.

She didn't say a word, but kissed him lightly.

"I'll take that as a yes." He tucked her hair behind her ear, exposing the spot he knew would make her come undone if he kissed her there again.

A faint smile played over her lips. "Ready?"

"What choice do I have?" He said goodbye to her little zoo of misfits before Lumiana led them into the spacious vivarium, which was yet another impressive feature of this beautiful house. In one large room, she'd recreated the natural habitat of each of her rescue animals so it housed a pond, a hay shed, a sofa, and even a freaking tree.

No way he'd ever forget her.

They held hands as they strolled down the long driveway a few minutes later. Johnny looked back at her house while Lumiana locked the gate. Its graceful symmetry, deep-set eaves and dark bare wood gave it the timeless quality of a Buddhist temple.

"It's beautiful, isn't it?" he heard someone say behind him.

"Mike." Lumiana gave the man a quick hug. "How is the cleanup going?"

"We're almost done. Took forever to clear the road. How about your house, all good?"

Mike had an accent too, maybe West African in origin.

"I haven't noticed any damage. Thank you for your hard work, Mike. Um, this is Johnny Graham. Johnny, this is Mike, our head of security. He is also in charge of making sure the land remains in pristine condition. Mike owns the house closest to the community gate."

Johnny shook Mike's hand before they said goodbye and continued on their way.

As Johnny and Lumiana followed the narrow gravel road, the sun was setting behind the mountains, painting them in hues of pink. He knew about the pink moment. Witnessing this phenomenon in person was the perfect ending to his accidental weekend adventure.

"Does all this land belong to your family?" He wondered if any of these houses were available. This would be the ideal place for a weekend home —or to record his album.

"One of my sisters inherited the Jonata reservation from her ancestors. She is a conservationist. Her house is the one over there next to Mike's." She nodded toward her right.

Johnny couldn't see much of the house because most of it was covered by some sort of vine with white blossoms that matched the window frames. "Any chance I can buy one of these houses?"

"Absolutely not. All six are occupied."

Well, it was a long shot. But as Oprah would say, 'you get in life what you have the courage to ask for.' And he subscribed to that philosophy.

They walked in silence for a while.

"I feel strange," Johnny said, slowing his pace. "Everything—where you live, you as a person, the past three days—it all seems surreal. I feel like I'm going to wake up tomorrow and find that none of this has actually happened."

"Maybe you lost too much blood."

"You're not taking me seriously," he said, stopping. "You don't feel weird at all?"

She stayed quiet for a moment. "We need to keep going, Johnny. Your car is waiting."

"That's all you have to say?"

"I don't know what to say. I feel... I don't feel anything."

"Okay, great!"

She pulled at her hair. "I don't understand what you are saying."

"This is not the ending I was going for," he said when Lumiana reached for him.

"Don't touch me, please. Let's just go." He started to walk briskly ahead of her. He could already see the red gate.

Lumiana ran in front of him and blocked his way, forcing him to look at her. "I apologize if I did something wrong. Please. I have difficulties reading social cues. You need to be specific when you talk to me."

"I can't believe you're that naive."

"Obviously I am. So please, spell this out for me."

Johnny bowed his head. He didn't know how to explain. "Meeting someone as remarkable as you, having this connection I think we have, that doesn't happen to me very often, if ever." He looked up at the sky. "I was hoping you might feel the same way about me, that you might want to see me again."

She didn't respond.

"Look at me, Lumiana, I'm pouring my heart out and you don't seem even a little sad about never seeing me again—"

"Damn you, Johnny." Lumiana clenched her hands into fists. "You are the first person since the love of my life passed away who has gotten this close to me. And although I don't want to admit this to myself, I enjoyed spending time with you. But I told you why I can't see you again and I need you to respect that."

He needed to talk to Adam. Maybe his best friend could shed some light on what was going on with Lumiana's family that she couldn't risk being seen with him. "You couldn't have led with that answer?"

"I could say the same about you."

They stared at each other for a long time before Lumiana reached for his hand. "I'm sorry," she said, gesturing toward the gate.

"Yeah, me too." He put his uninjured arm around her shoulders.

They walked the rest of the way without talking. There was nothing left to say.

"My bodyguard's here." Magnum had parked a little farther down the road on the other side of the massive steel gate, which opened when Lumiana signaled the guard in the small brick building next to it.

"Thank you, Linus," Lumiana said with a wave.

"You're welcome, Dr. Harding," Linus's voice sounded through the speaker.

They walked down the road but stopped a few yards from the car. Magnum stood leaning against the driver's side, his bulky arms crossed below his chest.

Johnny took her hand.

She blinked back tears. "Please, let's make this quick. I'd rather not cry in front of you."

He wiped the corner of her eye. "Thanks for everything, Doc." He gave her a long kiss, trying to memorize how she felt and tasted.

She cupped his face with her hands. "You should keep the stubble," she said with a small smile. "It suits you."

"I'll keep that in mind." Johnny gave her one more kiss before he joined Mag, who looked like he wanted to strangle him, probably because Johnny had been dodging his calls all weekend.

***

Lumiana ran all the way back to her house and up the stairs, falling face first onto her bed. She could still smell him there.

As she stripped the bedding, she saw the piece of paper lodged under her pillow. Johnny had given his address, email, and phone information, and then wrote:

Lumiana,

I've never met anyone quite like you. I admire how

you see beauty in everything, how strong you are even though life has put you through more hardships than any one person should ever endure. I feel blessed to be one of the few fortunate enough to know you, and I will always remember you for helping me rediscover my sense of wonder.

If you're reading this, it most likely means I wasn't able to convince you that we should see each other again. I wish you would reconsider. Even if we can't work together, I'd still love to be your friend, or at least an acquaintance, or a pen pal. I hope our paths will cross again. Until then, stay as amazing as you are.

Johnny Graham

Lumiana went back downstairs, pressing Johnny's letter to her chest. Curling up on the sofa, she wrapped her arms around the pile of clothes he'd worn, and wept herself to sleep.

PART 2

6

JUST LIKE A PILL

*"By going out of your mind,
you come to your senses."*

—ALAN WATTS

After Johnny said goodbye to Lumiana at the
Jonata community gate, he'd instructed his
bodyguard to drop him off at his ex-girlfriend's
house. Aside from shaking his head, Mag drove
him there without a word.

Yeah, I know, insanity. Johnny couldn't blame
the guy but was in no mood for a lecture.

As they arrived, Magnum quipped, "What,
five time's the charm?"

Johnny showed him the middle finger.

Mag snickered and threw him a military salute before he drove off.

Making his way up to Andie's penthouse condo, Johnny argued with himself that it was either this or getting chummy with a bottle of prescription pain meds.

It was a no-brainer really. Taking the meds brought back memories he didn't want to relive but that had been nagging at the back of his mind ever since Gus had offered him the Percocet.

When Parker died in his arms all those years ago, he'd sworn he'd never touch this stuff again. If he broke his promise now, he didn't know if he could get back up again.

"Johnny, hi, is everything okay?" Andie said when she opened the door. "You look like you had a run-in with a razor blade."

Andie looked stunning in a lacy beige dress with black accents that left little to the imagination. Her long, strawberry blond hair was curled over her shoulder, exposing her pale, delicate neck.

"If this isn't a good time..."

"No, it's good. I'm just surprised to see you," she said, gesturing for him to come inside.

Johnny took two strides, slid his hand into Andie's silky hair, and kissed her with such urgency their breathing grew labored before they even reached the bedroom.

"Take off your dress," he panted as he pinned her against the floor-to-ceiling window overlooking downtown L.A.

Andie turned around for him to unzip it. But because his arm was killing him, and he didn't want to bother taking off his clothes, he pushed her dress up and his pants down. Andie reached around to grab his right arm, and he cried out in pain.

"Are you all right?"

"Ah, yes, I just hurt my arm earlier."

"What happened?"

Talking was the last thing he wanted, so he gripped her hips and when she ground against him, he drove himself into her until he found the release he craved.

Spent, he fell onto her bed and into a restless sleep.

When Johnny woke up early the next morning, Andie was asleep next to him, her hand on his stomach. He kissed her forehead and eased out of bed. He shouldn't have come here, to take from her what the woman he wanted to be with wasn't able to give him.

Borrowing a pen and paper from her desk drawer, he wrote an apologetic note and left it on the kitchen counter.

The sun was coming up as Johnny lumbered out onto the sidewalk. Squinting, he tugged his phone from his pocket and scrolled through the contacts.

Fucking hell. His arm hurt so much, he flirted

with the idea of digging up the bottle of Vicodin he'd buried in his backyard. *Don't go there, man.*

Forcing himself to remember Parker's lifeless body, he called the concierge doctor he kept on retainer. And then he beat himself up some more, because the latter was what he should've done in the first place.

***

Lumiana woke at noon that day, her eyes burning as though she had stared at the sun for too long. Hearing the animals scratching at the door, she plodded over to the vivarium and let them out. They scampered around her as she headed for the kitchen, where she scraped the last few bites out of the casserole.

Her phone rang.

"Hi, *angelito*." Lumiana wanted to sound chipper but failed miserably.

"Are you all right, *mamá*? You sound sad."

"I'm fine, Ana," she assured her daughter as she fed the animals.

"Where are you? You're late."

She cursed under her breath. "I'm terribly sorry, Ana. I'm coming right away." How could she forget to pick up her daughter, especially after she hadn't seen her for a week?

Lumiana grabbed her keys and staggered into the garage, wearing only Jayjay's oversized UCLA sweatshirt.

Dammit, wrong keys.

Her vintage Peugeot wasn't in the garage. *It's still at the institute!*

Pressing her palm against her throbbing forehead, she muttered another curse and went back inside to get the keys for her battered SUV. As long as she didn't think about why her Peugeot wasn't where it was supposed to be, she'd be fine.

"Ana!" Lumiana ran over to her daughter, who was waiting in front of the rural Waldorf school, a fifteen-minute drive from home. Tears came to her eyes when she caught Ana in a fierce embrace.

"*Mamá*, you're suffocating me," Ana said with a soft laugh.

"I missed you so much." She kissed Ana on the forehead when she wrapped her arms around her neck.

"I missed you too."

Lumiana led Ana to the car, then held the door for her.

Once they buckled their seat belts, she asked her daughter about her class trip to a family-owned farm in Northern California. If there was one thing Ana excelled at, it was painting a picture.

"First tell me why you forgot to pick me up," her daughter demanded. "And why you sounded so sad on the phone. And why you are dressed like this. Where are your pants?"

At seven years old, Ana was a bright, quirky

kid with the soul of an old wise woman.

"I promise I will tell you, Ana, but I cannot do this right now. I have to concentrate on driving." Plus she needed time to think of a response.

Ana sulked for a moment before she launched into an account of her week-long adventure. Like Lumiana, Ana had the ability to captivate people with her colorful storytelling. She described in painstaking detail the birth of a calf and how everyone scrunched their noses because they had never smelled anything like it. And because Ana was the only one who had the guts to watch the whole procedure up close, she got to pick the calf's name. She called it Amaterasu after the Shinto goddess of the sun, who happened to be one of her latest obsessions.

Back home, their excited animals greeted them. Ana cuddled them one after the other while Lumiana went into her daughter's room to unpack her suitcase.

She frowned at the random items Ana had brought home: a fist-sized clover leaf, a snail shell with the snail still in it, and an old Christmas card of the Obamas. It wasn't the first time she'd returned with unusual souvenirs.

Last year, on their way back from a cruise to Mexico, port authority had stopped them because Ana had fourteen socks filled with sand in her suitcase. 'How do you explain this, young lady?' the officer had asked. With a sweet smile,

Ana had told them that she loved the way the Mexican sand felt between her toes, and that she wanted to have a small tub by her bed where she could enjoy it every morning.

"*Mamá*," she heard Ana shout from the living room. "Why are there clothes with blood on the sofa? And who is Johnny Graham?"

In her haste to pick up Ana, she had forgotten to hide the evidence of Johnny's visit.

Lumiana rushed over to the living room, where Ana was reading Johnny's letter out loud to the animals, who seemed to be listening attentively.

"Please do not read this." Lumiana yanked the letter out of Ana's hands.

"Why not?" Ana crossed her arms.

"Because I said so." And because she knew this t-shirt slogan wasn't a good way to handle the situation, she sat opposite her pouting daughter and apologized. "Something happened while you were on your trip, but I'm not sure how to tell you about it."

Ana took her hand. "Who is Johnny Graham, *mamá*?"

"Do you remember before your trip when I played you a few songs by a musician who wanted to work with me, but I said I was not interested? He came to see me a few days ago. He stayed here at the house."

Ana buzzed with excitement, then narrowed her eyes. "Is that his blood?" She pointed at the pile of clothes.

Lumiana nodded.

"Did you kill him?"

"Of course not," exclaimed Lumiana, torn between shock and laughter. "Why would you say that?"

"You said something happened. Why did he bleed so much?"

"He had an accident!"

Ana covered her mouth with her little hands, her eyes wide open. "Is he dead? Is that why you're so sad?"

"No. He cut his arm when he fell off the tree next to the rock."

"Is he your boyfriend?" Ana's eyes filled with what looked like hope.

Lumiana still found it hard to read faces, but after all these years she'd become quite adept at interpreting her daughter's. "Why would you think that?"

"He wrote you a very nice letter." Ana grinned. "Do you like him? Can I meet him?"

Lumiana shook her head, and Ana's expression turned somber. "Why are you disappointed?"

"I want you to be happy, *mamá*. I want you to have someone who can be with you when I'm not here."

Her daughter had too much insight for a child her age. Lumiana wondered whether it was genetics or history repeating itself. After all, she was raising Ana the same way her parents and Esperanza had raised her: surrounded by books and nature.

"I am happy, Ana. I don't need someone to take care of me, and it's not like you are moving out anytime soon. You're only seven years old."

"Is it because of *papá*? I'm sure he wants you to be with someone. Shawn said so too."

Lumiana made a mental note to scold her brother. "I love your father very much even though he's gone. I don't want to be with anyone else." She blinked at the tears of guilt bubbling up. She didn't *want* to want to be with someone else, but some part of her, if she were to be honest, wanted to spend more time with Johnny.

***

Once home in Calabasas, Johnny turned on the radio and undressed on his way upstairs to the bedroom. When Lenny Kravitz's "Again" blasted through the speakers, he felt like God was mocking him. Would he ever see Lumiana again?

He lay in bed for a while looking at the picture of her and her goofy menagerie on his phone. Until the one pill the doctor had given him finally worked its magic and he dropped like a stone.

Twelve hours later, Johnny woke up in the same dire mood. Because he didn't trust himself with pain meds—not even the over-the-counter ones, he poured the rest of them down the garbage disposal. Then he had two glasses of whiskey for breakfast and went back to bed.

When Johnny woke up again, he pulled a few napkins out of his jacket to see what he'd scribbled down at Lumiana's. They were fleeting thoughts, but one verse stood out:

You show me with the light in your eyes
What everybody else can't see
Things aren't always so black and white
Your secret colors call to me

Johnny picked up his guitar and worked on a melody to complement the lyrics. Once he got started, he couldn't stop. So he turned off his phone and barricaded himself in his house.

For ten days he did nothing but work, composing enough songs for a full album. Satisfied, dazed, amazed, Johnny decided to text his band mates to meet him at the studio later. When he turned his phone back on, he had hundreds of messages—but not one from Lumiana.

***

It felt unreal to finally be back in the studio, Adam thought later that evening. He grabbed a couple of beers from the fridge and joined the others in the lounge. They were at the end of an exceedingly productive day. Johnny's new material had energized everyone, and they'd worked tirelessly to take it to the next level.

"That was epic," Toni said, raising his bottle to toast them all.

"Yeah, man," Earl said to Johnny. "Where did that burst of creativity come from?"

"I spent some time on a reservation up north, reconnected with my inner child."

After an hour-long celebration, Adam found an excuse to ask Johnny to join him in the studio's back office. The room was full of boxes, papers, and unused equipment. They had to clear some space to sit.

"So, how did it go with Lumiana? And where the hell have you been all week? Jules and Ben have been hounding me because you dropped off the face of the earth."

Raising his eyebrows, Johnny took a sip of coffee. They'd decided to turn the session into an all-nighter and switched from beer to coffee to keep the creative juices flowing. "Why? Did you hear something?"

"No one could reach you for more than *a week*, Johnny! I called Shawn because the last thing I knew was that you were going to see his sister."

"And what did he say?" Johnny eyed him over the rim of his mug.

"That you had some kind of accident?"

Johnny set his mug down and pulled up his sleeve to show him the gash.

"Ouch. What happened?"

"I don't want to talk about it." Getting up, Johnny paced the messy room. "How is Lumiana, did he say?"

The way he asked gave Adam pause. "Shawn

hasn't mentioned anything." Adam studied his friend carefully. It was rare for Johnny to be so tight-lipped. "What's going on, man? Did you do something to her? Did she do that to your arm?"

"You're asking too damn many questions."

"You're answering too few."

Johnny sat back down, frowned into his coffee. "Let's just say it didn't go as planned."

Why was he being so damn cryptic? "Do I have to expect an angry call at some point? Seriously, man, Shawn is very protective of Lumiana. You don't want to get on his bad side."

Adam was fully aware of Johnny's track record with womankind—they worshiped him until they didn't. And whenever that happened it affected the band. If he'd actually felt something for them, Johnny got broody and secluded himself; if he felt indifferent about them, his girlfriends tended to seek revenge or turn into stalkers.

"Sorry," Johnny said, looking genuinely miserable.

Adam sighed. "I'm sorry it didn't go as well as you'd hoped." He patted him on the shoulder before he went to refill their coffee mugs. When he got back he asked, "So, what was she like?"

"You've met her, you should know."

"Yeah, but I never talk to her aside from, 'Hey, how is it going?' The usual small talk. She isn't exactly approachable."

A slow smile spread across Johnny's face.

"She's amazing, man. I've never met anyone like her. She's smart, she's cute, and she's crazy beautiful, from the inside out."

"She really got to you, huh?" Who would've thought? Lumiana looked nothing like Johnny's exes, and he didn't think he'd go for the prickly type. Shawn insisted that Lumiana was warmhearted and loving, but in Adam's experience, interacting with her was like touching a porcupine: approach with caution or get quilled.

"You have no idea," Johnny muttered. "But it doesn't matter how I feel about her. She made it very clear she doesn't want to see me again."

"It's her loss, man."

"No, believe me, it's not."

"Whoa!" Adam raised his hands. "Let me get this straight: the infamous ladies' man Johnny Graham, God's gift to women, thinks he isn't good enough for this woman?"

"I doubt there's a man good enough for her."

"I'll be damned," he laughed. "You got it bad!"

Johnny shook his head. "Let's go make some music. We didn't come here to chit-chat like a bunch of little girls."

Crazy to think that Johnny had a crush on Shawn's weird sister.

Adam got up, headed toward the door. "Does she know?"

Johnny rubbed the space between his eyes. "Can we please change the subject?"

"Fine, let's play some music."

Lumiana was having a hard time regaining her equilibrium. Whenever she closed her eyes, she was either swamped by memories of Jayjay, her parents, and Esperanza, or she relived her time with Johnny, which had woken her libido from hibernation.

Five years of abstinence, of believing she would never feel attracted to another person again, and then she nearly loses it after five minutes with a man who looked like some cock-sure playboy Disney prince.

Hoping to retain at least part of her sanity, Lumiana buried herself in work throughout the week and spent her nights contemplating exorcism—anything to get Johnny out of her system.

By Sunday, exhaustion surpassed her misery, and she was just about to fall asleep with her eyes open when Ana joined her in the living room.

"*Mamá*, you're so different." Ana hopped onto the sofa. Placing her hands on either side of Lumiana's face, she squished her cheeks together. "I want to know what's wrong with you."

"Nothing," Lumiana said through fish lips.

"No, you're still sad. I want to know why."

"There is nothing to know, Ana. It's time to get ready for bed." With a sigh, she freed herself and went upstairs.

Shawn had just finished talking with Adam when Ana called him. His niece pleaded with him to talk to her mom, who was acting stranger than usual. So Shawn stayed on the line while Ana went upstairs and handed Lumiana the phone.

"What's up with you, Lumi?" he said by way of greeting.

"I'm reading Eva Luna."

"You know what I mean. Ana is worried. She says you're not sleeping or eating or smiling, and that you're working nonstop."

"Shawn, please, I already told Ana, I don't want to discuss this."

"You've got to talk to someone, Lumi. If not to me, then someone else. But I wish you'd just talk to me. We tell each other everything, remember?"

Lumiana groaned.

"Come on, tell me what happened between you and the infamous Johnny Graham."

She didn't answer.

Gus hadn't been able to get the truth out of her either. And Adam had lucked out too with both Johnny and Lumiana. The latter didn't surprise him because Adam and Lumiana didn't know how to talk to each other. Which was funny considering they both spoke Japanese and both had been raised by elderly women. They had more in common than either of them cared to admit.

"I know something happened because you haven't been acting like yourself ever since he came to see you. Come on, Lumi, I can help."

Shawn growled inwardly when that didn't result in an answer either. He loved his sister dearly, but Lumiana tended to morph into a petulant child whenever someone tried to get her to reveal something personal. So he told her about his talk with Adam, who apologized for giving Johnny the idea to sign up for her course. "Adam said Johnny might've done something to upset you. Is that true?"

His sister kept silent.

"Did he hurt you, Lumi? Do you want me to beat him up?" That, at last, got a reaction out of her.

"No, Shawn. He didn't hurt me—at least not intentionally." After a pause, she asked, "Did Adam say anything else?"

"Only that Johnny couldn't be reached for over a week, and he didn't want to talk about what happened either. I've got to ask though, do you like him? And by that I mean, do you have amorous feelings for him?" He spelled it out for her because she might miss the meaning otherwise.

"What?" Lumiana's voice cracked. "Why?"

"I'm asking because Adam thinks Johnny has a crush on you, and knowing who you are and what happened with Jayjay, I'm thinking you might have feelings for him too, that you feel you can't act on."

"I hate him!" she blurted. "He was not supposed to come here. He messed everything up. I never want to see him again."

Oh, Lumi. "I think you do. I think you like him and when he got too close, you got scared."

And then it bubbled out of her. How she felt guilty for having feelings for a man that wasn't Jayjay. How she was afraid she wouldn't survive if she ever lost someone she loved again. And that even if she were to overcome the guilt and the fear, she and Johnny led such vastly different lives it would never work out between them.

"We can't choose who we fall in love with, Lumi. But to be honest, I can't see you two working out either."

What were the chances that Johnny would give up his fame to be with her, or that she'd leave her sanctuary behind to live a life in the limelight? Even if it wasn't about protecting the family, he knew Lumiana didn't like to be around strangers. Or have her picture taken. And that would be a given if she dated someone as high-profile as Johnny Graham.

Shawn sighed. "If people see you with him, they're going to come after you. They'll ask questions that will put us and the way we live in jeopardy." Johnny wasn't worth it. As far as Shawn knew, the man was king of on-again off-again relationships. "He also doesn't strike me as the type who'd like to share you with another man's child."

"He doesn't know about Ana, but I told him about Jayjay."

That was a major step for her. Maybe it was less about love and more about friendship. She had no one to talk to who wasn't family. And Jayjay had been part of their family too. They were hardly objective when they talked about him.

"And I *am* doing all I can to protect the family, Shawn. Nothing is more important to me."

"I know, Lumi. We all have to make sacrifices," he said mostly to himself. "But maybe it's time for you to put yourself a little more out there. I'm not saying go out and date," he added before she could protest, "but maybe try to make a friend at work or something."

"Everyone at work is much older than me."

"Okay, then maybe you can be friends with Johnny. Just make sure you guys hang out at your place."

"I cannot be friends with Johnny." She lowered her voice a bit. "He wants to have inter-course with me."

Shawn snorted at her clinical word choice. He was pretty sure Johnny Graham didn't have intercourse, the man fucked—and he'd be damned if Johnny got his thrill drill anywhere near his sister. "How do you know?"

"He said so."

"Did he now?" Go figure. "Okay, and do you want to have intercourse with him?"

"I don't plan on ever seeing him again."

Probably for the best. He hoped Lumiana would meet a kind man and get the happy ending she deserved, but he didn't understand why she liked Johnny. That guy had asshole written all over him. To his way of thinking, the farther Johnny stayed from Lumiana, the better.

**

Johnny couldn't believe that Lumiana hadn't reached out to him—not even for his thirtieth birthday. The tabloid press had a field day covering his elaborate party, which had included plenty of celebrities.

Surely Lumiana would've seen him on the cover of one of the magazines while she was waiting in the supermarket checkout line. But then again, she likely shopped at the farmer's market or one of those small-town grocery stores.

He contemplated stopping by the institute on a Friday, but there was a good chance she'd call security on him if he ever tried that again.

If Lumiana wanted them to be together, she'd have to come to him.

Three weeks later, Johnny stood before a crowd of two hundred people in the Grand Room of the trendy Tanahashi Hotel to celebrate the release of his new single, "Wonder," a song that wouldn't even exist if it weren't for Lumiana.

After giving their guests a preview of the song, Johnny and the rest of the band worked the room, chatting with the movers and shakers of the entertainment industry at their publicist's urging.

An hour in, he paused to check his phone, which had been vibrating nonstop for the past ten minutes. Six missed calls, a voicemail, and eleven text messages.

He stepped over to the wall to listen to the voicemail.

"Johnny, it's about your father... His housekeeper found him unconscious at the bottom of the stairs. I'm at Community General... It's bad. He's in the ICU. Please, you need to come. As soon as you can... please, hurry." His mother sounded so scared, he froze.

His drink slipped from his hand and shattered on the floor.

"Johnny, hey," said Toni, who'd been circulating with him. "What's wrong?"

"I... Emergency, I have to go."

"What? Go where?"

"Hospital. My dad... Cover for me, please." He rushed out before Toni had a chance to respond.

As Johnny waited for the valet to get his car, he read through his mother's increasingly desperate text messages, with her last one letting him know he should come to the stroke unit.

When his Porsche pulled up at the curb, he

jumped in and drove as fast as traffic permitted. Please be okay, he prayed, over and over. At the hospital, he abandoned the car and headed for the elevators, frantically hitting the call button.

By the time one arrived, he was wringing his hands. The ride up took too long. Johnny paced like a confined tiger until the doors finally opened, and he stormed out into the hallway.

"Johnny," he heard his older brother call. "Over here."

His heart was thumping so violently, he couldn't move.

Jason came over and wrapped his arms around him, holding him for a moment before taking him by the hand like he'd done when Johnny was seven. Back then they were visiting their mom after she'd lost the baby girl she so desperately wanted. Five miserable years later, their parents divorced.

Johnny hesitated at the door of the hospital room, until Jason nudged him inside.

His mom and his younger brother Jack were sitting by his father's bedside holding hands.

His dad looked as though he were made of fine glass, lying there unmoving, his eyes closed, his face pale as chalk. The machines attached to him beeped in the background.

This was all wrong. Jerold Graham was a strong, proud businessman who in recent years had taken a liking to teaching economics to young, impressionable minds. He was a rock star in his own right.

Johnny walked up to the bed and took his dad's limp hand. They hadn't been close for more than a decade, but since Lumiana had told him about the loss of her parents, he'd made an effort to reconnect. His dad had been so happy when Johnny took him out to dinner last week.

The doctor joined them, and Johnny pleaded with her to do whatever she could to save his dad—money wasn't an issue. She said she understood his frustration, but they had already done everything they could. Now they had to wait for his father to wake up while praying for a full and speedy recovery.

Two hours later, his dad briefly opened his eyes, but he looked confused and was unable to speak. It was too early to tell if the damage to his brain would be permanent, the doctor said, repeating that all they could do at this point was wait and see.

When Johnny left the hospital for the night, he sat in his car in the parking lot, staring at his trembling hands. Wait and see. *Wait and see?*

He pounded his hands against the steering wheel.

He didn't want to fucking wait and see, he wanted his dad to be better now.

In the haze of fear and frustration, Johnny drove around mindlessly for two hours until he found himself at the entrance gate of the Jonata community.

"Who are you here to see, sir?" asked the security guard, a lanky guy in uniform, a few years younger than Johnny.

"Lumiana Harding."

"Is she expecting you?" the young man said as another guard walked up to the car.

"Johnny?" Mike blinded him with a flashlight. "You all right?"

"I just need to see her, I—"

Mike turned to the other guard. "It's okay, let him through. He's Lumiana's friend."

The steel gate opened and Johnny followed the narrow gravel road.

He froze when he realized what he was doing. What was he going to say? Would she be alone? Would she even hear him out before she asked him to leave?

He rolled his shoulders and pulled up to Lumiana's estate. He shouldn't have come here, he thought as he got out of the car and plodded over to her gate. She'll probably kick me in the nuts.

Johnny punched in the security code he'd seen Lumiana use the day they met. The numbers were the year her first love died, he realized when the lock clicked open.

Leaving his car where it was, Johnny slipped through the gate and closed it behind him, his churning stomach forcing him to pause.

It's not too late to turn around, he told himself, leaning against the cool metal until the nausea passed.

When he straightened, his whole body felt as if it were covered in needles. Images of his father flashed before his eyes as tears swam behind them. How the hell was Lumiana doing it, moving on with her life after she'd been through this nightmare so many times?

Lumiana's voice pierced the quiet night. "Whoever you are, you have no right to be here! I'm armed and able to use force if I have to." She stalked toward him, carrying a long stick.

What the hell? What if he were an intruder with a gun?

"Hey, did you hear me?" she yelled, gripping the stick with both hands.

As Johnny strode toward her, she walked backward toward the house, stopping at the entrance like a warrior protecting the castle.

In the glow of the building's exterior lights, he could see Lumiana barefoot in a snug gray tank top and frilly miniskirt, wielding a wooden staff. She would've looked like a fairy if it weren't for her fuck-off posture. He couldn't decide whether he was more turned on by her appearance or afraid of her reaction once she recognized him.

"Do not come any closer," she warned, but he kept moving toward her. "Just because I'm a woman doesn't mean I don't know how to fight. You do not want me to hurt you."

Johnny stepped into the light the moment she

lunged.

7

JACKIE AND WILSON

*"Remember that everyone you meet
is afraid of something,
loves something and has lost something."*

—H. JACKSON BROWN, JR.

"Johnny?" Lumiana suspended the wooden staff in midair, her eyes wild with wonder.

His pulse was drumming in his ears as he stopped in front of her, an arm's length between them. "You're not going to hit me with that thing, are you?"

Letting go of the bō, she brought her hands to his chest.

"Lu—" He couldn't believe he was standing in front of her, so vulnerable he could hardly stand it.

Please, don't turn me away.

Her lips parted but no words came out.

He didn't know whether it was all the feelings he'd harbored since their parting or the adrenaline pumping through his veins that prompted him, but he yanked her toward him, his body taking over as he welded his mouth to hers.

He couldn't get close enough.

Clenching one hand in the back of her top and the other in the hair at the nape of her neck, he fitted her against him, capturing her soft moan as he pinned her between him and the wall.

Lumiana rocked her hips and slid her tongue against his until he could no longer think. It was everything he hoped it would be and more.

When she broke the kiss and wiggled out of his embrace, he worried that was it, that she'd come to her senses and was about to push him away.

Come on, Lu, please don't do this to me.

Much to his relief, she grabbed his hand and pulled him around the back of the house, where she hopped up onto the wooden patio table, and taking a fistful of his shirt, brought her hips back to his waist.

There it was, all that pent-up lust and passion he knew she had inside her.

She was so beautiful. And the expression in her eyes, hot and hungry. It felt like he'd waited a lifetime for this, for her.

"Touch me," she said, her voice husky. "Everywhere."

Best words she'd ever spoken.

Lowering his mouth to hers, he tugged down the front of her top and cupped her breast, rolling her nipple between his fingers.

She shuddered when he trailed his lips over her skin, and again when he drew the pebbled tip into his mouth, teasing her with his tongue and teeth until she shifted restlessly against him.

As he worshiped the other side, he slid his hand under her skirt and dipped his fingers into her panties.

He loved the feel of her, her scent, her silky skin.

When he eased a finger inside her, she moaned and trembled. *He* was doing this to her, he realized in awe. This strong, extraordinary woman, who'd become his muse, wanted him as much as he wanted her.

Bringing his mouth back to hers, he thrust and circled his fingers until her muscles contracted.

Lumiana, of course, wasn't to be outdone.

"Fuck, Lu," he rasped when she caught his earlobe with her teeth, nipping and licking her way along his jaw while her hand reached down to unbutton his jeans. She was by no means gentle, and he liked that, needed it even.

When she took him in her hand, he groaned out loud. The woman knew what she was doing, he noted appreciatively as he began to come apart under her touch.

"Easy, babe," he said, gritting his teeth when she picked up the pace. "If you keep that up, I'm not going to last."

The roguish smile she gave him almost pushed him over the edge.

With more impatience than finesse, he carried her over to a cushioned double chaise and set her down. While he hurriedly retrieved a condom from his wallet, she knelt in front of him and freed his jutting erection, her lips burning a trail up his neck as he sheathed himself.

The second he was done, she pulled him onto the cushion and devoured his mouth in a mind-numbing kiss.

Closer.

"More," she moaned against his lips before she fused her mouth to his again. He could never tire of kissing her, of looking into those piercing eyes.

As he slid his hands up her thighs, he bunched up the soft fabric of her skirt, guiding her on top of him. Their tongues clashed in a frantic dance as he gripped her hips to pleasure them with friction. What a thrill it was to have all her fervent energy directed to him.

Almost delirious with need, he rolled them over, his shaft sliding up and down between her folds until she bucked against him, ready to take him in.

As he plunged into her, over and over, her soft moans sounded like a melody—vibrant and sensual. This could easily become his favorite song.

When her hands clenched in the back of his shirt, he moved faster, burying his face against her neck and letting her scent fog his mind.

This was it, the wave that took him under.

Her nails dug into his ass, pushing him deeper. She came writhing beneath him, her long legs wrapped around his waist as he let himself go.

After, they lay there for a while, breathlessly clinging to each other until Johnny could no longer hold his weight. He shifted to his side.

"Well, that was…" Glancing down, he noticed both of them were still fully clothed. "I honestly don't know what to say… Please say something."

Lumiana tried to slip away, but Johnny pinned her under him.

Holding her hands next to her head, he leaned down to kiss her, slowly, unsure whether she wanted him to.

With a tilt of her chin, she closed the distance between them. Their tender kiss lasted until she pushed him off her so roughly he rolled onto his back. Before he could even utter a sound, she gave him a firm kiss on the mouth and got up, attempting to tame her gorgeous mass of jet-black hair.

His chest swelled when he saw her standing there, slightly off balance, a wicked smile on her face.

She was fucking perfect.

Johnny didn't get up from the chaise, so Lumiana extended him a hand. "Would you care to join me?"

He hesitated at first, but then took her hand.

She wondered why he'd come back, but to find out they'd have to talk, and she would get angry that he'd ignored her wish. Well, her conscious wish. Deep down, she had to admit that him being here, making her feel the way he did, was what she had been fantasizing about ever since she'd kissed him in the lake.

To prolong her current state of blissful oblivion, she quietly led Johnny into the house and up the stairs to her bedroom.

They stopped in front of the bed.

Lumiana ran her fingers over his chest, linking them behind his neck.

"Lu—"

She shook her head, and brushed her lips over his.

Once she helped him out of his jacket, she nudged him onto her bed.

When Johnny took off his shirt, she sucked in a sharp breath. There was something about the way he moved, the way he touched her—his scent, his taste—that filled her with such heat she wanted to scream.

As Johnny stripped away her clothes, his fiery gaze trailed over her. His hands explored each exposed curve, his hoarse voice humming his approval. This man awakened a hunger in her, a longing unlike anything she'd ever known.

Reaching around her, he cupped her bottom, bringing her closer.

She gasped when he slid his thumb further down to circle her most sensitive spot. At the same time, he flicked his tongue over her taut nipple, sucking and nipping until she quivered with need.

Then Lumiana did what she'd always done when someone inflicted intense pleasure or pain on her—she retaliated.

She pushed Johnny back onto her bed and lightly raked her nails across his chest, licking his warm skin on her way down. He was magnificent—solid and strong.

She wanted to touch him everywhere, explore each glorious inch. So she reached into his pants and stroked his hard silky length.

Mumbling something incoherent, Johnny took off his jeans and boxer briefs with shaky movements.

Lumiana straddled him, savoring their connection as she slid up and down. God, the way he looked at her—wrecked or in awe—she couldn't tell. It was breathtaking—raw and tender. She took it all in, hoping she would always remember.

Then she leaned over and retrieved a few things from her bedside table, the peaks of her breasts exquisitely rubbing against his chest when she leaned back.

He smiled when she tied his wrists with her cobalt scarf, moaned her name when she scooted down to tease him.

Extending her fingers, she grasped the smooth beaded necklace and rolled it over him. He really was stunning, she thought, amazed that he was here with her, letting her play with him as she pleased. There was something freeing about living out her fantasies.

A while later, they lay panting and sweaty on top of her rumpled sheets, a heap of tangled limbs. Only then did she realize how much she'd needed this intense connection with him. He brought a part of her to life that she'd buried a long time ago.

Dazed, she slipped out of bed and into the adjacent bathroom.

"Jesus, Lu, where did you learn all that?" Johnny asked from the bedroom.

"Where did I learn what?" she said, smiling to herself. He'd given her a nickname, one born in the throes of passion. Her family called her Lumi, but Lu sounded like a grown woman who knew what she wanted and how to take it.

"All the stuff you did to me just now."

She peeked around the corner. Johnny lay stretched across the bed, a mischievous smile on his face. "I'm an anthropologist, remember?"

"I didn't know being an anthropologist required that kind of skill set."

"It isn't a skill set, it's an inquisitive interest in human behavior, past and present. I've studied all kinds of mating rituals."

"Mating rituals?" he said with a snort. "Sounds romantic."

She came up to the bed and tossed a pillow at him. "You were the one who made it sound as though I tried some weird practices on you."

"I didn't say it was weird, I just noticed it was... I don't know, it felt different."

"Different how?" She sat near the edge of the bed, beginning to wonder if maybe it hadn't been as good for him as it had been for her.

"I'm not sure how to describe it." He got up and disappeared in the bathroom, but kept talking. "It was intense, especially for two people who haven't been together physically before. I expected something more basic."

"Um, okay, I apologize. I didn't..." she trailed off. She didn't know what he liked, so she had done what *she* liked. He'd seemed delighted when she used her silk scarf and the beaded necklace on him. Had her own arousal eclipsed her already impaired ability to read his cues?

Johnny came back into the room and joined her on the bed. "It far exceeded what I imagined it would be like. I'm trying to pay you a compliment."

She covered her face with her hands, feeling Johnny straighten in front of her. He pulled her up and close with his arm firmly tucked around her waist. Her stomach fluttered as she relished the heat of his skin.

"Why are you here?" she asked, and he released her.

Johnny sank onto the mattress, his eyes glowing with emotion. "I... Something happened. I didn't know where else to go. I didn't come here to have sex with you, if that's what you're asking."

His anguish was palpable. "Talk to me," she said gently.

"My dad, he had a stroke. He fell down the stairs. It's bad, Lu."

She hugged him, kissed his cheek.

Tears stung her eyes at the thought of her own dad, her mom, Esperanza... She didn't want him to go through the same thing—it had wrecked her.

"I just want to be with someone who understands, and I don't know anyone who would understand this more than you." Johnny clutched her so tightly, it hurt.

She held him until he composed himself.

Then Johnny went to take a shower.

Meanwhile, Lumiana padded over to the guest room and opened the nightstand drawer. There sat the box of condoms Shawn had brought with him when he lived with her for a month while his apartment was being renovated.

She took out a handful of condoms, but then

felt silly assuming Johnny was going to sleep with her again, much less multiple times. After all, he did say he didn't come by to have sex. So she put the condoms back. Then she reached in again to get one, put it back, took another handful, put them all back again.

She was so engrossed in her inner debate about the appropriate number of condoms that she didn't notice Johnny leaning against the doorjamb watching her—until he cleared his throat.

She jumped, and nearly fell off the bed. He was irresistible, she thought as he stood there, a towel wrapped around his toned midsection.

Smirking, he walked up to her, opened the drawer and took out a single condom. "How about we start with one?" he teased.

"I apologize, this is so inappropriate. I know you said you didn't come here for intercourse."

"I may not have come here for *intercourse* but I've been hoping this would happen." He ran his fingers across her burning cheek. "I have to say, I'm flattered you think I have this much stamina."

She smacked his arm. Then, bracing her elbows on her thighs, she cupped her forehead with one hand, and covered her eyes with the other. "This is certainly embarrassing."

Johnny took her hand and pulled her to her feet. "We all have needs, Doc." He led her to her bedroom and back onto the bed. "As much as I love doing this with you, I'm so freaking tired after the day I had. So don't get your hopes up too high."

"Managing expectations?"

He gave her an easy smile. "I might be up for another round as long as it's slow. Is that okay with you?"

She patted her hand invitingly on the mattress.

***

The next morning, Lumiana felt momentarily confused to see Johnny asleep next to her. She took a peek under the blanket to assure herself last night had indeed happened. It was painful to admit how much she liked him, how much she had longed to be with him, and how good it had felt when she allowed herself to get carried away.

Then she pushed all thoughts and feelings aside because today wasn't about her. This was going to be another hard day for Johnny, and she wanted him to sleep as long as possible.

Trying not to wake him, she eased out of bed, gathered the clothes from the floor, and headed over to the guest room for a shower.

On her way to Ana's room, Lumiana let the animals out of the vivarium.

Her daughter was reading in bed when Lumiana padded into the room and cuddled up to her.

"You are different, *mamá*. Are you feeling better?"

Lumiana gave her daughter a smacking kiss. "I have to tell you something." She felt like a love-struck teenager. "Do you remember telling me a few weeks ago that you wanted to meet Johnny Graham? Today you can. He is here."

"Ooh." Ana clapped her hands. "Is he your boyfriend now?"

"No, angelito. He came here last night because his dad is very sick."

Ana's face dimmed. "Oh no, that makes me so sad."

Lumiana folded her arms around her daughter. "We need to be there for him because we know how he feels. Can you help me do that?"

When Ana nodded, Lumiana gave her a kiss, and then went to make breakfast.

***

While her mother bustled about the kitchen, Ana checked the two guest rooms, eager to see Johnny. She loved meeting new people and was excited there was a man in the house who wasn't family or a close friend.

She found Johnny fast asleep in her mother's bed.

Ana padded over to him and examined the tattoos on his arm. She loved art, and Johnny had a colorful picture book right there on his skin.

Then she waited.

And waited.

After a minute, she got bored and poked him

in the forehead, flinching when Johnny woke with a start.

***

"Jesus, kid, you scared me." Johnny squinted repeatedly to make sure he wasn't imagining the little girl in the Star Trek pajamas.

"Sorry." Extending her hand, she introduced herself with a bright smile. "My name is Ana Jackson Harding. I am seven years old. And I live here."

Whoa, okay.

Johnny shook her hand. The girl looked pretty cute with her shiny black hair twisted into loopy buns like mouse ears on either side of her head. She seemed tiny for a seven-year-old. If she hadn't mentioned it, he would've thought she was more like four or five. "Pleasure to meet you, Ana Jackson Harding, I'm Johnny... Johnny Graham." He shook his head, still feeling a little fuzzy. "Is Lumiana your mom?"

"Of course she is, silly."

Funny, Lumiana had never mentioned that. The kid's hair and skin were dark like Lumiana's, but her facial features suggested she was of East Asian descent—Japanese, if their house was any indication.

"Who is your dad?"

"I don't have a dad. He died," she told him.

"Jayjay was your dad?"

Ana nodded. "Did you know him?"

"No, but your mom told me about him."

Ana climbed onto the bed, and Johnny pulled the blanket up to his chin, realizing he was naked underneath it.

"Are you in love with my mom?" She sat cross-legged atop the rumpled sheets.

"What, why would you think that?"

Ana looked at him like duh. "You are sleeping naked in her bed. My best friend Peyton said people hug in the nude when they are in love."

Johnny grinned. There had been a lot of naked hugging going on last night, he supposed. Fortunately, before Ana could ask him anything else, Lumiana walked in. Mortification spread across the woman's face when she spotted her daughter on the bed.

"Ana, I was looking for you. Why are you up here? Johnny, I'm terribly sorry. I had no idea she would go upstairs." Lumiana reached for Ana's hand. "Can you please go and eat your breakfast? I need to talk to Johnny."

The little girl tried to protest, but Lumiana shot her one of her scolding glares. Huh, and here he thought she reserved those for him.

With a defiant pout, Ana got off the bed and tromped downstairs.

Lumiana sat next to him, looking both radiant and thoroughly flustered. Probably not the best time to tell her how beautiful she was.

Johnny let go of the blanket, biting the inside of his cheek to keep a straight face. "So, I met your daughter. That was interesting."

"I am so sorry, Johnny."

"It's okay, Doc. That little girl of yours is just as cute as you are, and very outspoken." He smiled, unsure what else to say. "Why didn't you tell me?" It was hard to think of Lumiana as a mom because she possessed so many childlike qualities herself.

The question hung between them like a drop of tap water about to splash into the sink.

"I'm not in the habit of telling people I've just met about my personal life," she said eventually. "I barely know you."

That stung. Granted, they'd only spent a total of three days and three nights together, but the entirety of their time together had been so intense, it may as well have been three years. It was a sobering realization that she hadn't trusted him enough to tell him about Ana.

Rubbing the sleep from his eyes, he said, "You two don't look very much alike. She takes after Jayjay, I assume. Was he Japanese?" Johnny took an educated guess considering Lumiana's interest in the culture.

"She does resemble him, yes. Jayjay was half Japanese, half Xhosa. Ana's biological mother was Japanese as well."

That made more sense. But it wasn't just her youthful looks that made it hard to imagine her pregnant. There was something about Lumiana that he couldn't quite grasp yet.

Lumiana's lips pressed together in a slight grimace. "Jayjay met Ana's mother at a party his senior year. They had a one-night stand and Megumi got pregnant, but they never became a couple. She died in childbirth. That was three months before he and I got together. After Jayjay died, Ana stayed with me."

No wonder she hadn't told him about it—death seemed to follow her. "I'm sorry."

Lumiana joined him under the covers. "Ana turned out perfectly happy despite it all."

"She's feisty." That got a smile out of her. "Do you want to talk about what happened last night?" he asked, and laughed when Lumiana pulled the blanket over her head. "I know this is awkward—"

"Do you think?" she mumbled into the blanket.

Johnny pulled it down so he could look at her. He got a kick out of seeing her flustered. "Your daughter asked me if I'm in love with you because I slept in your bed, naked."

Lumiana muttered something foreign, a curse word by the sound of it. "Can you give me a moment while I pray to vanish into thin air?"

He kissed her forehead. "I need to use the bathroom anyway, so do whatever makes you feel better."

Lumiana was still lying in the same position when Johnny returned a few minutes later. He rolled on top of her, peeling her hands off her face. She closed her eyes.

"Come on, Lu, look at me," he said, stroking her cheek, but she shook her head. "Okay, then can you hold still for me?"

She nodded.

He kissed her softly. She tasted of the same spicy peppermint mouthwash he just used. "I've missed you over the past few weeks."

Lumiana didn't say it back, but she gave him a kiss that told him all he needed to know.

***

"You didn't know my music, but you know Bruno Mars?" Johnny said to Lumiana when he strolled into the living room twenty minutes later. She was sitting cross-legged in a lounge chair, playing "The Lazy Song" on the ukulele. Ana was singing along while their zoo of misfits danced around them. Their goose Doggie wasn't half bad, bobbing its head like the audience at his concerts.

"Bruno Mars is awesome," exclaimed Ana. "But you are awesome too. My mom played me some of your songs."

"Thanks, kid." Johnny dropped onto the sofa and petted Monroe. Ana scooted closer to stroke the dog's head.

"How are you holding up?" Lumiana asked him, her bare legs dangling over the right wing of the sculptural chair, close enough for him to touch her ankle.

"Barely," he said on a sigh. "I just talked to my mom. There's no change in my dad's condition."

Ana laid her small hand on his arm. "I'm sorry about your dad."

In the light, the girl's eyes were the color of his favorite scotch. He sure could use the drink. "Thanks, Ana." To Lumiana, he mouthed, "You told her?"

"I had to explain your surprise visit."

"My birth parents died too," the little girl told him.

"Ana!" Lumiana rebuked her.

Johnny put his hand over Ana's. "It's okay."

"Would you care for some breakfast?" Lumiana asked as she headed for the open-plan kitchen.

I'm not hungry, but thanks for offering."

"You should eat. My mom says it's important to have a healthy breakfast."

He gave her a pat on the head. "You're right, kid." Moving Monroe aside, he got up, so he could join Lumiana.

Johnny lingered by the kitchen counter and watched as Lumiana arranged fruit on a plate. She was quite the sight with her tousled hair, bare feet, and an oversized t-shirt emblazoned with a heart-shaped cupcake and the words 'love muffin.'

He strode over to her and hugged her from behind, nuzzling her neck. "How come you always smell like dessert?" Coconut and cocoa, that's what her warm skin smelled like.

Lumiana turned in his arms.

Before she had a chance to answer, he slid a hand around the back of her neck and kissed her. Because he didn't know how much time he'd get to spend with her, he wanted to make sure he savored whatever they had left.

"*Mamá!*"

Which wouldn't be easy considering they weren't alone.

Lumiana stepped away from him. "How long have you been standing there?"

"Long enough to see you kiss on the mouth." Ana beamed. "Does that mean you're girlfriend and boyfriend?"

Not only was that kid feisty, she also called it like she saw it. Johnny was so used to people trying to please him that it was refreshing when someone was as blunt as Ana. And wasn't that part of what had attracted him to Lumiana—her defiance and complete indifference to his fame?

"It's complicated," Lumiana said after a long, awkward pause.

"It's not all that complicated." Johnny cinched his arm around her waist. "To answer your question from earlier, Ana, I'm falling in love with your mom, but she doesn't want to be with me."

"*Mamá,*" Ana tugged on Lumiana's shirt, her eyes stern, "why don't you want to be with Johnny?"

"You are falling in love with me?" Lumiana uttered, her eyes improbably wide.

'Falling' wasn't the right word. *Plunging*. It felt more like a shock wave than the gradual trickle he usually experienced.

"Ana, could you give me a moment alone with your mom?"

The little girl nodded and headed over to the living room.

Lumiana continued to look at him as though he'd just announced he had swine flu. So he kissed her.

She pressed her hand against his chest. "You can't say things like that." She tried to pull away, but he held on to her.

"No, Lu." He tilted her chin so their eyes were level. "I want to be with you." He stroked his thumb over her cheek. "It's okay if you don't feel the same, but don't tell me what I can or can't say. I'm entitled to my feelings just as much as you are."

Johnny felt a tug on his shirt. "Your phone was ringing." Ana handed it to him. He had a voicemail and stepped out of the kitchen to check it, but he could still hear the mother-daughter conversation.

"*Mamá*, why don't you want to be with Johnny? He is so nice and I like his music. If we keep him, we can sing together."

"Ana."

"Please. Why don't you want him to be your boyfriend?"

151

"You don't understand. It doesn't matter if I want to be with him. I can't."

Can't? Yeah, right. They could find a way to address her privacy concerns. Besides, the paparazzi wouldn't follow him out here, Johnny thought as he walked back in. "I have to leave. I need to go to the hospital."

Ana touched his hand. "Do you want us to come with you?"

"You would really do that for me?" He held Lumiana's gaze. He'd love their support. Just the thought of seeing his dad so broken made his throat close up again.

"My mom said we need to be there for you," Ana told him, which Lumiana confirmed with a nod.

Because the two of them were still in their pajamas and hadn't had breakfast yet, Johnny gave Lumiana a quick kiss and asked them to meet him there, jotting down the hospital address before he rushed out.

8

STUCK IN THE MIDDLE
WITH YOU

*"Empathy is being with someone
and feeling with someone."*

—TAMARA LEVITT

Two hours later, Lumiana and Ana arrived at Community General Hospital. They'd been here before for a fundraiser because Gus was the hospital's top OB/GYN surgeon.

The staff had been informed they were coming, and Janice, a bubbly nurse with curly blond hair, helped them find Jerold Graham's room.

The door stood open, so they peeked inside. Lumiana held on to her eager daughter, touching a finger to her lips. Had she known Johnny's family would be here, she wouldn't have agreed to come.

It was too late now. She'd promised to be there for Johnny, and despite her body switching to flight mode, she was a woman of her word, so she would at least try. If only she knew how.

Hand in hand, she and Ana stood in the doorway. They were both dressed in white, Lumiana in her signature pencil dress and Ana wore a similar dress, but with frills along the hem.

Johnny's dad spotted them first. "Angels," he mumbled, but no one understood. "Angels," he repeated more clearly, pointing a shaky finger at them, and this time everyone turned toward the door.

"Hi," Ana said, tugging on Lumiana's hand.

A pale, elegant older woman, who had to be Johnny's mom, invited them to come in.

When Lumiana hesitated, Johnny strode over to them. He kissed her on the cheek, then crouched down to greet Ana because their height difference was enormous. Her daughter so easily rested her head on Johnny's shoulder—a sight that made Lumiana's chest ache.

Johnny pinched Ana's side, making her giggle, before he stood back up. "Lumiana, Ana, these are my parents Jerold and Eleanor, and my brothers Jason and Jack."

All the men's names start with a J. Why is that? Her mind latched onto the question and didn't let go.

"It's so awesome to meet you," Ana said cheerfully while Lumiana's brain recalled everything she'd ever read about child naming traditions from around the world. "I'm Ana Jackson Harding and this is my mom Lumiana."

When everyone smiled at them, Lumiana lowered her gaze to the floor.

Before she understood what was happening, Johnny asked his family to excuse them while he ushered her out the door.

***

They walked down the hall out of earshot. Something wasn't right, Johnny could sense it. It was as if Lumiana was trapped in her own head. She hadn't said a word yet, nor had she made eye contact with anyone.

"Are you okay?"

Lumiana just stared at him.

He placed his hand on her chest and felt her heart thumping. Her hand shot up to cover his. "Please tell me what's wrong, Lu. Something is obviously freaking you out."

To his chest, she said, "I'm glad your dad's condition has improved."

"Yeah, who would've thought. When they asked me to come back to the hospital, I imagined the worst. He's partially paralyzed though. It's too early to tell if it's permanent, but we're choosing to be optimistic."

Lumiana was struggling for words.

"I can see you're uncomfortable, but if you don't tell me what's going on I can't make it better."

"Being around strangers makes me anxious," she admitted. "I didn't anticipate meeting your family."

"I'm sorry. I didn't know they'd be here. But I don't understand, you're so confident in front of your students, why does talking to my family freak you out?"

"This is different." She averted her gaze. "At work I know what my role is and what I have to say. And I've practiced it a thousand times. But this is a completely new situation. I'm not good with social interactions."

He wondered whether her issues were a mix of nature and nurture—maybe she was born on the autism spectrum. It would explain a few of her peculiar behaviors, including what had happened back in the room.

Johnny ran his hands up and down her arms. "You also looked uncomfortable with me holding Ana."

"Please don't take this the wrong way, Johnny. It's just that Ana only met you a few hours ago and is already treating you like family. When I saw you with her it reminded me of Jayjay and her. I need some time to process everything. What we did last night, I enjoyed it very much, but I shouldn't have done it."

He took her hands. "We'll talk about it later. I

don't want to do this in a hospital hallway. Are you going to be okay if we go back to my dad's room?" She didn't move. "Can I do something to make you less anxious?"

"No. But you may want to apologize to your family."

"Apologize for what?"

"Ana and me being here, intruding on what is clearly a family affair."

"No worries. I invited you here, remember?"

"A-and for my behavior—I don't mean to be difficult. It's... I have... Maybe you have noticed—"

"That you have Asperger's?" It just made sense.

Clasping her heart-shaped locket, she nodded softly. "Meets the characteristics of 'autism spectrum disorder' is what I've been told. I don't get a clear-cut diagnosis because of my unusually isolated upbringing. My parents died when I was six, so I can't ask them if, and to what extent, I've always been this way." After a pause, she said, "Are you still..." Her face flamed, and she couldn't get the words out.

Wildly attracted to you? His lips tipped up, despite his best efforts to keep a neutral expression.

She pressed her hands to her cheeks before she let them fall back to her sides. "Are you going to treat me differently now?"

"Not unless you need me to." And because he was excellent at reading people, he dropped a quick, firm kiss on her mouth, answering the question she couldn't bring herself to ask. "And yes, I still have a huge crush on you. This doesn't change anything for me."

Taking her hand, he led her back to the room, where Ana was sitting on his father's bed, entertaining his family with a story about a pregnant cow.

"Your daughter is a fantastic storyteller." His mother smiled at Lumiana, who looked down at her feet.

He'd explain it to his family later.

"Ana told us the amazing stories of how you ended up with a dog named Monroe, a cat named Marilyn, who thinks she's a dog, a goose named Doggie, a pig named Kirk, and Walter the tortoise. Did I remember that correctly, Ana?"

The girl gave her two thumbs up. "Are you okay, *mamá*?" Contrary to her mother, Ana seemed positively comfortable sitting there, chatting with everyone.

It was a bit like *Freaky Friday*, as if Ana and Lumiana had switched roles.

Lumiana squirmed when all eyes turned to her. "I... I need to use the restroom. Excuse me." And then she fled the room.

Johnny rubbed his forehead. He had no idea how he was supposed to handle this situation. He had to read up on autism spectrum disorder later, so he knew what to do in the future.

"Please excuse my mom, she—"

"It's fine, Ana," Johnny assured her. "You don't

have to say anything."

"I don't want your family to think she's weird."

Johnny had a feeling this wasn't the first time Ana had to defend her mother's behavior.

"My uncle Shawn says that meeting many new people at once scares her because she had a hard time growing up."

"Oh, I'm sorry to hear that, sweetheart," his mother said.

"What happened to her?" asked Jason.

"Let's talk about it some other time. She might be back soon and I don't want to make her even more uncomfortable."

Jack cleared his throat, pointing to the door, where Lumiana was standing. The way she looked, she must've overheard at least part of their conversation. She promptly disappeared into the hallway.

Johnny headed for the door. "Excuse us for a moment."

"No, Johnny, wait." Ana got up. "We should leave."

"I don't want you to leave, Ana." He told her to sit back down. Until he had more information, he was going to play this by intuition. Autistic or not, Lumiana struck him as stubbornly resigned to her fate. "At some point your mom has to expand her comfort zone. She just needs a push, so she gets out of her own way."

***

Meeting Johnny's family reminded Lumiana of her first day of college. Being overwhelmed by the bustle on campus hadn't been her only challenge that day.

After her second class, she went to use the restroom. A group of young women started whispering the moment she came through the door. It wasn't even the first time that day that the other students had stared at her as if she were an alien invading their precious learning environment. Some of them giggled, others pointed at her.

"What's up with that hair?" she heard one of the young women murmur to her friends.

"And that dress! Did she steal her granny's nightgown?" whispered another.

"This is college, not high school," said a young woman washing her hands next to Lumiana. "At least pick on someone your own age."

The other women gave her a snotty look and left the bathroom, laughing.

"Don't mind those *idiotas*. Are you okay? I'm Candela, by the way."

Her kind brown eyes reminded Lumiana of Esperanza, except that the young woman had much lighter skin, a full set of teeth, and no wrinkles.

Lumiana nodded shyly.

"What's your name?" Candela was a head

shorter than Lumiana, with shiny brown hair, a sunny smile, and artfully painted nails.

Lumiana hadn't seen such a beautiful person since the last time she saw Äiti alive.

"*Mi nombre es Lumiana. No tienes que quedarte conmigo.*" Because Candela had a Spanish accent, Lumiana told her in Esperanza's native tongue that she didn't have to stay with her. "I'm sure you have somewhere else to be."

"*No te preocupes. No tengo más clases hoy.*" Candela wasn't in a hurry. "Let's go grab a bite to eat."

"I have to pick up the key for my room."

"*Dale, voy contigo.* I have no plans today," she insisted. "Where are you staying?"

When Lumiana told her about the old apartment building off campus, Candela shook her head.

"That place has a terrible reputation. It's not safe. I know a better place for you to stay. Get your backpack and let's go check it out."

Half an hour later, they stood in front of a beautiful Tuscan-style mansion. Lumiana had never seen anything like it. The plaque at the entrance read *Casa de Esperanza*—House of Hope. "What is this place?" she asked warily, her heart throbbing at the familiar name.

"It's technically an orphanage, but it doesn't feel like one. *Es mi hogar.*"—Her home. Candela beamed back at her.

Lumiana remained standing as though her feet were glued to the ground. She didn't know it then, but the moment Candela nudged her through the door she'd changed the course of Lumiana's life forever.

***

Johnny found Lumiana sitting on the floor at the end of the hallway, her head against her knees.

With a sigh, he crouched in front of her. "How's it going?"

"What do you think?" she replied without looking at him.

Patience, he reminded himself. "Come on, Lu, no one said anything you should be upset about."

She looked at him now, her eyes glimmering with unshed tears. "Your family is of the impression that I'm bizarre and damaged. And who can blame them? That's what I am after all."

He touched her knee. "Everyone comes with some sort of baggage. Considering what you've been through, you're doing remarkably well. You're different, not damaged." He got to his feet, held out his hand for her. "And besides, someone told me once that 'weird is just a side effect of awesome.'"

Her frown turned into a dazzling smile.

Christ. He took a deliberate breath to switch off The Flames' "Everytime," which popped up in his head whenever she smiled at him that way. "Come on, Doc, you can do this. My parents are pretty nice if you get to know them."

"I don't doubt that, Johnny." But that didn't

stop her from telling him it would be best for her and Ana to leave. Before he could respond, she said, "You have already spent too much time out here with me. Could you please tell Ana to meet me by the elevator?"

He shook his head. "If you want to leave, you have to go back in there and get Ana yourself. It's rude to leave without saying goodbye."

"You could say goodbye to them for me."

"Nope."

Lumiana groaned but followed him back.

"There she is," his mother said when they returned to his father's room. "Mr. Graham, Sr. would like to have a word with you."

Lumiana took a step back, hiding behind Johnny. If he didn't know she was genuinely overwhelmed, he would've laughed at her comical behavior like his brothers were about to do. They corrected their facial expressions when he shot them a warning glare.

"Don't be shy. We'll give you two some space." His mother shooed everyone but Lumiana out of the room.

There was no point in arguing. Both his parents were hardheads. His abnormal determination must've come from somewhere after all.

"Ma, what's going on?" Johnny said as they hovered in the hallway, curiously observing the copy machine-resembling robot that made its way down the corridor after telling them to please stand aside. "Why does Dad want to speak with her?"

"I don't know, sweetheart. I never understand what your father wants. That's why we're divorced, remember?"

Johnny started to go back into the room, but his mother held him back.

"It's okay." Ana clasped his hand. "My mom can handle one stranger."

"You're probably right. After all, she was prepared to kill me last night with this weird-ass Japanese warrior weapon."

"Johnny!" his mother barked. "Watch your language in front of the child."

"Sorry."

"What are you talking about, bro?" Jack stuffed his hands into the pockets of his pressed beige slacks. His brother had the prep school look down pat.

Johnny glanced at his mom and his older brother Jason who sported matching tailored suits. Seriously, how was he part of this family?

'If you weren't the spitting image of your grandfather, I'd think you were adopted,' his grandmother's bitter words crept into his consciousness.

"Johnny?" Jack's voice snapped his attention back to the present.

He told his brothers that Lumiana thought he was an intruder when he showed up at her house last night. "She came at me wielding this long wooden stick. Does she know how to use it?"

Johnny asked the little girl.

"Of course." Ana beamed at him with pride. "She has been practicing with my uncle Shawn since she was sixteen. The bō is her favorite. Shawn said it's the king among the Okinawan weapons."

Johnny and his brothers eyed each other. All three of them wanted to be Bruce Lee when they were kids. "I'd like to see her in action sometime. But I hope I won't be at the receiving end. She wrestled me more than once, and each time it ended with me on my back and her victoriously on top of me. Not that I'm complaining. It's pretty hot."

While his mother had been trying her best to cover Ana's ears, his brothers hooted with laughter while evading Eleanor Brent Graham's notorious glare. Taking pity on his mother who sometimes said she wished she'd had delicate daughters, Johnny wrapped an arm around her. Even if he was an eternal disappointment to the Grahams, he loved his parents and brothers.

***

Standing in Jerold Graham's doorway, Lumiana kept twisting a button on her dress.

What am I supposed to do?

She tried to recall her training while her brain tried to analyze the accent wallpaper. Her gaze darted back and forth between Johnny's dad and the sand colored nautical pattern on the wall behind his bed.

She was someone who found comfort in the predictability of her days, and this day was anything but predictable. And that was a problem, because whenever she was faced with a new situation, there was a decent chance she'd come across as odd or rude, or possibly both.

The ailing man signaled her to come in.

You can do this, Lumi.

Taking a big breath, she strode over to his bedside.

"Sit." He gestured for her to take the swivel chair next to him, then tried to reach for her hand; when she brought hers closer, he covered it with his.

She could see his resemblance to Johnny. Despite the different coloration, they had the same warm eyes and cheeky smile, although the father's was a bit uneven due to the stroke. But she could tell he was a charmer like his son. Lumiana began to relax—until Jerold Graham closed his eyes and seemed to stop breathing.

No, no, no, no, no. She sprang to her feet.

A crooked smile lit up his weathered face. "Still... alive."

Oh, thank God.

"Jerry," he uttered, pointing at himself.

"You'd like me to call you Jerry?" Lumiana smiled brightly at his nod. "I'm pleased to meet you, Jerry."

He lightly squeezed her hand. "Sunshine."

Where being around Johnny felt like touching a live wire, being with Jerry was like sitting by the fireplace.

"Johnny's fond... of you," Jerry struggled to form the words. "Take good care... of him." His eyes drifted shut again. "Please."

Lumiana doubted she could do this. As someone who stood by her word, it felt wrong to promise something she was most likely unable to keep.

"Promise," Jerry said, blinking his glassy eyes.

What if this is his last wish? "I promise I will attempt to honor your wish," she told him, thinking it was an acceptable compromise. He could hardly hold it against her if she tried and failed.

"Thanks." His eyelids fluttered.

"It will be okay." She stroked his hand, unsure whether she was consoling Jerry or herself.

After a prolonged silence, Lumiana stood once more.

He gave her a lopsided grin. "Going... to sleep."

Lumiana squeezed his hand. How much she wished she could've had a proper goodbye with her own dad. "Please don't die, Jerry."

"Promise," he murmured, a faint smile lingering on his lips as she left.

***

Lumiana stepped out into the hallway looking as if she was about to cry. Johnny's chest constricted instantly and all conversation died a quick death. After a moment of eerie silence, they all talked at once, bombarding Lumiana with questions, which only served to render her speechless.

Ana ran up to her and wrapped her arms around her mother. "Go to his room and see him yourself," the little girl said.

Without protest, the family rushed into the room, where Nurse Janice was standing at the end of the bed, blocking their view.

"Is he gone?" asked Jason. He was the most clear-headed of the Grahams.

"Oh no, he's asleep. He looks peaceful, happy even," Janice said as she moved aside. "Mr. Graham needs to rest. We'll call you if his condition changes."

They thanked her and filed out of the room.

Johnny scanned the hallway and spotted Lumiana sitting in the same spot as earlier, but this time her head was tucked against her daughter's neck.

Before he could join them, his mother grabbed him by the arm and pulled him in the opposite direction. "Johnny, can I talk to you for a moment?"

Once they were alone, she said, "What's going on with you and Andie?" At his questioning look, his mom added, "She called me and said the two of you had reconnected a few weeks ago, but she hasn't heard from you again."

"It's over between us."

"Why, Johnny? The two of you were so good together."

"It wasn't meant to be, ma." He didn't want to talk about his ex-girlfriend when he could see the woman he wanted to be with down the hallway, evidently not feeling well.

"I thought you were talking about moving in together, and now you're acting like it was nothing. You should call her. She'd want to know about your father."

"I can't deal with her right now. I've got other things on my mind."

"I can see that." His mother followed his gaze. "What kind of name is Lumiana?"

"She's from Finland," he answered curtly, his gaze never leaving Lumiana.

"Isn't she a little too... exotic looking to be from Scandinavia?"

"'Exotic' is for plants and animals, not people. Lumiana was born in Finland." Which he was pretty sure wasn't part of Scandinavia. "Her mother was Pardo Brazilian, her father was South African of Zulu and Dutch ancestry."

"Was? As in past tense?"

"They both died when she was six, which is why this is hard on her. Can we continue this conversation another time, please?"

"Fine, you can go as soon as you answer one more question."

"What?"

"What's going on between you and her?"

"Nothing, we're friends."

"Don't lie to me, Johnny. I see the way you look at her. And I heard your inappropriate comments earlier. You're more than friends."

"It's complicated." Johnny appreciated the irony that he was now the one using this clichéd ambiguous phrase. "As you can see, she has a hard time with social interactions. All I can say for certain is that I care about her and I'd very much like to go over there to make sure she's okay. We can talk about this some other time."

"Fine, go. Tell her goodbye from us. When you have some time this week, I want to hear the whole story and why your father wanted to talk to her."

He handed her the keys to his Porsche, because a "friend" had dropped her off earlier. Everyone knew she was sleeping with her accountant. Not that he cared. His mother could do whatever she wanted—the only freaky thing was that Jeremy Gardner resembled Jerold Graham a little too closely.

Johnny hurried over to Lumiana and Ana, who were getting ready to leave. "You all right?" he asked Lumiana. "I'm sorry my mom kept me for so long. I wanted to check on you right away."

"I'm fine, thank you," she said, walking past him.

"Hey, wait!"

Lumiana kept going but Ana grabbed his hand, pulling him along.

"Can you slow down, please?"

"No, Johnny. I need to get out of here."

He took a mental note to add 'not a fan of enclosed spaces' to the running list of all the strange and wonderful things that made up Lumiana Harding.

They walked in silence until they reached the parking lot. Lumiana leaned against her Peugeot. She closed her eyes and took deep breaths, while Johnny, who stood next to her, glanced at Ana, hoping she knew what to do.

Shoving him as hard as she could, the little girl managed to push him into Lumiana.

"What did you do that for?" Lumiana asked. But to his surprise, she tucked her arm around his waist and rested her head against his shoulder.

Johnny was so proud of her public display of affection, he almost launched into a happy dance. This was no doubt purely reflexive, but it felt like a step forward.

Ana leaned against his other side. "Johnny said that all it takes sometimes is a push." She grinned when he patted her head. He really liked the kid.

Lumiana pulled away. "Let's go before someone recognizes you."

"Relax, Lu, I'm not that famous." That someone recognized him was a possibility though. It was mostly young women who came and asked to take pictures with him. Some of the nurses had recognized him too, but they'd been friendly and professional. Thankfully, so far most interactions with his fans had been pleasant.

Lumiana unlocked her convertible, then raised an eyebrow when he opened the passenger door. "Aren't you going to take your car?"

"My mom took it. She needed a way to get home."

"I can't drive you home. It's too risky," she protested. "What if someone sees us together?"

He wanted to say, 'So what?' But went with, "I guess you'll have to take me to your place then." Which was where he wanted to be anyway. "If you're okay with it," he said when Ana clapped her hands in approval. "I don't want to be alone right now."

Lumiana agreed.

He knew that line would work on her. She wasn't the kind of person who left a friend in need—or an acquaintance in need, if that's what he was. Just because last night was special for him didn't mean it was special for her. Johnny put his hand on her thigh, experimentally.

"Under one condition," Lumiana told him. "You ride in the back with Ana." When he frowned, she pointed at his hand. "You are a distraction."

Johnny grinned. He stayed where he was, but retrieved his hand.

***

From the parking lot, Janice watched the Peugeot drive off. She'd gone outside to follow Johnny and the woman and child with him, ducking between cars to take a picture. Then she called her roommate.

"Ruby, guess what! Johnny stopped by the hospital today. And get this: he left with some woman, and it wasn't Andie Woodhull—thank God. They seemed close though. She put her arm around him, but I can't tell if they're a couple. It would surprise me if they were—she has dark hair and brown skin. Not his type."

Ten years earlier, when they were both thirteen and Johnny made a splash with his first album, the two of them had founded an unofficial Johnny Graham fan club. And they'd never fully outgrown their adolescent crush.

For the past six years they'd been running a website dedicated to all things Johnny Graham, posting about everything from his outfits and tattoos to rumors about his love life. They went to every concert they could and waited afterward to get his autograph. One time they even showed up at a meet-and-greet where Johnny posed with them for pictures.

And now Janice had his father as a patient, how unbelievably lucky was that?

"Did you take a picture?" Ruby asked.

"I took one, but it's blurry. I was too far away. I don't want to post it though. They had a little girl with them, and you know how I feel about paparazzi taking pictures of children."

"I want to see it," Ruby insisted. "Maybe we can use it but crop out the kid."

"I'll send it to you later. I need to get back inside before my supervisor notices I'm gone. Oh, by the way, I took your suggestion and told Johnny and his family that they should consider Mansfield for his father's rehabilitation, assuming he pulls through." Ruby worked as a nurse at Mansfield Park, an upscale clinic that offered its high-profile clientele discretion and first-class treatment, at a hefty price.

"Good job, Jan. Let's hope he does survive. Imagine the possibilities if Johnny's dad becomes a resident at Mansfield."

9

YOU'RE NOBODY 'TIL SOMEBODY LOVES YOU

"You are absolutely, maddeningly, irrevocably perfect."

—ARIANA

Back home, Lumiana prepared lunch while Johnny and Ana sat across from her at the kitchen island, talking. She still couldn't believe he was here. Or that she'd slept with him, and that she wanted to do it again.

"Why do you have so many pictures on your arm?" Ana asked him.

"They are reminders of important events and people in my life."

If Lumiana had to pick one, the *nana korobi ya*

oki tattoo would be her favorite. *Fall down seven times, stand up eight*—they were words she lived by.

Ana made Johnny explain every tattoo on his arm. "Do you have more?" Her daughter loved hearing stories as much as she enjoyed telling them.

Johnny took off his sweatshirt to show her the tattoo on his shoulder blade. The black tank he wore underneath clung to his muscles—and impaired Lumiana's ability to chop vegetables, which she realized when she nicked her fingernail with the Japanese chef's knife.

When Johnny caught her looking, Lumiana bit her lip. Of course he smirked. And what did it say about her that his smugness stimulated her libido?

Johnny told Ana that the *Toji San Bijin*—Three Beauties of the Present Day—represented the three women who raised him. His grandmother Margaret, who basically despised everything he stood for. His mother Eleanor, who'd spoiled him as much out of love as she had out of competition with his dad. And Mineko Tsukino, Adam's grandmother, the strongest, wisest woman he'd ever known. The elderly Tsukino was also the one who'd designed his tattoos.

Lumiana recalled with a smile that Adam's grandmother owned a vintage record and tattoo shop in Los Angeles called Johnny B. Goode.

After they covered all of Johnny's tattoos, Ana

focused on the four-inch scar on his right arm. "Is this from your accident when you came here the first time?" She traced the ragged line with her little finger.

Johnny told her all about his fall, and Ana's eyes brightened when he portrayed Lumiana and Gus as superheroes that came to his rescue. The man was a natural with Ana, Lumiana thought, relishing the warmth spreading through her chest.

Wanting a moment alone with Johnny, she sent Ana outside to pick fresh basil from the garden. "Can I see it?" she asked when her daughter was out of sight. Although she had seen him buck-naked last night, she'd been too distracted to get a good look at the scar.

Johnny stretched his arm across the kitchen counter.

When she leaned in to take a closer look, he took advantage of her position and touched his lips to hers. She sighed when he lingered, his fingers stroking along her cheek and neck. At least they had one area, aside from music, where they were compatible.

"I've been meaning to do this all day," he said. "Thanks for being there for me."

She ran her finger along his scar. "I'm sorry about your arm."

"Don't be. I don't mind the scar. It makes me think of you whenever I look at it."

She kissed him with all the affection she

could muster—it frightened her how much there was.

Then she saw her daughter and instantly drew back, her chest constricting as a wave of guilt washed over her.

Ana smiled. "You don't have to stop because of me."

Lumiana blew out a long breath. "I can't do this." She hurried outside and ran all the way to the end of her property, then climbed the tree and lay down atop the rock, panting. She knew she was in trouble when her desire to be in Johnny's arms outweighed her need to push him away.

***

Johnny was sitting alone at the counter, wondering what the hell just happened.

Ana had left the kitchen right after Lumiana, slamming the door to what he assumed was her room.

He let out a heavy sigh, then stretched his neck.

He might not have a handy reference manual to explain how the Harding women functioned, but he was beginning to see a pattern. Like a startled baby bird, Lumiana flailed and fled whenever she felt overwhelmed. And Ana either sulked or tried to fix things, depending on how much her mother's behavior interfered with her own needs.

It wasn't an ideal situation, but not a deal breaker either. He loved spending time with them. And what Lumiana gave—affection, fun, stimulating conversation, hot sex, and musical prowess that matched his own—far outweighed the issues that came up because of her trauma and autistic tendencies. The more time he spent with them, the easier it would get to navigate these situations.

After giving the kid a couple of minutes to cool off, Johnny went to check on her.

Ana lay on her canopy bed, her face burrowed into a pillow.

The room was spacious, well lit, and decorated in sunset colors. There were painting supplies by the window, and huge white shelves filled with books next to a tidy desk.

Johnny noticed the framed picture on the small table next to the bed. It was the only photograph on display in the entire house. He picked it up and sat next to Ana.

"Is this you and your parents?" he said, knowing the answer. Lumiana looked impossibly young and was gazing lovingly at the smiling man who cradled his infant daughter. They looked like one of those perfect families that came with commercial picture frames.

Ana sat up, nodding as she wiped her eyes.

He set the picture back on the bedside table and put a hand on the girl's shoulder.

"Hey, it's going to be okay."

Ana wrapped her short arms around his neck. He held her tight, wondering what it would be like to have a family of his own. Two years ago when Jack's twins were born, the mere thought of settling down gave him the hives. He loved being an uncle though. And now he felt like being a dad might be something he'd enjoy, especially if he could make a kid as awesome as Ana.

Johnny held her for a while, noticing that Ana and Lumiana both hugged as if they were trying to crawl inside him.

They needed someone to love them with the same fierceness. Someone who could fill the void in their hearts. And he wanted to be that person for them if they would have him.

But that was a big *if*. He could tell Lumiana was scared of her feelings for him, and he could understand why. She just needed to let him get close enough for long enough, so he could prove he was reliable, and that he wanted to be all in.

"Is my mom ever going to change?" Ana peered up at him through her wet eyelashes.

He gave her a kiss on the forehead.

If he were in Lumiana's shoes, he doubted he'd be able to work, much less maintain a family. Despite her challenges, Lumiana was a remarkable woman, and he wanted Ana to know that. "Your mom is super strong and brave. And I can tell how much she loves you."

Ana nodded, rubbing her eye with her fist. "I just want her to have someone when I'm too old to live with her."

"You're only seven. There's still plenty of time for her to meet someone."

"But I want it to be you." She tightened her grip around his neck.

Christ, right in the heart. He wished he could promise the girl the world, but they needed to be realistic. "Your mom and I live very different lives. The odds that we can work things out between us aren't great." He sat Ana down. "I can promise you this though. Even if it turns out that I can't be with your mom, I can be your friend. I'll scare all the boys when you're starting to date."

"But you need to wear short sleeves, so they can see your tattoos and your muscles."

"Of course. I'll be very scary."

Giggling, she shook her head. "You don't look scary. You smile too much."

He mimicked Edvard Munch's *Scream*.

"You're goofy, but not scary," Ana said, laughing.

Johnny got up, strolled over to her desk, and scribbled his phone number and address on a sticky note. "You can contact me anytime," he assured her. "Friends?" He held out his hand.

"Friends!" Ana shook his hand with such enthusiasm it made him feel ten feet tall.

"All right, kiddo, let's check on your mom and get something to eat."

They couldn't find Lumiana anywhere, so they ate lunch without her.

Half an hour later, Ana went to her room to do homework, and Johnny headed for the infamous rock. He remembered what Lumiana had told him the day he injured his arm and figured she might be up there trying to find some peace of mind. He brought food and water with him, unsure in what condition he would find her.

**

Johnny found Lumiana up on the rock, stretched out on her back with her eyes closed. She looked so serene he wished he had his phone with him, so he could capture it on camera.

Johnny sat next to her, but she didn't move. "Hey." He touched her cheek.

She woke with a start.

"You were sleeping?"

She sat up with a yawn.

"How are you feeling?"

"How is Ana?"

"She's fine. Are you hungry?" He handed her the bag he'd brought.

She smiled at the sight of the empanadas and dug right in. "Thank you," she said between bites.

Johnny rubbed the back of his neck. "At some point we have to talk, Lu. And I think now would be a good time. No one's going to disturb us up here."

"What about Ana?"

"She said you'd be fine with her being alone

in the house as long as you're nearby. So, no more excuses." He held her gaze until she nodded. "Last night—what are your thoughts?"

She bowed her head. "Why do we have to talk about this?"

"You told me you weren't going to have sex with me and then you did it three times in one night. I want to know what changed your mind." He couldn't wait to get his hands on her again.

"I don't know…" She fiddled with the water bottle. "I never expected I'd miss you as much as I did."

Johnny took her hand. "How do you feel about me now?"

"You already know."

"I'd like to hear you say it."

Sighing, Lumiana got up and dusted off her clothes. Johnny did the same and waited her out, but she didn't speak.

Then she pulled him close and gave him a thorough kiss that made his heart beat a little faster. "This should tell you all you need to know." She turned around and was about to walk away when he grabbed her and kissed her so vehemently it left them panting.

"We're not done yet."

"Johnny—"

"Please, I need to know where we go from here."

"Do you want to be friends?"

"With benefits?" He'd take friendship if that

was his only option, but he wanted her in his life any way he could have her.

"I don't need your money, and I don't wish for gifts," she said with her chin held high. "I'm doing extremely well for myself."

He burst into laughter, then gave her a smacking kiss. "Lu, that's not what friends with benefits means." He had to do a better job of remembering that she was a foreigner with no sense of pop culture past the Victorian era. He feathered kisses along her neck. "Friends don't do this, right?" He slid his hand down her back and curvy behind, pressing her against him.

Johnny was about to let go of her when she swiftly covered his hand with hers. With her other hand she cupped the back of his neck and drew his mouth down to hers.

He swept her off her feet and carried her over to a rise in the rock, pushing her up so her legs came tightly around him. He loved her right there, wrapped in sunlight, surrounded by breathtaking landscapes.

"Now that you have experienced the benefits," he said afterward, "is this something you'd be interested in?"

She looked at him with a furrowed brow.

Part of him considered backing off, but his gut told him to push forward. He took her hand. "Do you really want to live your life like this? Void of meaningful relationships because you're scared of getting hurt?"

She didn't answer.

He studied their linked hands. "Pain is part of living a full life, Lumiana. Otherwise, most people would never explore what can be."

He knew facing fears was easier said than done. He'd struggled with depression and would choose a life without it in a heartbeat, but it had also taught him to savor the moments of joy more consciously.

"And who knows, if we shift our thinking from 'this is never going to work because of our differences' to 'let's try and find a solution so we can make it work,' we might find a way. I know I'm a lot to take on. But I want to give this a try."

She let out a huge breath. "Okay."

"So you're in?" He couldn't contain the smile and leaned in to kiss her, but she stopped him.

"I'm willing to give this a try." She kept her hand pressed against his chest. "But promise me you won't put too much pressure on me all at once."

Johnny saw the fear in her eyes and embraced her.

"Promise me," she insisted.

"I promise. We'll take it one day at a time."

***

Half an hour later, sitting around the patio table overlooking the rolling hills of Las Espitas, Johnny and Lumiana told Ana they wanted to keep seeing each other. Johnny felt as nervous as

Lumiana looked, but the little girl jumped with excitement at their news, hugging them both.

It would've been a moment of pure joy if it weren't for the words that left Lumiana's lips right before Ana ran off to play with the dog.

"Even if I want to spend more time with Johnny, I will always love your dad."

This made him itchy. He'd seen the family picture. Jayjay had been her everything. Maybe it was absurd to be jealous of a dead guy, but Lumiana's feelings for that man were still very much alive.

He hoped to God she didn't fantasize about Jayjay when he slept with her. Hadn't she said she felt bad for using him as a substitute when they first met?

Johnny pulled at the thin black elastic around his wrist and let it snap against his skin; he hadn't used it in a while, had almost forgotten it was there.

The past three months he'd curbed his obsessive worrying with booze, sex, and weed. But now that he was going to spend more time with Lumiana and Ana, he needed a more sensible way to cope. Might be time for an appointment with Dr. Sobel.

Lumiana stopped his train of thought when she tilted his chin toward her and pressed her lips to his.

He could kiss that woman for hours—

"Um, excuse me," a voice startled them.

"Sorry to interrupt your little matinee."

"Marisa!" Lumiana jumped up and ran over to a pretty woman holding a small package. She gave the woman a hug so energetic it nearly sent the package flying.

When Johnny got up to join them, Lumiana said, "This is Johnny, my friend with benefits."

Say what now? Johnny gave her a nudge.

"What?" Lumiana murmured to him.

"You can't say that to people," he whispered back.

Marisa's rosy lips twitched with humor. "It's nice to meet you, Johnny. I'm Marisa, Lumiana's aunt."

They looked nothing alike, except for height. They were both about five foot eight, but Marisa was pale and slender and wore her chestnut brown hair in a curly bob.

"They delivered the herbs and tea leaves you requested," Marisa said, handing Lumiana the package. "Are you coming to the family get-together Monday afternoon?"

Lumiana sniffed the box. "We'll be there."

"Are you coming too?" Marisa asked him. "It's quite the event. Very high energy."

Johnny took Lumiana's hand. "I'd love to come, as long as you don't introduce me as your friend with benefits."

"You were the one who used this term earlier."

"As a joke," he said with an apologetic glance

at Marisa. "You were asking me to be friends, Lu, which isn't quite the accurate description of what we are."

"Fine, then what do you want me to call you?"

"I don't know," he said sheepishly. "You're the one who sets the parameters of our relationship. You decide." He had several relationships over the past two decades but this one felt like his first. Probably because Lumiana was so different from what he was used to, and the environment was different too.

Marisa beamed at him. "You must be special to her regardless of your relationship status, because Lumi never brings a date, or a friend to meet her family."

He couldn't say that surprised him. Imagining her on a date put a smile on his face.

Johnny draped his arm around Lumiana's waist and kissed her temple. He still couldn't believe he got to touch her now whenever he felt like it. That alone made him stupidly happy.

"I assume you told him how important discretion is," Marisa said to Lumiana. "No phones or cameras."

Johnny shot Lumiana a questioning look, but before she had a chance to speak, her aunt said, "I'll leave you two to it. It was fun meeting you, Johnny." Marisa gave Lumiana a kiss on the cheek, then nipped across the lawn to say hi to Ana.

"What was that about?" Johnny asked as they

returned to the patio.

Lumiana put the package on the bamboo table before she faced him. "I told you my family isn't like other families."

He folded his arms. "Yes, but you didn't give me the specifics."

"If you think what I've been through is tragic, you don't want to know what happened to some of my siblings before Emma and Fernando took them in. At least no one wishes to take my life," she said before he could ask her to clarify.

Trying to get Lumiana to open up was like digging up state secrets. But she finally revealed there was one case in particular that could be a serious threat to their safety if the wrong people found out who the Arendt-Garcías were, and where they were hiding Lumiana's sister Ayana.

Johnny wondered if her sister was around here somewhere, because the Jonata reservation wasn't even on the map. He had to send Magnum the GPS coordinates to get here.

Johnny scratched his cheek. This was just getting better and better. First the dead love of her life, then the kid, and now some complex web of family secrets. Mix that in with their different lifestyles and his apparent inability to make relationships last, and you have one glorious recipe for disaster. Maybe he was getting more than he'd bargained for.

"Is this the real reason why you didn't want to meet me?"

"Yes, because I have to keep a low profile at all costs while your life is all about being heard and being seen." The wariness left her eyes, and determination took its place. "I cannot change who my family is. And in order to protect them, you can't tell anyone who I am to you or where I live."

So they were hiding Ayana here.

"Not even your family and friends can know about this, unless you are absolutely certain they can be trusted. But to be honest, I'd rather you told no one."

He shook his head. *How the hell is this supposed to work?* That meant they could never be seen in public together, or at least not in a way that appeared attractive to the media. But even if he'd be okay with hiding their relationship from the public, he could never keep his girlfriend from his band mates or his family.

"Do you really want this, Johnny?" There was a challenge in her voice. "Now everything is new and exciting, but after a while you might wish to bring me to an event or share this," she gestured to encompass them and their surroundings, "with others, but you can't. Not until this case is closed, and even then we'd have to be careful. Do *you* want to live your life like that?"

Who in their right mind would want to live like that? "This is just great," he muttered, raking a hand through his hair.

"I apologize, Johnny. I understand if you wish to part ways now." Lumiana closed her hand around her locket. "Please say goodbye to Ana before you leave."

"Just give me a moment, okay?" He tried to imagine what life with Lumiana would be like if they couldn't be seen together in public. Did it mean their entire relationship would be confined to Jonata?

***

They sat without speaking for a while. Lumiana wasn't sure what to do. This was the reason her family kept to themselves.

All of them, whether deliberately or accidentally, had been abandoned by their birth families, so trust was something that didn't come easy. Jayjay had been an orphan too, and he and Ana quickly became part of her family because they fit right in.

But with Johnny it would be different. Not only was he famous for his music, he was also born into one of California's wealthiest families. People were interested in him and who his girlfriends were.

She needed to be cautious if she wanted to be with him, provided it was something he still wanted after discovering that her family was hiding a small army of skeletons in Casa de Esperanza's closets.

Johnny still didn't look up but was absently playing with the black elastic on his wrist. He'd snapped it earlier. She didn't know why he was wearing it, but she knew people used it as a coping mechanism to stop compulsive thoughts and behaviors.

Lumiana couldn't stand his silence any longer. It was strange to see him so quiet, so still, because he was usually the opposite. He liked to talk, and she liked listening to him. The sound of his voice was like a rich, velvet melody that touched something deep within her.

Inhaling courage, she placed her hand over his. "I apologize that I haven't been more forthcoming with you. But I think you wouldn't have tried to get to know me had you known all of this about me and my family from the beginning." And this wasn't even all of it. They'd barely skimmed the surface.

He remained silent but turned his hand so her palm touched his.

"Deep down, part of me hoped you wouldn't stop trying. I can admit that now." She kept staring at her feet. "Please, say something."

He sighed, but after a few more moments, he said, "It's not a good feeling, is it? Not knowing what's going on in someone else's mind when you feel you really need to know?"

"Are you attempting to teach me a lesson?"

He scrubbed a hand over his mouth. "I think I'm actually teaching myself a lesson. It may not feel good if you can't get an answer out of someone when you need one, but it's also hard when you're the one who has to find the right words and talk about stuff that's difficult."

She nodded. "Do you need more time?"

"No." When she lowered her head, he closed his hand around hers. "To be fair, you repeatedly told me to leave you alone, and it was my decision to ignore it, so you're not really the one to blame here. And you're right, had I known how the nature of your family would affect our relationship, I probably would've stayed away."

After thinking for a moment, he said, "No, you know what, knowing how I am, I would've tried to get you to work with me anyway. You have a voice I could never forget. I knew I had to meet you."

That made her smile. His sheer determination was something she was able to connect with. It was the thing that kept her going no matter how many times life tried to beat her down.

Giving her hand a squeeze, he added, "I'm glad I didn't stay away because I haven't felt this alive and inspired in a long time."

She touched her lips to his, but he broke the kiss right away.

He drew his bottom lip into his mouth. "I have to be honest with you though. I'm not sure I can do this." He motioned between them.

There she was, finally daring to open her heart a crack to see if she might be ready for a new adventure, and the door shuts right in her face. But because she'd made it this far, she would at least attempt to pry it open. "I understand,

Johnny, but—"

"I don't think you understand, Lu. I'm someone who tends to overshare," he said before she could finish. "I understand this whole secrecy thing is necessary, and I hope with time you trust me enough to get into more detail about your family situation. But I can't promise that being with you only when we're at home, no matter how beautiful this home is, will be enough for me."

She wished things were different, and hopefully one day they would be, but for now they needed to be careful.

Johnny tipped her chin up and kissed her gently. "If it's meant to be, we'll find a way."

10

FEVER

*"You don't have to attend every argument
you're invited to."*

—UNKNOWN

Before dinner, Johnny, Lumiana and Ana climbed
up the moon bridge and watched the sunset
paint the hills in hues of pink. Lumiana had
made this visual reminder to appreciate the
beauty all around them an integral part of their
evening ritual. And what a beauty it was, Johnny
thought as he admired the stately oak and ash
trees, which stood scattered about the landscape
like dancers frozen in time.

He loved this place, really appreciated the
serenity it offered. In theory, he knew how differ-

ent his way of life was from Lumiana's, but every hour he spent with her he could *feel* the difference. The peace he experienced here was something he'd rarely felt throughout his life. First because his family fell apart, and he wasn't able to live up to their expectations, and then because of all the media attention. Those damn paparazzi were always waiting to capture his next mishap and constantly pried into his love life.

He needed a break. He needed *this*—and at the worst possible time because of his impending album release and the required promotional tour.

Just then Johnny's phone vibrated. He'd kept it on him this time in case it was his mom or the hospital. Sliding it out of his pocket, he squinted at the screen, and then dismissed the call, but not before Ana, who sat next to him, saw the caller ID.

"Who is Andie?" she asked.

"Ana," Lumiana scolded her, "don't be so nosy. If Johnny wanted us to know, he would tell us."

"Let's just enjoy the sunset," he said, stretching his neck side to side.

"Was that your off-on girlfriend Andie Woodhull?" Ana practically had stars in her eyes. "She is *so* beautiful and everyone loves her. My best friend Peyton is her biggest fan. She has a huge poster of her."

Johnny glanced at Lumiana, who kept staring into the distance. "How do you know this, Ana?

Andie is not my girlfriend anymore. It's called on-again, off-again. If you say 'off-on' it sounds like we're still together, which we are not," he stressed the last word to make sure Lumiana understood he wasn't two-timing her.

"I googled you after I found the letter you wrote to my mom," Ana told him. "We have Internet at school."

"Great," he muttered. "I wish you hadn't done that, Ana." He was fully aware of all the true and false shit people wrote about him. The thought that Ana may have read it not only embarrassed him, but also reminded him that if he had kids one day, they might read it too.

Lumiana cleared her throat. "How about I go back inside and prepare dinner while you two talk?" She climbed down the moon bridge and disappeared into the house.

Man, a couple of hours into their relationship, and he was already messing this up.

"Ana, please know that the things people say about me aren't necessarily true."

"I know that," she assured him. "My mom always asks me, 'What is your source?' when I tell her something." Johnny gave the kid points for nailing Lumiana's intonation. It was a little freaky that Ana looked more like a preschooler than a seven-year-old but sounded almost like a teenager. "It's very annoying because sometimes I can't remember the source, and then she makes me search for it or I have to admit that it's not a fact but *especalation*."

"You mean speculation?"

"Yes, speculation. You don't know what it's like to have a mom who is a scientist. She wants proof of *everything*."

He smiled, thinking that Lumiana was like comedy and tragedy combined into one beautifully wrapped package. So what if she felt irked or jealous hearing about Andie? At least his ex hadn't been the love of his life. He was the one who had to measure up to the great Jordan Jackson.

"But Andie Woodhull was your girlfriend until not so long ago. There are photos of the two of you together that prove it."

"You're right. Andie was my girlfriend until recently."

"How recently?"

He went with the truth. "About a month before I met your mother." Okay, not the whole truth. Ana didn't need to know about the one night he'd spent with Andie after his life-altering weekend with Lumiana. Had he known there was a chance for him and Lumiana to be together, he never would've done it.

"And how long were you boyfriend and girlfriend?"

"On and off, about a year."

"Why aren't you together anymore?"

"Ana, why do you want to know all this? You sound like my mother."

Her brows crinkled. "I don't want my mom to get hurt."

"You do know your mom is already upset, right?"

"Why?" she said, reminding him she was a kid after all.

"You'll understand when you're older. But for the future, please don't talk about Andie in front of your mom. And to be clear, I don't see your mom as a rebound, if you're worried about that."

"*Mamá*, what is a rebound?" the little girl asked when Johnny and Ana returned to the house a few minutes later.

Lumiana was in the kitchen, whisking eggs in a bowl. She scowled at him.

Johnny drew a deep breath. He knew his past would come to bite him in the ass, he just didn't think it would be so soon.

"A rebound is when something bounces back after striking a hard surface, like when you throw a ball against a wall," Lumiana explained.

God, he loved the way she pronounced *thr* with a roll of her tongue. He could listen to her all day. Unfortunately, she wasn't much of a talker.

Ana turned to him. "I don't understand what you meant with my mom and the rebound."

"Lucky for me, your mom doesn't know what it means either."

Lumiana put down the bowl. "Enlighten me."

"I'd rather not."

She grabbed her phone and sent a message.

Johnny and Ana had just taken a seat at the counter when Lumiana's ancient iPhone buzzed. He'd love to get her the latest model but was pretty sure she'd take offense if he tried.

"Shawn says, 'a rebound means you quickly move from one relationship to the next to avoid the pain of a breakup,'" she read aloud. "Is that what this is, Johnny, a rebound relationship?"

He pressed his palm against his forehead. "I told Ana that I do *not* see you as a rebound."

Lumiana shrugged and ignored him throughout a very quiet dinner.

When the napkin he asked for landed on his plate, he said, "That's enough, Lu. Can we talk please?"

She got up and carried the plates over to the kitchen, ignoring him.

Ana gave him a rueful look and told him she'd go to her room.

Once they were alone, Johnny strode over to the kitchen, where Lumiana continued to evade him until he lost his patience.

Despite her protests, he gave her a fireman's lift up the stairs to the guest room because it was closest to the staircase, and she had her mind set on making carrying her as difficult as possible. She nearly made him stumble when she pinched his ass.

Johnny closed the door behind them and dropped her on the bed. He could see she was poised for a fight—not with words, but an actual wrestling match.

"Please talk to me, Lu."

She kissed him instead. Good thing he liked it rough, because the woman was relentless. A second later, taking advantage of his inattention, she threw him on his back, straddled him, and cuffed his wrists with her hands.

"Those self-defense classes really paid off, huh?"

She smiled triumphantly and was about to have her wicked way with him when his phone vibrated again.

Johnny freed one wrist to fish it out of his pocket but Lumiana kept a tight grip on his other wrist. Biting his earlobe, she slid her free hand down his jeans and fondled his erection.

"Ah, sorry," he said through clenched teeth. "I have to check who it is in case it's the hospital."

But it was Andie.

Again?

He dismissed her call and put his phone on the nightstand.

Rolling over, Lumiana tried to get off the bed, but he managed to catch her by the arm.

"Where are you going?"

"Why don't you just talk to her?" she shot back.

"Right, because it's not at all inappropriate to talk to my ex when I'm trying to have a moment with you. Isn't that what got this whole thing started?"

Lumiana propped her hands on her hips. "It's obviously important. She has called twice in one hour. Talk to her. I will go to my room. I could use some time to myself." She smiled mischievously. "Maybe I'll wait for you. Maybe I won't."

He groaned at the thought, but let her go. She was right, Andie wouldn't call unless something was up.

***

When Johnny padded into Lumiana's bedroom ten minutes later, she was bundled up on the sofa, absorbed in a book. She ignored him, but made no effort to prevent him from touching her, until he trailed kisses along her neck.

"I'm attempting to read here," she said, but angled her head, so he could continue.

"Do you want me to stop?"

Taking a fistful of his shirt, she pulled him onto her.

He was devouring her mouth in a heated kiss when a knock on the door interrupted them.

"Dammit." He covered his hard-on with a pillow because he didn't want this to turn into an educational moment.

Lumiana gave him a cheeky smile before she told Ana to come in. "Is everything okay, *angelito*?" she asked the little girl who crawled into her lap like a love-starved puppy.

"I don't want you to fight because of me."

Johnny took Ana's hand. He hadn't meant for her to feel at fault. "We didn't have a fight." Just an uncomfortable moment of which there'll probably be a shitload more.

Ana held on to his hand. "Can you come downstairs for storytelling?"

Lumiana smiled at him. "Would you like to witness another Harding family tradition?"

The three of them went downstairs, where they said goodnight to the animals, then huddled on Ana's bed.

"Have you brushed your teeth?" Lumiana asked her daughter.

Ana showed off her pearly whites. Johnny smiled at the typical mother-daughter moment.

Nightly storytelling was a routine Lumiana and Ana had perfected. Rather than Lumiana reading to Ana from a book, the two of them made up their own story as they went along. Johnny appreciated their hilarious impressions of the different characters and Lumiana's skill at ending the story with a moral.

"I'm so happy you're here, Johnny," Ana said when they tucked her in.

"You and me both, kid." He kissed her on the forehead, then led Lumiana back upstairs.

***

They sat on the sofa in Lumiana's bedroom, both leaning against an armrest, so they were facing each other but with only their legs touching.

They didn't speak, and since she needed to re-group, she was grateful he didn't try to fill the silence.

Despite the stress of meeting Johnny's family and the discomfort she felt earlier, it had been an incredible day. She loved that Johnny had this way of making Ana feel special, like he genuinely enjoyed having her around.

He was good with *both* of them.

Surprisingly, Johnny hadn't changed his mind about being with her. According to Shawn, Johnny was infamous for being the life of the party, attracted to all things glossy, which appar-ently extended to the women he dated, who were supermodels and actresses. Women who were the polar opposite of her.

But for some reason he appeared happy and relaxed around her, like he belonged here with them.

And she loved having him around, even though it was different from the way it had been with Jayjay. Jayjay had never challenged her like Johnny did. Johnny actually liked butting heads with her, she thought with a smile. He touched her with a passion that was raw, almost feral. And because he was wild with her, she was able to unleash her own wildness. It was liberating in a way she hadn't felt since childhood when her parents and Esperanza had let her run free.

"What is it?" Lumiana said when Johnny looked at her with an intense expression she couldn't interpret. It prickled her skin.

"You're incredibly beautiful."

She couldn't help but laugh.

Johnny poked her with his foot. "Has no one ever told you that you're beautiful? This is not the way you're supposed to react."

She tapped her lips. "I bet it's something you say to all the women. If you feel compelled to compliment me, I'd appreciate it if you could make an effort to be a bit more original."

He scratched the back of his neck. "Even if it *is* something I've said a hundred times to a hundred women, I didn't say it to you for the fun of it or in hopes of sexual favors. I said it because there are moments when I look at you and it feels like someone reaches into my chest and squeezes my heart. You make me feel things I haven't felt before—when you smile, when you scowl at me, when you're so engrossed in something that the world vanishes around you. So when I said you're beautiful it wasn't just about the way you look, but about the way you are."

She jumped him like a leopard does its prey, making them tumble off the sofa.

"You okay?" he mumbled against her shoulder.

"Yes," she said, grinning. "You?"

Johnny pointed at his head. "I think I hurt myself."

Lumiana came closer so she could examine him.

When he pulled her down and kissed her, she squealed and swatted at him. "I was so worried!"

Laughing, he flipped her over on her back and kept kissing her, his mouth traveling all the way south.

As he bunched her dress up, he nipped the inside of her thigh, his fingers stroking over the cotton of her underwear. When she arched her back, he hooked her legs over his shoulders and pushed her panties aside. His breath on her skin made her toes curl in anticipation.

Sliding one hand up her torso, he palmed her breast, squeezing lightly. As his tongue flicked her most sensitive spot, her eyes drifted shut, her breathing growing more labored with each skilled movement of his hands and mouth.

So good.

She dug her fingers into his hair as the pressure built in her core.

So close.

With an appreciative growl, he stroked her inside and out. When he pressed his tongue against her once more, Lumiana saw a kaleidoscope of stars, leaving her so light-headed it took her a moment to figure out where she was.

Bathed in soft beams from the lights in the ceiling, she blinked a few times until she saw Johnny smiling at her.

Her instinct was to cover her face, but he took hold of her hands.

"I hate you," Lumiana grumbled, failing to

keep the smile off her face.

Johnny laughed with his heart, which only added to his beauty. "How are you feeling otherwise?"

"Why did you do that to me?" She touched her forehead, hoping she didn't look as feverish as she felt.

His grin was that of a naughty boy. "I admit, I love seeing you flustered, but there's no reason to feel embarrassed. I'm impressed you can let go like that. And I did it because I wanted you to feel good, and because it's fun to play with you. Why do you ask? You'd rather I didn't?"

And make myself miss out on earth-shattering orgasms? No, thank you. She closed her eyes. "Do you give encores?"

"If the audience cheers loud enough I certainly will."

Much to Johnny's amusement, she staggered a bit as she got up.

"You know what you could do for me, Doc?" he said as they headed toward the bathroom to get ready for bed. "Cut your damn fingernails."

They weren't particularly long, but they were strong and sharp.

Lumiana came to a halt, but before she had a chance to react, Johnny tipped her over his arm, kissed her, and swooped her back up. She would have run into the wall hadn't he grabbed her shortly before impact. "Watch where you're going," he said, laughing.

The next morning, Johnny met his mother at Community General, and congratulated himself for actually making it there.

Crazy, the amount of willpower it had taken to get out of bed earlier.

After he and Lumiana had been up half the night rolling around in the sheets, he'd selfishly wanted her to stay in his arms. But instead of letting him hold her for all eternity, she'd kicked him out of her bed, served him the world's most delicious omelet, and then topped it all with a mind-numbing blowjob in her rainfall shower.

It was a miracle he'd made it through traffic alive.

"Where have you been?" his mom huffed when he ran into her in the hallway.

"Sorry, ma, I've been out of town. It took a while to get here." He couldn't get used to the sterile smell of the hospital. It was as though the walls were calling his name: *You're next, Graham.* The faster his dad got out of here, the better.

"You didn't tell me you were going on a trip. I thought you stayed with a friend."

"I stayed with a friend who lives out of town," he said because he wanted to prolong his happiness. If he told his mom about his relationship with Lumiana, she'd find a way to spoil it for him, most likely by attempting to talk him out of it. "How's Dad?"

"He's doing better. He's been waiting to see you."

Janice, the attractive blond nurse, spotted him from across the hallway and waved. It still baffled him that he was falling in love with someone so different from the women he was usually attracted to. Maybe his shrink could shed some light on that.

Johnny returned Janice's wave. If he hadn't just met the woman who rocked his world like no other, he might've asked her out.

"I talked to Andie," his mother interrupted his thoughts. "She says she has something important to tell you. Why haven't you gone to see her?"

"She won't tell me what she wants over the phone and I've been busy doing promotion for my single." His publicist had called earlier to tell him she'd lined up some additional promo gigs. He still couldn't believe "Wonder" debuted in the Top 20. "Ma, I'd really like you to stop bugging me about Andie. I've moved on, and so should you."

"What about what's her name... Lumiana?"

"What about her?"

"Is she the friend you've been staying with?"

"What does it matter?" He didn't mean to sound snippy, but his mom liked to poke around in places that were none of her business, which made her an excellent attorney, but often an annoying mother.

Why was she even still talking to Andie?

His family hadn't been fond of her in the

beginning either. To them, modeling, much like singing or acting, wasn't an actual career but a hobby. However, once they learned that Andie was the daughter of a wealthy Catholic business-man, they took an interest in her, which eventually turned into genuine affection.

Even Grandma Margaret, according to his mother, had been "deeply dismayed" by their breakup. He'd bet his beloved Porsche she was most upset over the lost opportunity to grow the family fortune.

His mom pinned him with her lawyer gaze. "Why are you being so secretive lately?"

There was no point in arguing, so Johnny sucked it up. It was what they did in his family —that and diligently sweeping things under the rug until they formed a bulge so big someone tripped over it. "I have to figure some stuff out for myself. I promise, I'll talk to you when there's something to tell."

Although she kept frowning, she did agree to leave him be.

11

NEXT GENERATION

*"It's not our differences that divide us.
It's our inability to recognize, accept,
and celebrate those differences."*

—AUDRE LOURDE

Johnny arrived an hour late at Casa de Esperanza,
the Italianate mansion that had been Lumiana's
home during her college and grad school years.
Although it was only a fifteen-minute ride from
his own childhood home, he didn't know this
place existed.

The spacious parking lot was right past the
entrance gate and held an eclectic mix of ve-
hicles from motorcycles, sports cars, and station
wagons to battered pickup trucks, sleek SUVs,

and an Airstream travel trailer.

It was beautiful here, quiet. The only sounds he heard were chirping birds, the hum of an approaching car, and the gravel crunching under his shoes. He could see why Lumiana had been happy here.

Strolling up the unpaved driveway, Johnny felt the same sense of peacefulness settle over him that he experienced at Jonata.

The exterior of the house and the landscape surrounding it looked sunny and cared for, but not manicured like his parents' and grandparents' estates. This place had character. The slightly weathered terracotta brick building, and the pin-straight cypress trees that lined the path, reminded him of the villa his parents had rented in Tuscany on the last vacation they took as a family.

Lumiana's aunt Marisa Arendt arrived at the same time and welcomed him with a hug. Johnny wondered if it was a family thing because Lumiana and Ana had been equally affectionate with him from the get-go. Being around them was like getting CPR for the soul. Perhaps he wouldn't need Dr. Sobel after all.

Marisa opened the door for him. "Are you ready for this?"

"As ready as I'll ever be." Taking a deep breath, he crossed the threshold.

Marisa patted him on the shoulder. "Meeting the family for the first time can be nerve-racking, but we're open-minded, so don't be nervous."

Johnny knew it only took one Google search to figure out he wasn't a saint. "I hope you're right," he said as she led the way through the house.

The light suffused interior of the building was stunning. The tall, moulded walls were painted in warm colors ranging from coastal beige to autumn red, and just like in Lumiana's house, hundreds of books lined the floor-to-ceiling shelves.

Johnny followed Marisa out to the gorgeous backyard, where the party was in full swing. He stopped mid-stride when he saw the crowd.

There were at least a hundred people, many dressed in indigenous clothing, probably reflecting their countries of origin. Small flags of different nations hung in the olive and cypress trees, and he could hear guests speaking in foreign languages. It felt more like an international summit than the average family get-together.

"You like it?" Marisa said, beaming with pride.

"Not at all what I expected."

"It's our annual celebration of cultures. Didn't Lumi tell you?"

"Nope. Unless it's about anthropology, literature, or music, I have to work hard to get any kind of information out of her."

"She's like that with everyone." Marisa gave a good-natured shrug. "In the beginning she barely talked at all. Yes and no was all she said whenever someone asked her a question. Her brothers used to call her NTY—'No, Thank You,' her favorite response. They adore her, and always have, so no bad blood there."

"Yeah," he said with a chuckle, remembering the dynamic between Lumiana and Gus. "She hasn't told me much about her past. Every time I've tried asking her about it, she got upset."

The light in Marisa's eyes dimmed. "Some of her story will always hurt. But it's important for you to know these things about her. It'll help you understand her sometimes rather odd behavior. And she's also stronger than she appears."

It felt reassuring to get some encouragement from someone who knew her.

Marisa took two Bellinis from one of the passing waiters and handed him one.

"Cheers," he said, raising the champagne flute to toast her.

Before Marisa clinked her glass to his, she told him, "It's customary in German culture to look each other in the eyes while toasting because legend says it's seven years of bad sex if you fail to do so. Right, Justin?" Marisa winked at the guy who'd just joined them on the patio.

"I'm British, darling. We always have bad sex." Justin gave her a kiss on the cheek and disappeared into the house.

Johnny took another sip of the fruity drink. "Can I ask you something?"

"Sure."

"Lumiana has a large family she's very fond of, so why are there no pictures of loved ones displayed around her house, except for the one in Ana's room?"

"Self-protection," Marisa said with a sigh. "She's afraid to get too attached to people and things, because in her experience, they get taken away from her sooner or later. That's why she has so little stuff and prefers to keep it that way." Marisa finished her glass, set it on the table. "She has one picture of her birth parents, which is in the locket she wears. The necklace, her mom's diary, and her white dress are the only heirlooms she has." Marisa gave his arm a sympathetic squeeze. "Let's go find her. I think she might be getting ready for her performance."

"Her performance?"

"Oh, you're in for a treat." Marisa told him that every year for this celebration most of the adopted siblings put on a show where they performed something that represents their origins. Lumiana usually did some kind of medley to honor her diverse roots. "Lumi is amazing, so prepare to be dazzled."

She better be singing because it had been too long since he'd heard her sing. During the weeks when he thought he'd never see her again, he'd nearly begged Adam to send him his recording of her.

Ana joined them just before Lumiana's adoptive father Fernando García took the stage. The man, who reminded Johnny of Lenny Kravitz with the aviator shades and the rock star air, welcomed everyone. Then his son Gus and a few of his other kids performed an upbeat mix of reggae and ska from Gus's native Jamaica. When Fernando grabbed the guitar to accompany them, the crowd went wild. And damn, was he good—the man could teach him a thing or two.

Johnny was even more surprised that he recognized some of the faces. "Is that Bruno Mars and Philip Lawrence?" he asked Ana as she pulled him through the crowd. "Hey, wait, I know this guy—Adam?" He let go of Ana's hand.

"Johnny?" Adam shot him a skeptical look. "What are you doing here? And how's your dad?"

"He's doing somewhat better." Johnny brohugged his friend. "What are you doing here?"

"I'm tight with Shawn, remember? This is his family's *Fiesta de las Culturas*. You're the last person I expected seeing here after whatever happened between you and—"

"Are those two over there Helen Green and Jimmy Noel?" Johnny interrupted. "We're scheduled to appear on their shows sometime this month, right?"

He waved, and Helen and Jimmy came over.

"Johnny Graham?" Helen said by way of greeting. In her fifties, Helen had the energy of a woman half her age. "This is a surprise!"

Jimmy gave him a pat on the shoulder. The man was about a decade younger than Helen, but he too had a youthful energy that defied his age. "How are you doing, Johnny? Really looking forward to your performance next week. I hear the album is your best one yet."

"Thanks. Didn't expect to see either of you here. I thought the Arendt-Garcías were trying to avoid media attention at all costs…" The cumbia performance momentarily distracted Johnny. He gazed at the colorful traditional Colombian dresses swaying gracefully as the dancers swiveled across the stage.

"We're close friends with the Arendt-Garcías, and this is indeed a private event," Helen told him. "We've been supporting their work for years. CDE—*Casa de Esperanza*—is not only their home, it's a charitable community project." Helen bent down to greet Ana, then asked, "What brings you here, Johnny?"

"Yes, Johnny, what are you doing here?" Adam teased, giving him a pat on the shoulder.

"I thought I was here to spend some quality time with my girlfriend. This," he gestured around, "wasn't what I expected." He actually had no clue where Lumiana was.

"Andie is here? I had no idea you two got back together." Helen had interviewed Johnny numerous times, as had Jimmy, and they knew all about his string of famous exes.

"Johnny is my mom's boyfriend," Ana announced, and then ran off to play with the other kids.

Helen and Jimmy stared at him, while Adam's mouth formed a silent 'seriously?'

"You're dating Lumiana Harding?" Jimmy asked with raised brows.

"'Dating' isn't the right word." Even 'girl-friend' somehow didn't feel like an adequate description. Those words sounded too cute, too frivolous to reflect the intense nature of their relationship.

"Please don't take this the wrong way, Johnny," said Helen, "but how in the world does someone like you end up with someone like her?"

Looking around in hopes of spotting Lumiana somewhere, he mumbled, "I've been asking myself the same question."

"Are you sure we're talking about the same person?" asked Jimmy. "Unusual eyes, sunny smile?"

Adam gave him a wide-eyed stare. "When you said something happened between the two of you, I didn't think you meant *that*."

He scratched his temple. "I *didn't*. We got together this weekend, which is why I haven't had the chance to tell you about it. But you knew I have feelings for her, so it shouldn't be that much of a surprise."

"Lumiana, really?" Helen's gaze darted around as if she was trying to spot a hidden camera. "How did you two meet?"

"Adam gets all the credit. First he played me a recording of her singing, and then he suggested I sign up for her course. I just wanted to chat with her about the possibility of a musical collaboration, but, well—things went in an unexpected direction."

The drumming sounds of the cajón on stage echoed the sudden tension Johnny sensed in Helen and Jimmy.

"Johnny, if you're messing with her, you better believe in Jesus because he's the only one who can save you if you break that woman's heart," warned Helen. "Do you know what she's been through? She doesn't deserve to get hurt again. And believe me, you don't want all these people here coming after you. They might seem harmless, but if you hurt one of their own, all bets are off."

"What she said," added Jimmy. "They have friends in powerful places, Johnny. I'd be careful with this one."

Johnny felt the heat rise up his throat. "I know I haven't been a fucking angel, okay? Thanks for the reminder. But I'm making a real effort here. Do you honestly think I'd be with someone like her if I wasn't dead serious about her? Sure, she deserves better than me, I'll give you that, but she's also a grown woman, and she chose—"

"Stop it, all of you," Lumiana snapped, her face flushed.

Only then did Johnny realize that a number of people around them were listening in.

Fuck it.

His own family was judgmental enough. He didn't need this. Scrubbing his hands over his face, he turned to leave. Ironic, because that was something his family excelled at as well: running from problems. Like his grandfather had done two decades ago, then his parents, and ultimately, he realized now, it was what he himself had done in every relationship he'd ever been in.

Lumiana pulled on his arm. Part of him wanted to push her aside, so he could leave, but that she wanted him to stay even though he'd caused a scene kept him frozen in place.

Lumiana tightened her grip on his arm as she faced Helen and Jimmy. "I know you want to protect me, and I appreciate it, but please refrain from doing it in a way that scares him off. We are not the Corleones."

Go Lumiana—a pop culture reference from this century! Who knew she had it in her.

She turned to him. "Johnny, I apologize. This is certainly not how I envisioned the introduction, but—everyone, this is Johnny, my boyfriend."

Yeah, not the right term. He wanted to be her partner, possibly her spouse one day. Even 'significant other' sounded more accurate.

All eyes turned to him.

He gave a weak smile.

"Johnny, this is my family."

There was a moment of uncomfortable silence before Lumiana's family members welcomed him. Helen and Jimmy apologized, although Johnny was convinced they had meant every word.

A few minutes later, the party resumed and Johnny grabbed a moment alone with Lumiana, who said she was sorry before he even said anything. She cupped his face with her hands and kissed him like she meant it.

Sighing, Johnny stroked her cheek. "Thanks, Doc. I needed that."

"Why do you think I deserve better than you?"

His fingers went cold. "You're everything I'm not, Lu. Which is a good thing," he said while she continued to frown. "But it also makes people think, and that includes myself, that you deserve to be with someone who's more like you... pure of heart—"

"Johnny, I'm not pure of—"

He shook his head. "No, please let me finish. If the past has proven one thing, then it's that I suck at relationships."

Now she was the one shaking her head. "Everyone, including you, is hinting at me that you are somehow a bad person."

"Not bad per se, but—"

"*But*," she repeated, "all the time we've spent together, and even the day we met when I was cross with you, there was nothing indicating that what you say about yourself is true. Sure, you are a bit smug, annoyingly persistent, and here is a big word just for you, *loquacious*—"

Her taking a dig at him for being an English

literature minor with a propensity for eloquent speech put a smile on his face. "Thanks."

"But you are also kind, compassionate, and very patient with me. And I see how great you are with Ana. I trust my instincts, Johnny." She laid a hand on his cheek. "I can't imagine I'd be falling in love with you if you were a bad person."

"You're falling in love with me?"

Lumiana nodded.

Sliding his hand in her hair, he gave her a long kiss. "You know I'm crazy about you, right?"

When she smiled he sang the first verse of The Beatles' "She Loves You," bringing out her beautiful laughter—a sound he loved hearing as much as her singing.

***

Adam still couldn't wrap his head around Johnny's news. *Johnny and Lumiana? How?* he thought when Lumiana took the stage and sang "The Girl From Ipanema" in sultry Portuguese, honoring her birth mother's Brazilian roots. It wasn't until she launched into a lambada that the spectators left their seats and danced along with her.

Adam gave Johnny a nudge when Lumiana swirled across the stage, the short skirt of her yellow dress resembling a spinning top. "Damn, your girl can move!"

Johnny smiled at him. "I had no idea she could dance like that."

"Yeah, she never struck me as the seductive type." Adam liked to think of Lumiana as an asexual robot with laser eyes and a few loose wires. It was hard to reconcile Shawn's weird sister with the enchanting singer dominating the stage as if it was where she belonged. There was no denying she was a phenomenal artist.

"Someone like her doesn't need to act seductive," Johnny told him. "She got me without doing any of those things women normally do."

How? Lumiana and Johnny were like water and oil. They should repel each other. At least that had been the whole point of this fiasco.

Not in a million years did he think they would fall for each other. The only reason he'd encouraged Johnny to convince her to work with them was to teach Johnny a lesson in modesty—and to light a fire under his ass to get him out of his creative slump.

How was he supposed to know his friend would be turned on by blatant rejection?

"By the way," Johnny pointed a finger at him, "why didn't you tell me she has a kid and that the dad is no longer among the living?"

"Because it wasn't my place to tell you. I already told you more about her than I should've."

Being a former foster child of the Arendt-Garcías, Adam was one of the few outsiders who'd earned their trust. And because CDE had become a second home to him, he was careful not to jeopardize that trust. They might not be the Corleones, but the Arendt-Garcías had influence in places where it counted.

When Adam was nine, their lawyer, the elusive Jonathan "Big G" Specter made sure his grandmother got custody of him. It was the best thing that ever happened to him. "She's pretty cool, huh? The kid, I mean."

"They *both* are," Johnny stressed, smiling adoringly when Lumiana twirled her daughter around on stage. "You don't like Lumiana?"

"It's not that I don't like her, it's more that I don't know her, which is her fault. She doesn't talk. Try getting to know someone when that person only gives one-to-three-word answers and never asks you anything back." Adam scratched his chin. "What are you guys even doing when you're together? I mean aside from sex. With Ana around, I imagine it probably doesn't happen as often as you'd like."

"It's nice you're not holding back." Johnny gave Adam a slap on the back. "Believe it or not, I'm learning to appreciate silence. And we do manage to have conversations. I admit it's hard to get her to open up, but it's worth it. She's smart and cute, and she makes me laugh."

Adam could see it in Johnny's face—the adoration, the happiness—he even looked younger, more carefree.

"She makes me feel things I've never felt before and things I haven't felt in a long time."

"Spoken like a man head over heels in love."

Adam nudged him with his shoulder. "I've always wondered what kind of woman it would take to bring Johnny Graham to his knees. In a good way, that is." It was meant as a quip, but Johnny didn't object. That man was a goner. "You're going to marry her or what?"

"You're seriously asking that after I've been in a relationship with her for two days?"

"When you know, you know."

Johnny shook his head and smiled, but the way he smiled told Adam the thought had at least crossed his mind.

**

Three hours later, Johnny and Lumiana were relaxing in the Jacuzzi inside her garden lodge, which resembled a ridge-roofed tea house. Just like Lumiana's house and backyard, the space conveyed serenity with its floor-to-ceiling bamboo paneling and lush indoor greenery.

Ana was in bed. Marisa hadn't been kidding when she said their family reunions were high-energy events. By the end of the evening the little girl was so exhausted she fell asleep while she stood leaning against him.

"I wish I'd grown up in a family like yours," Johnny said as he replayed Lumiana's family get-together in his head.

"I was very fortunate to end up in this family. I wouldn't be where I am if it wasn't for their unconditional love and support."

Johnny gave her a gentle kiss. He might as well ask her about her past now since they were already on the subject of what had made her who she was. He needed to figure out what her triggers were. Knowing what the minefield looked like would at least give him a fighting chance to try and step around it.

Girding his mental loins, he said, "When I think about what happened to you as a child I wonder how you feel about Esperanza. I mean, I get that she rescued you, but she also kept you away from the rest of the world. In a sense, she held you hostage for a decade."

Johnny could see Lumiana's shoulders stiffen.

"At what time do you have to be in the city tomorrow?"

So he'd poked the beehive and now she was trying to get rid of him? "Look, I'm sorry I brought this up. I didn't mean—"

"It's fine. I'm asking because I think I need to show you something."

He blew out a breath of relief. "I have to be back around noon for a radio interview. What do you want to show me?"

"You'll see." She splashed water at him. "If you feel uncomfortable tomorrow, remember you brought that on yourself."

They soaked in silence for a few minutes. He really was learning to be comfortable with quietude. "This is the good life."

She grinned. "I'm glad my wellness oasis has

the intended effect."

Pulling Lumiana close, he fondled her sexy ass.

"Don't even think about it."

He kissed her anyway, nice and slow.

Pressing her hand against his chest, she said, "Please, let's continue this somewhere else."

"Fine." He released her. "But why?"

"This is my sanctum sanctorum, where I come to relax and meditate. If we have intercourse here I'll think about it every time I'm in here and that defeats the purpose."

"*Intercourse?*" He propped his arms on the edge of the pool. "Let me get this straight, wherever we make love—have sex—fuck each other into oblivion," he supplied some great alternatives, "you'll think about it whenever you're in that spot?" He smiled, and so did she. "Good to know."

Johnny climbed out of the hot tub, picked his jeans off the floor and took a condom from his wallet. Then he reached for her hand. "We still have a lot of ground to cover, so we better get started." He pulled her outside.

"Where are we going? I'm freezing."

"You'll see, and you won't be cold much longer." He led her to the moon bridge.

"Oh, I hope you are kidding." Her gaze bounced back and forth between him and the steeply arched bridge. "You want to do it up there?"

"Come on, Doc, it's a challenge, but it's going to be fun."

It proved to be both.

12

I HAVE THIS HOPE

*"Swim out until you can't see land,
and then drop down deep
to where there is nothing you've ever known."*

—JESSICA GRAHAM

The next morning, Lumiana took Johnny on a trip. They had five hours before she had to teach, but she drove her snug Peugeot 403 as if some invisible Terminator was chasing them.

The woman's car was a relic, a beauty in Grecian green. It suited her, Johnny decided. Lumiana had an appreciation for the old that rivaled his dad's. They'd get along great, he thought as he watched the endless line of trees they passed through the passenger window. Lumiana and his mother, on the other hand, only time would tell.

As they turned onto a dirt road leading into the woods, Johnny got a funny feeling in his gut. Abandoning the car, they followed a shallow creek winding through a maze of pine trees.

Lumiana marched ahead like she was on a mission, which reminded him of the day they met. There was no trail here either, but she navigated the wilderness as if she could do it in her sleep.

Half an hour later they reached a small, run-down cabin half hidden by shrubs and weeds.

No way. "Lu, is this where Esperanza kept you?"

"Yes. You are very deductive." She linked her hand with his and let out a long breath.

The place looked like she'd described it in her lecture, with the flat roof, the rickety porch and the shrubs in front of it, the sweet smell...

Squeezing his hand, Lumiana took another heavy breath. Either she'd developed a sudden case of asthma or she was close to having a panic attack.

"You okay?" he asked, easing her chin up.

"Yes... no... kind of... I don't know... It's strange being back here after all this time, but even stranger to have you here with me." She looked at him like she thought she might be dreaming. "I don't come here often and only by myself. The last time I was here was five years ago."

After Jayjay died, he supposed.

Her gaze darted around like she was calculating something in her head.

"Why did you decide to come here today?"

"You asked me how I feel about Esperanza," she said, her voice barely audible. "Marisa said I have to tell you more about me and my past so you understand me better."

Bless her aunt. "You could've just told me. You didn't have to bring me here."

"Do you wish to leave?" She squeezed his arm, her sharp nails biting into his skin.

"No, Lu, I don't mean it like that. I appreciate you bringing me here. This must be hard for you."

He wanted to hug her, but she took two steps back.

"I brought you here because I want you to get a sense of what it's like to grow up isolated." With a tense expression, Lumiana began to tap her foot.

"What is it? Do you want to leave?" He spun around, almost expecting another black bear to appear out of nowhere. Well, not *nowhere* seeing that he and Lumiana were the ones traversing bear country.

How many black bears had Lumiana encountered growing up, he wondered. How much time had she spent exploring these woods? Lumiana understood animals and nature better than anyone. The woman had a free-spirited wildness in her that both fascinated and scared him.

"Could you please step a bit to the side? You're standing on Esperanza."

"Wait, what?" He moved as if bitten by a snake.

"A little more, please. Now you are on my *äiti*."

"What the hell?" He moved to stand behind her, gripping her upper arms. "You're freaking me out, Lu. And what's an *äiti*?"

Shrugging him off, she spun around. "*Äiti* is my mother," she said, appalled at his ignorance.

"Then speak English. I don't understand Scandinavian."

"*Suomi!* Finland is not Scandinavia. Scandinavia comprises the three kingdoms of Norway, Denmark, and Sweden. Finnish is—"

He held up his hands. "This is not the time for a lecture, Doc. I just found the skeletons in your closet—and Jesus, Lu, how many people have actual skeletons? You buried your own mother and the woman who rescued you—here?" He motioned toward the spot he was standing on just moments ago.

"You have been to my introductory class," Lumiana reminded him. "Why are you surprised?"

"Yes, but in your lecture you didn't go into those details. I would've remembered something freaky like this." Now that he thought of it, she hadn't used names or specified where and when it all happened—and she definitely hadn't mentioned that she dug holes in the ground and buried people in it like a freaking serial killer.

"Of course I couldn't go into all the details, I can't risk people poking around. It is already a gamble to tell my story at all."

As crazy as it all sounded, she was right. It's not like she had a choice in the matter. Seeing loved ones die and being responsible for finding them a resting place at such a young age must've been traumatic.

"I'm sorry I'm making you remember all the painful stuff from your past." He drew Lumiana into his arms and buried his face in her hair.

"I can't change my past, Johnny. It's part of who I am. And because it still has such a strong hold on me, it's important for you to know the truth so you understand what makes me think and behave the way I do."

Taking his hand, she led him inside the shabby cabin.

It was exactly the way she'd described it in her class: dark and chilly like a cave, but in addition to the old, moldy smell, it now contained an obscene number of spider webs.

The wooden floorboards creaked under their feet, raising the hair on his skin.

"I told you this might make you uncomfortable," Lumiana said as she lit a lantern.

"I had no idea how terrible this place is." He looked around, trying to ignore the claustrophobic feeling in his chest. At six-foot-three, he was a tall man, and the ceiling was uncomfortably low.

The cabin was just one room crammed with

dusty old books. In its center stood a small wooden table with two chairs that looked like they'd fall apart if someone dared to sit on them.

"No kitchen or bathroom?"

"There is a stone oven outside. We didn't have electricity or running water." Lumiana went through what appeared to be Esperanza's closet. It held five floral dresses and a frilly off-white apron. "You aren't the first person to suggest that Esperanza held me prisoner for a decade."

Her gaze met his, and Johnny nodded.

"I still remember it like it was yesterday, every little detail." She tapped her head. "My *äiti*, her name was Malia, she wouldn't wake up." Her voice faltered. "I was looking for help when I came across this cabin. I was frightened, but also so hungry. I hadn't eaten all day."

She closed her eyes as she continued. "The scent of cinnamon lured me onto the porch. And there I saw it, this wooden plate filled with warm cookies. I slipped one into each pocket and was nibbling on a third when I heard a squeak."

Lumiana stomped her foot and the floor creaked, a spooky sound he was sure would haunt his dreams tonight. "The door opened and an old woman with wild white hair poked her head out and glared at me. I ran away from her, but she hobbled after me, shouting in a language I didn't understand. '*Äiti!*' I cried out for my mom, tripping and falling over a tree root. I flailed when the old woman cast a shadow over me."

Johnny watched Lumiana as if in trance. It wasn't just her voice, her whole body was telling the story. It was why her students hung on her every word.

"The old woman sat next to me and spoke calmly in a husky voice. I remember her warm smile—toothless and almost comical. 'Shh. Don't be scared, little girl,' she said. Not understanding, I sat up and stuck my tongue out at her. The old woman mirrored my gesture and said, 'My name is Esperanza. What's your name, dear?' To me it sounded more like '*Mah nei sberanzu, wut nei, der*,' and that is what I repeated back to her."

Lumiana's smile was contagious.

"Esperanza's eyes crinkled when she smiled. The old woman raised her arm and gestured at her body, head to toe. '*Es-pe-ran-za*,' she said slowly, then pointed at me. I indicated my own little body and said 'Lumi.'"

"Like Tarzan and Jane," Johnny said with a chuckle.

"Right." She grimaced before she continued. "Once I found the strength to get up, I began to hike down the narrow trail I'd come on. Esperanza followed me until we arrived at our campsite. My *äiti* was sitting slumped against a tree."

Goosebumps bloomed on Johnny's skin.

"'*Äiti*?' I placed a hand on either side of my mother's face and shook her. '*Äiti? Oletko siellä, äiti?*' *Mommy? Are you there, Mommy?* Esperanza leaned over my mother, touching her neck and wrist. Then she looked up and shook her head. 'I am so sorry, Lumi,' she said, 'Your *äiti* is gone.'

I didn't know the words then but understood her gestures. I pushed by Esperanza. '*Äiti? Oletko siellä, äiti?*' I shouted, shaking my mother's head. Esperanza reached for me. I lashed out, but she managed to pull me onto her lap and hold me tight. 'Shh, *angelito*,' she murmured, stroking my arm with a hand that was soft as plush and brown like my own. I burrowed into her and listened to the strong beat of her heart while she sang to me."

Lumiana sang a passage in Spanish so hauntingly beautiful it tightened his throat. She amazed him. How strong she had to be to keep moving on with her life, to find happiness despite it all.

He remembered her words from the weekend they met: *I choose to be happy and therefore I am.* He didn't know if it worked like that, but he liked that she saw happiness as a choice independent of one's circumstances. That anyone could be happy if they decided to be.

Tears were streaking Lumiana's cheeks as she sang. She swiped at them with the backs of her hands, but they kept coming.

Johnny swallowed to relieve the pressure in his throat. He recognized the Mexican folk song.

"La Llorona."

There were different interpretations of the

song, but he knew *The Wailing Woman* was a rather disturbing ancient legend about a woman who drowned her children and mourned their deaths for eternity. As a ghost, she haunted her lover and foretold death.

Johnny didn't need to understand the lyrics to understand the sorrow, the pain. It was one of those songs that stuck with you and made you feel something whether you wanted it or not.

"When Esperanza found me and took me in I was all alone in the wilderness in a foreign country where no one even spoke my language. I was so frightened. I didn't know what to do or where else to go." Lumiana came across an old nightgown and smiled at it. "That's why I didn't run away. She never locked me up. On the contrary, Espe took good care of me. She was patient and taught me everything she knew."

Lumiana paused while Johnny batted away a cobweb. She didn't seem to mind them, but they freaked him out. This whole place made his skin crawl.

"I was a curious child, in many ways similar to Ana, but I grew up without my family or contact to the outside world. Espe made sure there was always something for me to explore and discover. I was quite happy here."

Then her shoulders slumped. "I don't know why my mother died. But now that I have seen your dad and how his face droops on one side, I remember that her face was a bit off too. Maybe it was a stroke, or a spider bite or some other infection that affected her brain."

A shiver ran down his back. "The two women are really still buried here?" It was heartbreaking to think this had been her life, to imagine how she must've felt when she laid Esperanza to rest —once again alone in the world.

"I haven't told anyone where the cabin is. To be sure no one came looking, I said I was too traumatized to remember. I expect you to take this secret to your grave."

"Jesus, Lu—" He pressed his palms to his face, softly shaking his head.

"Promise me you won't tell anyone."

"Of course, I promise." No one would believe him anyway. "Now tell me more about Esperanza. Why did she live out here in the middle of nowhere?"

Lumiana plodded over to a shelf crammed with books and gingerly ran her fingers across the weathered spines. "Esperanza had her own sad story. She was an immigrant with no formal education, although she was a very intelligent woman. She was originally from Colombia, like my adoptive dad Fernando."

Johnny couldn't imagine how they had managed to live here for so many years. Fending off another bout of claustrophobia, he sat on one of the filthy beds, although bed was an overstatement. It was a small metal wire frame covered with dusty rags.

"Like so many people, Esperanza came to the U.S. with hopes and dreams of a brighter future. She was a beautiful woman and attracted the attention of many men. Among them was a much older, wealthy American gentleman who promised her a better life if she married him."

Lumiana opened a drawer and handed him a crinkled black and white photo of a stunning young woman in indigenous clothing. "He invested in her education, especially to rid her of her accent, which he claimed made her sound primitive. But life did not get better for her. He came to see her as a possession, finding pleasure in torturing her when no one else was around. Espe was infertile, which she once told me made her useless to her husband. He was a *monstruo*."

Wiping her forehead with the back of her hand, Lumiana took a step back.

Sensing her distress, Johnny urged her to take a break.

"No, I need to finish this," Lumiana insisted, her face stern. "A year into their marriage, Esperanza's husband began beating her more often and more violently, until she couldn't take it anymore and escaped. He found her and promised to be a better man. But he did not become a better man, he became more evil.

One day, he came home drunk and threw a bottle at her face. When she lay on the floor bleeding, he bent down and started punching her. She managed to grab a candlestick and hit him over the head with it. He fell onto the sharp edge of the coffee table. Even as he lay on the floor, his mean eyes were still laughing at her, so she hit him again and again.

Then she cleaned herself up, took all his gold and money, and ran away as far as she could, so no one would ever find her again. This," Lumiana swiveled around, "is where she found peace."

Johnny wondered how anyone could feel at peace in this hole, but then again, anything was better than living with someone who abused you, stripped you of your dignity, dehumanized you.

"There is a village not so far from here where she would buy the bare necessities, but most of what she needed she either stole or made herself. Almost all the books you see here were from flea markets, but some were stolen. Espe was resourceful: she always went to town on different days, never talked to anyone, and made sure no one ever followed her. She became an urban legend. Decades passed before she found me out here, stealing her cookies…"

Lumiana stared at her shaking hands, clutching them to her stomach. "I only did it because I was so hungry."

Johnny got up and took her in his arms, held her for a while.

"Espe saw it as a gift from the heavens that after all those years she was finally given a child. She called me *angelito*, which means little angel."

Johnny remembered that his dad referred to Lumiana and Ana as angels too.

"I know I meant the world to her. Espe put everything she had into providing for me. She was the one who taught me how to play the guitar. And she had a beautiful voice too. Espe made me learn every popular Colombian folk song there is."

Lumiana pointed at the dusty guitar leaning against a stack of books—a tiple with copper strings. He itched to pick it up.

"I was almost sixteen when Espe took me to the village for the first time. She wanted me to get a formal education, so I could manage alone when she could no longer take care of me. She went straight to Las Espitas' mayor Frederick Truman and convinced him to have the school test me to see which grade I should be in.

But because I had done nothing but study for the ten years I stayed with her," she gestured at the hundreds of books surrounding them, "it turned out I was too advanced for high school. So I took the SATs. When I got a perfect score, Mayor Truman helped me get a full scholarship to UCLA. Espe died shortly before my first semester there. She was ninety years old."

"So you loved her."

Lumiana nodded. "I understand why she did what she did, even though at first I longed to go back home to Pernoo. In the end, I saw life with her as a blessing, because my parents had been first-generation immigrants themselves and I had no family left in Finland."

Lumiana kissed the old photo of Esperanza she'd been holding and put it back in the drawer. "After Espe's death, which I kept secret, I went to see the mayor, and he told me there were problems with my paperwork. Lumiana Alves, the six-year-old Finnish girl, and her mother Malia had been legally declared dead on December 19, 1992."

Johnny's skin prickled at those words.

"So not only did I not exist anymore, I was also an undocumented immigrant. But Mayor Truman took pity on me and introduced me to a lawyer that everyone called Big G."

Lumiana eyed him for a moment. "You remind me a bit of him, actually. Big G's specialty was, and still is, immigration and family law. Today he is one of my parents' most trusted employees. He is in Ethiopia at the moment, otherwise you would have met him yesterday."

Lumiana circled the little wooden table. "Casa de Esperanza was always more than an orphanage. My parents sometimes took in foster children. Adam was one of them. Big G was the one who ensured that Adam could live with his grandmother. And he also pulled a lot of strings in order for me to begin my college degree and receive citizenship without anyone learning what really happened.

This is why it's important that no one finds

out. I still go by Lumiana Harding. Delani Harding was my father's name. My parents weren't married. But my American passport has a different date and place of birth. And I have another ID under my adoptive parents' last name."

Johnny rubbed his eye. "So my girlfriend is an illegal immigrant with fraudulent documents." If that ever got out, Grandma Margaret would disown him.

"You can't tell anyone, Johnny. I trust you. Don't make me regret telling you." She gripped his arm again.

"Relax, Lu. I won't tell anyone. Besides, Helen and Jimmy already warned me that your family would go to extreme lengths to protect you. And you have a kid. I'd never do anything that would hurt Ana."

"There are still things I can't tell you." She looked him straight in the eye. "But my family has crossed lines, and they would do it again if necessary. I know you think I'm pure of heart, but listen carefully," she came closer, her face showing resolve, "there is nothing I wouldn't do to protect them."

And here it came, that tingling sensation coursing his body.

Her brows furrowed. "Why are you looking at me like that?"

"Like what?"

"It's similar to how you sometimes look at me before you..." She looked down, met his gaze again.

"Before I... what?"

She pressed her hips to his. "You are aroused."

Closing his eyes, he shook his head. What was he going to say? They were standing in the creepiest place he'd ever known, and he was ready to tear her clothes off. "I have issues. I'm sorry." He stepped away from her.

"What kind of issues?"

She took a step toward him. He took another one back.

"There are things I can't tell you either, not yet anyway."

"You can trust me," she said, touching his arm.

He pinched the bridge of his nose. "It's not that. It's that how I was, how I am, and how I want people to see me don't match."

"I suspected as much."

"How?" Johnny pulled at his shirt—suddenly it felt too tight. "Can we go outside, please?"

Taking his hand, she led the way.

Outside, Johnny leaned against the porch railing, relishing the warm, clean air.

Lumiana kept her distance. "Did you think I wouldn't notice that it both frustrates and arouses you when I defy you or demonstrate my strength in some way?" She put her hands on her hips. "Isn't that why you came to see me even though I said I wasn't interested in working with you, and why you followed me into the woods the day we met?"

Johnny scrubbed his hands over his face, letting them rest there.

He hadn't thought about it that way. But she was right. He was a rebel, and seeing that same rebellious nature in Lumiana attracted him to her on a visceral level. He was addicted to the challenge, he supposed. It's what had been missing in his life ever since his last album went platinum.

Same with his love life. Andie, as sweet as she was, had been accommodating, his for the taking from the beginning. Never had to chase her. But she hadn't loved him. She loved a romanticized version of him that he could never live up to and that he'd come to resent.

With Lumiana things were different. She saw him—all the rough edges and broken parts—and still wanted him.

And then there was the challenge: the different way her brain worked, their very different environments and lifestyles, the kid, the mystery surrounding her family, and her wild spirit. Seeing who was going to end up with the upper hand day-to-day was a thrill he couldn't get enough of. Sure, they'd probably end up driving each other crazy half the time, but they would make each other happy too.

Lumiana came up to him, took his hands, and kissed him hard on the mouth. "Please don't pretend with me, Johnny. If our relationship is not a place where we can feel safe to be loved and accepted for who we are, then there is no point for us to have one."

He hugged her with such force he could hear her spine pop.

"Thank you for dislocating my vertebrae."

"If anything, I put them back where they belonged." He gave her a swift kiss. "Thank you."

She smiled at him. "Do you feel as though you understand a bit better now why I can't be your girlfriend in public?"

He nodded. It meant a lot to him that she trusted him enough to share the stories from her past, and so he vowed to never tell her secrets to anyone.

Lumiana took his hand and led him behind the cabin to show him the spot where she spent hours on end lying on the grass, reading. "Other times I would run through the woods and explore—climb trees, spy on wild animals, collect leaves and stones or whatever caught my eye. That is how I got most of my scars."

Lumiana rubbed the marks on her arm. "They are reminders of my adventures and the lessons I've learned." Then she pushed up his sleeve, exposing his scar. She traced her finger over it. "And that's why I like your scar. It is a reminder of our first weekend together, and I hope it taught you not to climb while angry."

Wrapping an arm around her waist, he kissed her. With a content sigh, he said, "I think it was more than that. It taught me to be more mindful and accept what is, and that acceptance doesn't mean resignation. I really see that in you. You spend more time in the now than anyone. And despite your past and your struggles you keep pushing your boundaries."

Smiling up at him, she said, "I was at a point in my life where stagnation had gotten very comfortable. And then you showed up." She patted his chest. "You're the match that starts a wildfire."

Grinning, he pinched her in the side, and they headed back to the car. Just as they were about to reach it, he grabbed her hand.

"Lu, I need to tell you something."

Pursing her lips, she lowered her brow.

"Since the moment I first heard your voice, I couldn't shake the feeling that I had to meet you. And ever since I met you, I've felt so inspired by what you say, the way you live, and how you are. When we had to go our separate ways, I shut myself in the house and made music all day every day for ten days straight. In the end, I came up with enough songs for a full album. I didn't mention you by name, but the album is a tribute to you and our time together."

He paused, gauging her reaction. She just stared at him. "I thought you should know in case you or someone in your family ever listens to it. But this is not the only reason I'm telling you. My new album is going to be released next week and I have to do a lot of promotion. I'll have to go out of town with the band too—New York, London, Cape Town, Sydney. So for the next six weeks, I won't have much time to spend with you."

Lumiana remained silent.

He took her hands. "Please say something."

"I can't believe you dedicated your work to me." Her eyes grew big and teary. She pushed him against the car, and much to his delight, expressed her gratitude with rousing actions rather than words.

13

MAKE YOU FEEL MY LOVE

"Life is short. Kiss slowly, laugh insanely,
love truly and forgive quickly."

—PAULO COELHO

Two weeks later, Johnny and his band were scheduled to appear on Helen's daytime talk show to promote his new single "Wonder."

Johnny was pacing backstage as if he'd had one too many coffees when Adam came and put a hand on his shoulder. "Relax, man. It's going to be fine. Just try to think before you speak."

"Thanks, how reassuring," Johnny scoffed. Usually he enjoyed being interviewed by Helen, but after their heated exchange at Lumiana's family reunion, he wasn't sure what to expect.

Then it was time. He said a prayer and sauntered out onto the stage. As soon as the mostly female audience spotted him, they cheered wildly.

Looks like Lu was right about keeping the stubble, he thought, brushing his hand along his jaw.

Johnny gave the audience a wave and breathed easier when Helen kissed him on the cheek.

He sat in the crisp white armchair and tapped the armrest.

"You seem nervous." Helen called him out on it.

"I am. Especially after our last conversation. 'Serious Helen' is a force to be reckoned with."

She grinned with a glint in her eyes. Tugging at the lapels of her plaid blazer, she told the audience, "Johnny and I coincidentally ran into each other at a party last week and I gave him a piece of my mind that, in retrospect, was a little strongly worded. But in my defense, I had a good reason and I meant it in the most loving way."

"Right. Out of love for someone else though."

"Do you mind if I give the audience some context?"

He knew Helen was sworn to secrecy, so he trusted her not to mention Lumiana by name.

"I'd love to hear your side of the story," he said, shifting in his seat.

"So, Johnny here has dated quite a few celebrities, most recently the wonderful Andie Woodhull."

The audience cheered for Andie, the most famous of his exes.

"Imagine my surprise when I found out that he's now with someone I consider family. And she's a remarkable woman in her own right—incredibly smart and sweet, and she has a very special way of making sense of the world. I feel protective of her, so when I found out he's involved with her, I told him to treat her well."

"I believe your actual words were, 'you better believe in Jesus because he's the only one who can save you if you ever break her heart,'" he said in a voice that mocked Helen's tone.

"True." Helen chuckled. "I just wanted to make sure you were serious about her."

"I am very serious about her. I've never met anyone like her, and that's also what inspired 'Wonder.'"

"Tell us about the story behind it. Is it true that you wrote your upcoming album in a matter of days?"

He touched his throat. "In all honesty, I wasn't sure I had another album in me, which is why it's been taking so long. And then I wrote the entire album within ten days of meeting her. It just poured out of me and I couldn't stop. I still can't believe it. That woman both challenges and inspires me in the most unexpected ways. She even took me rock-climbing."

Johnny pulled up his sleeve to show off his

scar. "I thought I'd lose the arm, but now I have this in common with her. She has a lot of scars," he told the audience, "but a great way of looking at them. She sees them as reminders of her adventures, as lessons learned. And that is what the song is all about: the way we make sense of the world and life, and realizing that our way isn't always the right way, or the only way."

Helen smiled warmly. "You really love her, huh?"

Johnny felt the heat burning his cheeks, and nodded.

Helen patted his arm. "I hope you two work out, I really do. You're good for each other."

They chatted for a few more minutes before Helen announced, "Let's hear Johnny's new single 'Wonder.'"

***

That night, Johnny showed up unannounced at Lumiana's, but this time she knew it was him. She recognized his car and the way he walked with a slight swagger that she found annoyingly attractive.

Please don't let it be his dad, she said a silent prayer before she opened the door for him.

Without preamble, Johnny pulled her close and kissed her with an urgency that had her gasping for air.

Before she could regain her senses, he said, "I'm sorry for showing up here like this, but I need to tell you something. I…"

He looked down, fiddled with the zipper on his bomber jacket before his gaze swept back to hers. "I'm sorry if this is going to freak you out. But I can't help it. I'm fucking in love with you, Lumiana. And I want us to last. I'm in this for the long haul, if you and Ana will have me."

She stood still as his words pattered out like Rimsky-Korsakov's "Flight of the Bumblebee."

He took her hands. "I know this is the opposite of taking it slow, but when you know you know, and I—"

She cut him off with a long, deep kiss, then punched him in the arm.

"Ow!"

"Damn it, Johnny, you upset me. I thought something happened with your dad."

She could see the relief in his face.

He folded her into his arms and kissed her temple. "My dad's actually going to be moved to an assisted living facility tomorrow."

She hugged him tighter, wishing they could stay like this. He was a phenomenal hugger. And his scent—she loved that he didn't mask it with cologne. If anything, he smelled like a spa—tranquil and serene, like white bamboo and lotus flower. "Would you like to come in?"

"I'd love to, but I have to go back to the city. I need to be in Burbank early tomorrow morning for another TV interview."

"So you came all the way here just to profess your love to me?" Her chest burned as if it were launching fireworks. He wanted to be hers —*theirs*. She wished it were that simple.

"I've been meaning to do it earlier, but I was afraid of your reaction." He rubbed his arm pointedly.

When she kissed him again, she poured all her love into it, hoping it would tell him what she couldn't put in words.

"I wish I could stay, but this week's going to be crazy. My publicist scheduled back-to-back interviews and performances for the next couple of days. I'll call you tomorrow."

"I might not be available until the evening. I have a lot of work." Ever since they became a couple, she'd been falling behind in her professorial duties. Now that Johnny was busy she could catch up before anyone noticed.

"Right. We'll figure this out." He kissed her goodbye, but she held on to his shirt. "Unfortunately, you have to let me go," Johnny said as she drew him closer. "Okay, one more for the road."

They kissed again. Then he headed down the driveway toward his car.

"You are a good man, Johnny Graham," she called after him.

Johnny turned around, grinning from ear to ear. "I'm trying."

***

Johnny spent the following day in the Burbank

Studios, meeting with one entertainment reporter after the other. Dealing with the press was his least favorite part of the job, because being asked the same questions over and over bored him.

This time was even worse. After Helen's show aired that morning, reporters were eager to find out more about his new girlfriend. He cursed to himself every time they asked for her name.

On the bright side, his candid interview had made him look like a good guy for a change—or as his publicist Juliana had put it, "more human, and less asshole."

After he finished talking to *Hollywood V.I.P.*'s Vicky Puentes, Juliana finally gave him a break.

"You have fifteen minutes," she told him. "Fifteen, Johnny." She pointed a warning finger at him when he groaned.

Closing the dressing room door behind her, Johnny leaned against it. His head was throbbing, so he grabbed a bottle of water from the catering table and lay down on the suede leather couch. After a few minutes of blissful quiet, he called Lumiana.

"I'm so happy to hear your voice," Johnny said with a yawn.

"You sound exhausted."

"I'm okay, just tired. How about you?"

"My students presented a project today, and they all did well, even Kevin."

"Ah, Kevin... the guy who spends more time

imagining you naked than listening to your fascinating insights into the evolution of humankind?"

"He does no such thing."

"I've been to your lecture, remember? He was drooling when you cleaned the top of the blackboard and your dress hiked up a little."

"Are you certain you aren't talking about yourself?"

"Believe me, Doc, I enjoyed the show as much as Kevin."

"Is that why you always stand behind me when I unload the dishwasher?"

He knew she was trying to lift his spirits and loved her all the more for it. "You have nice legs and a prominent derrière." He gave a dramatic sigh. "Hell. Now I'm turned on and you're not here to enjoy my appreciation for your anatomy."

"At least you sound like yourself again."

"Thanks for cheering me up."

"Anytime. How did it go with your dad?"

"The transition from the hospital took a toll, but Mansfield Park seems like a great place for him to relax and take his time to heal. He asked about you and Ana. He's hoping you come visit him sometime."

"Can you text me his address when we hang up?"

There was a knock on the door. Juliana came in and said, "Time's up."

Johnny groaned. "I have to go. I'll call you

later," he said, and hung up.

"Your girlfriend?" Tossing him a fresh shirt, Juliana gave him a pleading look.

"I'm not telling you her name." He texted Lumiana the address for Mansfield Park, then changed his sweaty shirt.

"What's with all the secrecy, Johnny? I'm your publicist, dammit. I want to know who we're dealing with in case this blows up like all your other relationships."

"I told you, she doesn't want anything to do with this part of my life. I haven't even told the guys about her. I need this relationship to work, Jules. Let me hang on to what little privacy I have, and when things are more solid with her, I'll introduce you."

"Meh." Juliana shrugged. She was a petite blonde with freckles and a pixie cut but that cute exterior fooled no one. The lady was a shark—a lovable one though. "Let's go. We're two minutes behind schedule."

Johnny mocked outrage.

"Don't get cute with me, Graham. I take my job seriously, and so should you." Juliana signaled Magnum who was standing in the door, ready to roll.

God, I want to go home, Johnny mouthed at the ceiling as he followed Juliana and his bodyguard down the hallway. Only five more hours.

***

The next day around noon, Jerold Graham sat in bed with pillows propped up behind his back, staring daggers at the soup bowl in front of him. The thing was fucking mocking him! *You want me, old man, but you can't have me*, it said with a derisive laugh when a melodious knock sounded on the open door.

"Angel," he said, smiling at Lumiana who stood in the entrance of his spacious suite, sporting the same white dress and golden locket she'd been wearing the first time he saw her.

This was a pleasant surprise.

He liked that woman for his son. And he also knew it was because of Lumiana that Johnny was speaking to him again.

This time around his relationship with Johnny would be different—supportive, fun—everything he'd hoped it would be when his son was a little boy. Johnny was exceptional at what he did and making music made him happy. If he'd pursued his passion like his son had done instead of what had been expected of him, maybe he would've led a happier life too.

"Hi, Jerry, may I come in?"

Lumiana smiled when he waved her inside.

And what a smile it was. The whole energy in the room shifted. And the light in her eyes... Johnny was a lucky man. He hoped his son could see that.

"Sunshine. Always... a pleasure."

Lumiana stepped inside and kissed him on the forehead just as Nurse Ruby came in with fresh lilies.

Funeral flowers, how appropriate, he grumbled.

"Is this your daughter, Mr. Graham?" the nurse asked with a curious glance in Lumiana's direction.

"Not yet... someday, I hope."

Ruby smiled at him before she replaced the wilting flowers on the glass table.

"You are funny, Jerry," Lumiana said, squeezing his hand.

"My son... loves you... You... love him."

"He makes me happy."

Jerry was relieved to hear his son had been treating her well. Johnny was good at a lot of things, but making relationships last wasn't one of them. And that wasn't entirely his son's fault.

It weighed heavy on his heart that his boys had witnessed how their parents and grandparents had made each other miserable. Whereas Johnny became a serial monogamist, Jason apparently didn't date at all. Only Jack, the youngest, seemed to be unaffected by his heritage—he married his college sweetheart Linda, and they appeared to be happy raising their little twin boys.

Nurse Ruby gave him another warm smile before she left the room.

Lumiana eyed his gourmet lunch, which sat on the tray table in front of him, untouched. "You don't like your meal, Jerry?"

He averted his gaze.

"What is it?" she asked, her expressive brow knitting in concern.

"I… I can't…" He tried picking up the spoon, but his hand was too shaky.

"Oh, I see. Would you care for assistance?"

"I'm not… a baby," he protested despite his growling stomach.

"Jerry," she scolded him as she got up to get the spoon. "This is not the time for hurt pride. You will be able to eat by yourself again, but for now it is what it is. You better get over it. Nutrition is important, otherwise you won't have the strength it takes to rehabilitate."

"Fine." He was so hungry he didn't have a fight in him.

Lumiana spoon-fed him the cream of wild mushroom soup while she distracted him with recounts of her students' presentations, and because she knew he was a part-time professor himself, she asked for his opinion. He deeply appreciated that she didn't give him time to feel sorry for himself.

When Chief Nursing Officer Tamra came in to make sure he'd taken his medication, Lumiana suggested a walk in the park.

"Is it okay if we go outside?" she asked Tamra, who helped heave him into the wheelchair.

Lumiana had a delightful little accent that he couldn't place. A mixture of accents, perhaps.

Johnny had mentioned that she was born in Finland to a Brazilian mother and a South African father, and that her adoptive parents spoke in their native languages German and Spanish. Both the way she looked and the way she sounded were a beautiful blend of different cultures.

Jerry took a profound breath when the entrance door opened. It felt liberating to catch the fresh air and a few rays of sunshine. "Thanks, angel."

Lumiana enchanted him with her colorful stories while they explored the gorgeous park with its vast flowerbeds, freshly cut grass, and ornamental trees.

By the time they returned to his room, Jerry felt energized. Johnny was right about Lumiana's calm yet upbeat demeanor being contagious. He thoroughly enjoyed her company, so it made him happy when she promised she'd be back the next day.

**

Ruby Kyle was sitting on a Victorian bench in front of the cream white brick building when Jerold Graham's visitor left.

Could she be Johnny's new girlfriend?

Although Ruby had only seen the young woman briefly in Mr. Graham's room, she had a feeling it was the same woman Janice had seen at the hospital. But Janice was right, Johnny was known to go for skinny blondes.

Maybe Mr. Graham, Sr. was talking about one of his other sons when he said he hoped the woman would be his daughter-in-law one day—weren't there three Graham boys?

***

During the next ten days, which included a hectic three-day trip to New York, Johnny didn't have time to see his dad or Lumiana. They tried calling each other a couple of times, but one or the other was always busy.

By Friday, Johnny began worrying that his relationship with Lumiana was doomed to fail just like his previous relationships because they were too caught up in their work to make time for each other. And it wasn't like she lived around the corner. An hour's drive each way proved to be another hurdle on their already rocky path.

While Lumiana spent Friday night hosting Candela's birthday bash, Johnny had to attend an A-list party, where he had three too many drinks and ended up chatting all night with an easygoing French model named Antoinette. When 'Annie' offered to take him up to her hotel room, he politely declined. As much fun as 'easygoing' was, he preferred exploring the enigma that was Lumiana Harding.

Saturday morning, Johnny woke with a hangover ten minutes before he was due to meet his family at Mansfield Park. He took a quick shower, ran a red light, and managed to arrive only nine minutes late, which still earned him a raised eyebrow from his mother.

They met Jason and Jack in the elegant lobby and Chief Nursing Officer Tamra showed them to his father's suite, where his dad was sitting in an armchair reading on a Kindle.

"Look at that, Jase, Dad finally unpacked your Christmas present," Johnny teased, leaning down to hug his father. Jerold Graham was suspicious of technology. By the time his dad adopted an innovation, everyone was already moving on to the next big thing.

There was a knock on the open door.

"Hi," his dad's pretty nurse, Ruby, greeted them with a warm smile.

She reminded him of Andie. Same slender figure, same pale skin and light hair but where Andie looked more on the Dutch side, Ruby appeared more Icelandic with her almost white blond hair.

Johnny smirked when Ruby's gaze slid over him, slow and shameless, like she wanted to do the same with her hands.

The woman liked what she saw. This was going to be interesting.

***

This must be my lucky day, Ruby thought as she sauntered into Jerold Graham's sitting room to bring him his meds.

Johnny gave her one of his dazzling smiles, and she used the opportunity to congratulate him on the success of "Wonder," which had made its way into the Top 10 on the charts. Whoever he'd written that song for was one lucky girl. She wished it were her.

On her way out, Ruby dropped the empty pill container. Johnny picked it up and handed it to her.

With his day-old stubble, ripped jeans, and the tight gray v-neck shirt that showed off both his defined muscles and his artful tattoos, he had bad boy written all over him. Just the thought of touching him made her nipples strain against her blouse.

A few years ago, she'd mailed Johnny a photo with those nipples on prominent display, but his publicist had probably tossed it before Johnny could see for himself how desirable she was.

Ruby swayed her hips on her way out, praising herself for parking her cart right next to the door, because it allowed her to listen in on the Grahams' conversation.

"It's amazing how much progress he's made in just one week," Johnny's mother said to Tamra, who was checking in on Mr. Graham. "When he left the hospital they were much more dire about his prospects for recovery."

"I'm sure it has a lot to do with the lovely young lady who's been keeping him company," Tamra said. "Is she coming today, Mr. Graham?"

"A lovely young lady, huh?" said Johnny's brother Jack, his tone teasing.

"Don't know," Mr. Graham said to Tamra before she left the room.

"Who is this lovely young lady?" Johnny asked.

"He calls her Angel," Ruby told them as she returned to change Mr. Graham's sheets. Housekeeping wasn't in her job description, but with Johnny around she went the extra mile to prolong her time with him. How could he fall in love with her if he barely got to see her?

Ruby leaned a little further down while she made the bed to give Johnny a prime view of her plunging neckline. It gave her a jolt when she saw the smirk tugging at his lips.

Damn, those lips. She wanted to sink her teeth in them and imagined how it would feel when they explored her body. Soon the pleasure of his touch would be hers, she was sure of it.

***

"Wait, Lumiana has been visiting you?" Johnny said, smiling at the smug look on his father's face. *How about that?* His girlfriend seemed to care more for his dad than his own family.

Right, his girlfriend, he reminded himself when Ruby sashayed over to the side of the bed where he was sitting. She gave a slight wiggle of her apple bottom as she smoothed out the sheet. Her fine ass came so close he wondered if she was trying to give him a lap dance.

"I don't understand," his mother said, a muscle ticking in her jaw. "If you didn't talk about it, how did she know where to find him?"

Johnny shifted in his seat. If Ruby continued her little seductive dance, he'd be in need of a cold shower. "I told her that Dad would be happy to see her again, so she asked me to send her the address. But I didn't know she'd already been visiting him." That was the thing with Lumiana. She took people's words literally, which also caused the majority of arguments between them.

Johnny watched as Ruby swayed out of the room, flashing him a cheeky smile. That nurse knew how to play the game. And she played dirty —his favorite kind.

"Don't you think it's weird that your friend is visiting your father without telling you?" his mom said once they were alone.

Why was she still on this subject? With a sigh, he decided he might as well share the news now. "I need to tell you something." He glanced at the open door to make sure they didn't have an audience. "But first you have to promise me to keep this to yourselves." When they all agreed, Johnny went on. "People might start asking you about this, so it's better if you hear this from me. Lumiana and I are more than friends."

Shaking a finger at him, his mother said, "I knew it! I can't believe you lied to me."

"I didn't lie to you," he countered, rolling his

shoulders back. "When you met her she wasn't my girlfriend. I didn't want to say anything until I was sure it's the real deal."

"Whoa, 'the real deal?'" said Jason, looking at him like he'd just announced he'd be the first celebrity to take flight in Elon Musk's SpaceX rocket. "You're thinking of marrying her?"

"You can't be serious," his mother interjected before he could respond. "She is not the right woman for you, Johnny. You're supposed to be with Andie. Lumiana obviously has a lot of issues—don't tell me you want to deal with that for the rest of your life."

For once the thought of forever didn't scare the hell out of him. "Yes, things are complicated, but she's worth it. She makes me happy." He folded his arms across his chest. "The thing with Andie and me is that we're too much alike. That's great when you want to be friends, but no friction often means no passion. It's different with Lumiana. She keeps me on my toes, and she couldn't care less that I've got money and fame, which makes her one of the few people who aren't afraid to call me out on my crap. I like that she could outsmart me in a heartbeat, it forces me to step up my game. Being with her is very... stimulating."

"I don't know, Johnny," his mom said, tapping a finger to her lips. "Isn't she a bit young for you? What is she, eighteen?"

"She's in her late twenties, ma. I don't do

underage girls." And that one time he flirted with one was by accident; she looked much older with all the makeup, not to mention her fake ID. "Lumiana is a respected anthropologist. She teaches at the California Institute of Natural and Social Sciences, but she also contributes to the UCLA Center on the Everyday Lives of Families."

"She is a professor?"

His mother had a soft spot for academics. Johnny knew she considered her college years the happiest of her life, and despite their eventual divorce that included meeting his dad while they were both students at Harvard Law.

Johnny spent another fifteen minutes with his family, then took off for Jonata to see Lumiana.

***

After her shift was over, Ruby lingered in her car, waiting for Johnny to leave. From the parking lot she had a good view of Mansfield Park's entrance. While she waited, she called Janice.

"I have bad news, Jan. The mystery woman is Johnny's new girlfriend. Her name is Lumiana."

"Are you sure it's the same woman?"

"Positive. But he flirted with me, so maybe they're not that serious."

"She has met the family, Ruby. I think that's serious. And you're very attractive. They could be married, and he'd still check you out. You're his preferred type."

"I don't know." She drummed her fingers on the steering wheel. "God, he's so hot—really, could he be any more perfect? You should've seen the way he looked at me, Jan. I think he's starting to fall for me. I just need to find a way to spend more time with him. Mark my words, his next girlfriend's name is Ruby." She straightened when she saw Johnny leaving. "He's coming out."

"What's the plan?"

"I'm going to follow him, see if we can find out where he lives or if he's rendezvousing with her. I'll call you if I get a picture of the two of them."

"What if you lose him?"

"In that case we'll focus on his girlfriend. I overheard her tell Tamra that she'll be back on Monday. It's always good to know your competition."

Maybe if Lumiana kept coming around, she could befriend her and see what it was about her that led Johnny away from glamorous blondes. And once she gained Lumiana's trust, it would be so much easier to get rid of her, especially when Lumiana learns her boyfriend is cheating on her with her new best friend Ruby.

14

GIRL ON FIRE

"Storms make trees take deeper roots."

—DOLLY PARTON

Johnny stared at Lumiana's door for a full minute, working up the nerve to ring the bell. He hadn't managed to talk to her in four days and now he was showing up at her doorstep unannounced yet again.

Probably should've brought her flowers or something.

He stretched his neck, worrying how Lumiana would take the news that he'd told his parents and brothers about them. The shocked expression on his mom's face had been expected. She hadn't liked Andie in the beginning either—a fact she'd conveniently forgotten. His happiness mattered to her though. So hopefully with time his mother would get used to Lumiana and root for them.

Ana answered the door and jumped on him like a monkey. She weighed nothing, he thought when he threw the giggling girl over his shoulder. He knew Ana had a healthy appetite, but he couldn't shake the feeling that something wasn't right with her physical development. She was too small and babyish looking for a seven-year-old.

Johnny gave her a kiss on the temple and set her down. "Where's your mom?"

Ana clung to his leg. "She's reading outside."

He ruffled her hair. It wasn't just affection. He felt as protective of Ana as of his 1948 Gibson hollow body guitar. Spending time with her was like being a dad in training, but without the weight of responsibility.

Johnny followed Ana into the living room, where a large sheet of recycled paper covered in drawings lay atop the bamboo floor.

He crouched next to Ana. The girl had incredible talent, he thought as he admired the faces she was drawing. The one on the right closely resembled her uncle Gus.

"Do you want to draw with me?"

"I'd love to, but I have to talk to your mom." And he'd rather not embarrass himself. Compared to Ana he drew like a three-year-old. He couldn't wait to introduce her to Adam's grandmother, who was the greatest artist he knew.

Johnny gave Ana a peck on the head before he went outside, where he paused to take in the gorgeous view of the fields, woods, and mountains. The peacefulness settled his nerves.

Lumiana was sitting on one of the large sofas, surrounded by books. Monroe was dozing on her lap, and she absently stroked the dog with one hand while holding the book in the other.

"Hey, Doc," he said, startling her.

When she turned and looked at him, her face lit up with such joy it knocked the air out of him. Reaching for his hand, she pulled him onto the sofa and brought her soft lips to his.

As he kissed her, Johnny moved the books out of the way and lowered her onto the seat cushion. Pinning her under him, he propped himself on his elbows.

"I missed you," she murmured, cupping his face.

He gave her a lingering kiss. "I'm sorry I haven't called or stopped by."

"You told me you'd be busy with interviews and performances."

Great that she was so understanding but at the same time it worried him that she seemed to have no trouble being without him for so long. At least she said she'd missed him, and the look she'd given him—he wished he could get one of those every time he got home.

"I told my family about us today."

"How did it go?" Her forehead creased and he smoothed a finger over it. "Did you tell them they can't tell anyone about us?"

He nodded. "It went okay."

Pushing him aside, she sat up. "That doesn't sound like it did."

"Don't worry about it." He pulled her back down, but she sat right back up.

"I know your dad and your brothers approve of me, so I presume your mother does not?"

He put a hand on her knee because she wouldn't give him her hand. "My mom never liked any of my girlfriends the first time she met them. And you said it yourself, you often make an odd first impression. She'll come around once she gets to know you better and accepts that Andie and I are over."

Lumiana slumped backward onto the sofa cushion, covering her face with her arm.

Johnny rolled on top of her. "We're going to make this work, Lu. I'm not letting my mom or anyone get between us." When she brought her arms around him, he said, "You didn't tell me you've been visiting my dad."

It took a while before she replied. "You were busy, and I didn't think it would be a problem. You said he would be happy to see me again. And he was." He felt a twinge of guilt when she added, "It's not like you or your family came to visit him. What is a problem, I think, is that everyone is treating him like a coma patient. It's not helping him if your family acts as though he isn't in the room. Just because he cannot talk or move at a normal pace, doesn't mean he is incapable of thinking and feeling."

Tamra, Mansfield Park's Chief Nursing Officer, had told them earlier that Lumiana was helping his father and a few other patients practice eating. He knew that volunteering her time and skills had been a value her adoptive parents had instilled in her.

His own childhood couldn't have been more different. What his family had cared about was teaching him about stock options and compound interest. There was a silver lining though: he'd invested his allowance since he was twelve and then ten percent of his income from after-school gigs. So even without his current success or his sizable inheritance he'd be living a comfortable life.

Johnny took her hand. "I'm grateful for what you're doing for my dad. It means a lot to me."

"Only the first visit was because of you. Now I visit him because I like your dad and I enjoy talking to him. He is an interesting man."

"He's very fond of you too," he said, and harrumphed theatrically. "Not as fond of you as I am, of course."

Lumiana leaned closer for a long, lush kiss.

"Can I ask you something about Ana?" he said when she released him.

She sighed. "I apologize. I know she has boundary issues. It's just that to her you are the 'coolest' person she knows. She adores you so much I have to remind her every day that she cannot tell her classmates about you. But I can talk to her if she makes you uncomfortable."

"No, Lu, it doesn't bother me. Ana is the coolest kid I've ever met." The little girl had been rooting for him since the moment they met. Ana surely was one of the reasons why Lumiana had agreed to give their relationship a try.

She didn't seem convinced. "You need to tell me if it gets too much."

"I adore her, so please don't worry. What I wanted to ask is if everything is all right with her. She seems way too small for her age."

Lumiana traced a scar on her knee. "Her pituitary gland doesn't produce enough growth hormone." Climbing onto his lap, she put her arms and legs around him. "Ana receives treatment, but she may never exceed five feet."

"What she lacks in height she makes up for in intelligence and attitude." He was about to kiss her when Lumiana's brother came out of the house with Ana on his shoulders.

"Looking cozy," Shawn remarked, a challenge in his voice. The man was built like a rugby player and looked vaguely Irish with pale skin, copper brown hair, and impossibly blue eyes.

"I forgot," Lumiana said, moving off Johnny's lap. "I apologize, Shawn. I got distracted."

"Yeah, I can see that." He set Ana down. "Still wanna go a round?"

"I do." Lumiana stood, straightening her dress. "Especially today."

"Okay then," Shawn said, his eyebrows raised.

Lumiana hesitated. "Johnny, would it be okay if I left for half an hour?"

"No worries. Take your time."

Johnny went inside to get some water. He could tell Lumiana's brother was suspicious of him. He just wasn't sure if it was Shawn's natural instinct to protect his sister or if there was more to it.

***

Seeing Lumiana and Johnny together was so weird that Shawn could barely suppress the snide comments hanging on the tip of his tongue.

Johnny was nothing like Jayjay. The whole dynamic between Johnny and Lumiana was different. He couldn't remember her ever being so openly physical and playful with Jayjay.

He'd witnessed it at the *Fiesta de las Culturas* too. Whenever Johnny and Lumiana were near each other, they touched, and half the time without realizing it. Although it was almost always Johnny who initiated it, she always reciprocated. And she looked like she cherished it, her face lighting up like she was grateful someone was touching her.

And that hurt, because it shouldn't be this way. Jayjay shouldn't have died, and she shouldn't have had to be without him. But as much as he wanted his sister to move on and fall in love again, seeing her with another man felt wrong.

"I never thought you'd go for a guy like that," he said as he and Lumiana marched over to the lodge to change into workout clothes.

"A guy like what?" She opened the door, motioned him inside.

"Famous, rich, model looks, incapable of commitment. But maybe that's it, huh, because you don't want to commit either."

"None of that is why I'm with him." Lumiana undressed. "Johnny is a good man."

He found that hard to believe after following the guy's career over the years, which he'd only done because Adam was in his band. Johnny had a tendency to say and do things that made him look like an ass. But he got away with it because he was a remarkably gifted musician. That, and it probably didn't hurt that he looked like he could be the protagonist in every girl and gay man's wet dream.

Shawn slipped into a pair of sweats. "I worry he's going to hurt you, Lumi." And he wouldn't hesitate to snap the guy's arm like a twig should it ever come to that. "You deserve to be with someone who loves you and has your best interest at heart."

Lumiana put on a threadbare UCLA t-shirt and black yoga pants. "And what makes you think he doesn't?" She gestured to the bōs next to the door. Shawn took two and followed her outside.

"There's just something about him that rubs me the wrong way." They set up on the lawn. Shawn could see Ana and Johnny out on the patio. They were cute together, their mutual adoration palpable—he gave the man credit for that. But to think Johnny touched Lumiana with the same parts that had touched god knows how many women before her, gave him the creeps. "It's just that with Jayjay—"

"No," she said, attacking him with the bō. And with that his sister was on a roll, hitting him harder than she usually did, forcing him to move quicker than he wanted to.

"Why did you say you needed this especially today?" Shawn panted as he circled her.

Shaking her head, she lunged at him. This time he stepped up his game and succeeded in ridding her of her bō, then launched into another round *mano a mano*.

When he managed to wrestle her to the ground, Lumiana said, "Johnny's mother is of the opinion that I'm not an adequate match for him because of my issues."

"*Excuse me?*" Shawn hauled her to her feet. "She should be thrilled and amazed that her son was able to get his filthy hands on you. And if one of you isn't good enough for the other, it's him."

"Shawn—"

"No, Lumiana. I know you're in love with him, but no one gets to make you feel bad about yourself." He jutted his chin in Johnny's direction. "He better have stood up for you."

She smiled. "He said he wouldn't let anyone get between us."

"Good for him." Shawn wiped his forehead. With this intensity and speed they'd be black and blue by the time they were done. "I need you to tell me if he doesn't treat you right."

"So you can beat him up like you did Jayjay that time?" She gave him a shove and resumed a combat stance.

He'd forgotten about that. When he was younger he didn't know where to put his anger, so he pounded on everything and everyone that got in his way. One day when he saw Lumiana wiping at her eyes right after Jayjay had talked to her, he jumped him from behind. Jayjay kicked his ass, and then Shawn found out Lumiana had been crying because of a misunderstanding, which was entirely her fault. But Jayjay earned his respect that day, and they'd been like brothers until his death.

"I miss that bastard."

"Shawn, I can't think about it. I feel like a cheater if I do."

"God, you've been on your own for years, Lumi. You deserve to enjoy your life, and if

Johnny is what you need right now, that's okay." When he saw the tears in her eyes, he hit her hard. He didn't want her to go to that painful place again that he knew all too well himself. "Step it up, sis," he urged, and grinned when she did.

***

Johnny's mouth hung open as he witnessed what looked like a fight sequence from a martial arts film. He tried to cover Ana's eyes, but she pushed his hand away. When Lumiana repeatedly lashed out at her brother, Johnny started biting his nails. She was right, he thought. She could've seriously injured him when she mistook him for an intruder.

"It's okay," Ana assured him as they watched Shawn throw Lumiana to the ground. "They know what they're doing. They've trained together since they were teenagers. It's like a dance. They won't hurt each other."

He was pretty sure they were hurting each other. Those jabs and kicks hit their target, which meant they'd be covered in bruises later.

Lumiana and Shawn went another round, then lay on the grass, holding hands. Adam had mentioned they were close and that Shawn would stop at nothing to protect her. Now that he'd seen what the man was capable of, Johnny had no doubts. Not that Lumiana needed much protection. She was clearly more than capable of defending herself.

Eventually, and with visible discomfort, Shawn got up and helped Lumiana to her feet. When she linked her hand with Shawn's, leaning her head against his shoulder, Johnny felt a pang of jealousy. Did Shawn have a thing for her? They weren't blood relatives. Maybe Shawn had taken an instant dislike to him because he wanted Lumiana for himself.

"All right, Lumi, that was painful, also kind of fun," Shawn said as they came up the stairs to join Johnny and Ana on the patio. "But let's go back to the basics next time."

"You're getting old," Lumiana teased, stretching her limbs like she'd just finished a yoga class instead of an audition for *Kill Bill: Volume 3*.

"Let's see how you feel tomorrow, sweetheart." Shawn caught Lumiana in a fierce embrace and kissed her on the mouth.

To be fair, it was a peck, but still.

Ana followed her uncle back into the house, giving Johnny a moment alone with Lumiana.

She winced when he tried to pull her close. "I'm a bit sore from my workout."

He reached out to touch her, but she scooted farther away.

He gave her a smoldering look. "Can you hold still for a sec?"

She hesitated at first, but then let him pull up her shirt. She had streaks and bruises emerging on her shoulders and torso. "When I saw you and

Shawn go all Jackie Chan on each other, I was worried something like this might happen."

"I've had worse." She moved onto his lap, bringing her arms and legs around him. Which made him think of her and Shawn again.

"You and your brother are very close."

"Shawn is my best friend," she said with a gleam in her eyes.

"You and him, it seemed like you're more than that."

She tugged on her ear. "What do you mean?"

"Your body language, you were very affection-ate with each other. I'm not used to seeing sib-lings kiss on the lips and stuff. I mean, you're not blood-related so technically it would be possible without being too weird."

That made her laugh. "Shawn and I would never ever be lovers."

"Why not? He's good-looking, seems to be a pretty cool guy." He tried to sound nonchalant. 'Tried' being the operative word.

"But so are you, and we are together. Why would I be interested in someone else? And why my brother?" She thought for a moment, then smiled as though she solved a mystery. "You aren't jealous, are you?"

"I'm only human. So yes, a little, I guess."

"There is no need, Johnny. You should know by now that my family and I are affectionate with each other. It was a peck, not a sexual kiss whatsoever. Shawn is my brother, as much as he would be if we were born to the same parents. And even if he wasn't my brother, he isn't attracted to women that way."

He felt like such a jerk. "I'm sorry, I had no idea. And please believe me, I didn't mean to imply that not being related by blood makes you less of a family. I know you love Ana as much as if she were your biological daughter."

Lumiana gave him a peck on the lips.

"Very funny." He nipped her ear.

Then Lumiana gave him a kiss so passionate it made his stomach flutter. "Just making sure you know the difference."

"It's a real pity you're so sore." He slid his hand under her shirt and up her back. "How long until I can touch you without hurting you?"

"Is this your way of saying you wish to have intercourse?"

He cupped her ass to draw her closer, his hardon rubbing against her center. "It's my way of saying I want to fuck you six ways to Sunday." He loved the flushed look on her face. "Could you please stop calling it intercourse?"

"That's what it's called," she said, her voice husky. "You make it sound like I invented the term."

Johnny pushed her up against him once more. A soft moan preceded her next words. "It looks worse than it is. Most of the bruises are on my arms and legs, so if you don't squeeze me too hard, it won't be a problem."

With a chuckle, he tangled his fingers in her hair and tugged lightly. "You need to work on your pillow talk, Doc." He closed his eyes appreciatively when she trailed her lips up his neck while her hand moved expertly between them.

***

Johnny thought he'd be nervous seeing Andie again, but when he knocked on her door, it felt like visiting an old friend. An old, clingy friend. He'd tried ignoring her calls, but she kept bugging him about needing to talk, so he figured the easiest way to put an end to it would be to talk to her in person.

A sweet smile graced Andie's face when she let him in. He gave her a kiss on the cheek and followed her into the living room, where they sat on her gray Art Deco sofa. Andie was a fan of the eclectic style with its bold geometric shapes. And he liked it too, although her striped wallpaper made him queasy when he looked at it for more than thirty seconds.

Inching closer, Andie stroked her hand up his thigh.

Was this why she wanted to see him? To start over?

He stopped her wandering hand. "I'm sorry, Andie. I'm seeing someone."

Her face fell.

Shit.

Sighing, she pushed her hands through her

strawberry blond hair. "That's unfortunate, and the worst possible timing. I thought this would go differently..." She got up. "Do you remember coming over a couple of weeks ago?"

"Yes, and I'm sorry." Slumping forward, he put his face in his hands. It sure hadn't been his brightest moment. Sadly, severe pain and an epic case of blue balls could do that to a man. Still, it was a shitty thing to do, and he'd regretted it ever since.

"Don't sweat it, Johnny. We both needed it. But that's not what this is about." Andie left the room, and when she came back, she handed him something he did not expect.

"This is the result of our little reunion."

Johnny stared at the positive pregnancy test in his hands, then up at Andie.

She combed a hand through her hair, brushing it to the side. "Aren't you going to say anything?"

He couldn't hear her over the buzzing in his ears. "I... I thought you were on the pill."

"I am, but I've been flying back and forth so much. With the time difference it's easy to miss one. It happens. And the way you jumped me that night, I didn't really have time to think."

He shook the stick as if it were a pen running out of ink. "Ah... Are you sure this is correct?"

"It's peeing on a stick. It's pretty straightforward."

"Funny. Did you see a doctor to confirm?"

"Do you think I'm making this up?" she snapped. "I'm not a liar."

He didn't think she was lying. He just wanted the facts. "Considering the impact this is going to have on our lives, I think it's fair to ask questions." He braced himself. "Are you sure it's mine?"

"I have an appointment on Monday but I haven't had my period in weeks," she grumbled. "And I'm not sleeping around like you." Propping her hands on her hips, she began to pace. "We only broke up a short time ago."

Not that short. Or at least not as unreasonably short as she was implying. And Lumiana just happened. He hadn't been looking for a new relationship when he met her.

Propping his elbows on his thighs, he massaged his temples. "I'm not sleeping around."

"You said you're seeing someone."

"Yeah, but it's *one* woman, singular, and I'm serious about her. I'm sorry."

Andie picked at a loose thread on one of her shimmering throw pillows. "Let's see how she feels about you when you tell her you're having a baby with someone else, because I'm keeping it. You know I'm Catholic." She put her hand on his thigh again, but this time it wasn't sexual. "She's not going to stay with you, Johnny. You haven't been together for long, unless you cheated on me."

"I didn't cheat on you. I've never cheated on

anyone." He got up, held her gaze. "I met her only three days before this happened." He waved the stick. "I wasn't with you then and I wasn't with her yet either. And you don't know her. You can't possibly know how she will react."

"Oh, Johnny," she laughed without humor. "I can't think of a single woman who'd be happy to hear her boyfriend is having a baby with someone else."

They stared at each other for a moment. He prayed Andie was wrong.

"Where does this leave us?" she asked, chewing on her bottom lip.

He looked past her at the foggy Los Angeles skyline, hoping for some sort of sign. "I don't know, Andie. This is a shock. Can I have some time to wrap my head around this?"

"Fine, I guess that's fair. It was a shock for me too. Call me when you come to a decision. I'll have this baby, with or without you." Andie kissed him on the cheek and told him to show himself out.

***

Johnny had promised Lumiana he'd call her that evening, but he couldn't bring himself to do it. Nor did he feel any better the next day or the day after that. He ended up avoiding her all week, which was astonishingly easy. She wasn't the controlling type, and she accepted that traveling across the States to promote his new album was part of his job.

Friday evening, Johnny decided he had to tell Lumiana about his impending fatherhood. He plodded up her driveway feeling like he was about to appear in court. When Ana opened the door instead of Lumiana, he relaxed a little. She jumped into his arms and showered him with kisses.

"I missed you so much," she declared, putting her head on his shoulder.

"I missed you too, kiddo." More than he'd realized. It was fucking ironic that being with the little girl had made him want to be a dad, and now he might become one.

Be careful what you wish for.

Why, God, did it have to be with the wrong woman?

"Hey, stranger," Lumiana's voice sounded from afar, raising the hair on his skin in a delicious tingle.

He missed her, but knowing he was about to hurt her made him want to run for the door.

Johnny watched her come down the wooden stairs. She was wearing a short, floral-patterned balloon skirt, a cream-colored sweater, and a bright smile that warmed his chest every time he saw it. Her long black hair was tied into a loose braid.

Johnny carried Ana over to the bottom of the staircase, where Lumiana gave him a quick kiss, then tickled her giggling daughter.

"You look lovely." He smiled at her, hoping she wouldn't notice the storm brewing inside him. "Where do you get these clothes?"

He wasn't ashamed to admit he liked fashion. Having VIP access to runway shows was one of the perks of his job.

And seeing Lumiana like this was a rare sight. Most of the time she wore the white pencil dress or the UCLA sweatshirt, but when she didn't, she sported an array of clothes that looked like they were made for her. Her style reflected her nature: playful and sensuous.

"I don't get them." She winked at him, leading the way toward the living room.

"She makes them," Ana whispered.

Of course she does.

They headed for the kitchen and Ana dashed outside to collect her toys.

Johnny took a seat at the counter. "Ana told me you're making your own clothes."

"My adoptive mom taught me how. My siblings and I often meet with her on Sundays to brainstorm ideas or work on something. It's fun and the clothes fit well because they are tailored to our individual bodies." Reaching across the counter, she laid a hand over his. "Would you care for a cup of tea?"

Johnny nodded. He hadn't drunk much tea before meeting Lumiana, but it seemed to be her solution for everything from physical ailments to awkward silence.

"What is your mood like?" she asked to determine what tea would suit him best.

"Do you have something that goes well with bad news?"

A small frown creased her eyebrows. "Let's go with lavender."

"It's cute that you believe drinking tea is going to make things better."

"Never underestimate the power of tea." As she prepared it, she asked, "How bad is it? Do I need to worry?"

Sighing, he braced his elbows on the counter. "What I've been told is that we're going to break up over this, so it's pretty bad."

"Why would we do that?" Reaching up, she placed her hand over her locket. "I know I'm not easy, but I am trying. I'm even practicing using sexier words than intercourse. And I prescribed myself a daily dose of *Fifty Shades of Grey*. It's rather fascinating."

He chuckled at the image of Lumiana reading erotica in between Toni Morrison and *Stone Age Economics*. "Lu, you make it sound like I'm breaking up with you, which I assure you I'm not. You're not the problem at all. I am. I've done something I shouldn't have done and that action had serious consequences."

"You didn't tell anyone else about us, did you?"

He covered her hand with his. "No, again, it has nothing to do with you."

"Then what is it? You're making me nervous, and not the good kind."

He dropped his head, his gut twisting at the thought of losing her. How could he be so irresponsible? It hadn't even occurred to him to ask Andie if she was still on the pill, much less whether she'd had sex with anyone else since their breakup. STDs were no joke either. "Can we have tea first? Actually, do you think it can wait until after Ana goes to bed? I'd like the chance to say goodbye to her."

She reached for the Lionel Richie mug. "I'm not sure I can stand the suspense much longer."

"Please."

Lumiana checked the time, and because Ana was about to go to bed anyway, she agreed to wait.

After saying goodnight to Ana and closing the door to her room behind him, Johnny leaned against the wall. He recoiled when Lumiana touched his arm.

"This is harder than I thought," he said, rubbing his face. "Where would you like to have this conversation? And keep in mind you might want to yell at me."

Grabbing a lantern and a picnic blanket, Lumiana led him out the front door. They walked hand in hand to a big oak tree near the gravel road.

Lumiana spread the blanket out under the tree and sat down, gesturing for him to join her.

Johnny touched a hand to his churning stom-ach.

"You didn't kill anyone, did you?" Lumiana asked, and made him laugh.

He sounded hysterical. "God, no. It's the op-posite actually."

Come on, man, you can do this. Just say it al-ready.

He scrubbed his hands over his face and through his hair. "The last day of the first week-end we spent together—you know, the same day I injured my arm—I was upset and in pain not only because of my injury, but also because I thought I was never going to see you again. So after we said goodbye at the gate, I had my body-guard drop me off at my ex-girlfriend's house to let off some steam... You know what that means, right?" With Lumiana he was never sure if she was able to read between the lines.

"You fucked," she said experimentally.

He laughed, despite himself. "That just sounds wrong coming from you. And in this case I prefer calling it 'intercourse' because it was just a means to an end. As you might remember, she called me a few times because she had something she wanted to tell me, so I met her earlier this week—"

"Is that why you didn't call or wanted to see me?"

"I'm sorry, Lu. I needed some time to think and work up the courage to talk to you. I... My ex... she's pregnant."

Lumiana stared at the flickering lantern. He waited for her to say something, but she didn't.

When she finally did make an attempt to talk, no words came out.

"I kind of expected you might have something to say about this."

She looked right through him with a blank expression. It wasn't until he snapped his fingers in front of her face that she said, "Just to make sure I understand this, you are telling me you had sex with your ex-girlfriend after we spent that first weekend together, and now she is pregnant from that one time?"

"Yes. I didn't cheat on you, in case that's what you're thinking."

She made a noise in her throat before she said, "Okay."

"Okay?" His relief that she didn't yell was short-lived, because her calmness made him wonder whether her feelings for him weren't as strong as he'd hoped. "Don't you feel even a little angry, or sad, or disappointed?"

Breaking eye contact, she gripped her elbows. "Of course I do. But what I feel doesn't change anything. And this might be a good thing if you want to have children."

His mouth went slack for a moment. "Are you saying that if we stay together you don't want to have children with me?"

"We'd have Ana," she said, scratching at a scar

on her arm. "I never considered having biological children. I didn't even think being a mom would be a possibility for someone like me until Jayjay and Ana came into my life. But if you want a child, you should be happy you got what you wanted."

He dropped his head. "What I want is to have a kid with the woman I love and want to spend my life with, which is *you*, not my ex. And I love Ana. I would've been fine if my family consisted only of the three of us for the time being." He didn't realize the magnitude of what he was saying until he looked up and saw Lumiana's face. "I'm so sorry, Lu. Please don't cry. I—"

Her lips met his in a fervent kiss. Hands groping, they rolled across the cool grass in the deliciously futile attempt to melt into one. He learned then what had been missing in his previous relationships: this overpowering need to connect on a level that transcended all reason.

15

JOHNNY

"Pain is real. But so is hope."

—UNKNOWN

When Andie went to the OB/GYN two days later, she learned life could be a nasty little bitch.

In the morning Johnny had called her to say he would be there for her, giving her hope that once he saw his baby growing inside her, he would forget all about his latest floozy.

But now there was no baby, just bone-deep humiliation. *A false positive from an ovarian cyst. How?*

It wasn't fair.

Johnny was still the man she loved, the person with whom she had most in common, who shared and accepted her lifestyle. Sure, they had problems coordinating their schedules. She was an international supermodel, and Johnny, although significantly less well-known, was an award-winning musician who lived for his art. There were long periods when they hardly saw each other, but for her, it didn't justify the breakup.

When Andie got home, her best friend Claudia was sitting in the moss-green velvet armchair, a martini in one hand, a script in the other. Claudia Jean McAllister had wanted to be a TV actress ever since she fell in love with secret agent Angus MacGyver in the spring of 1992. Hollywood hadn't embraced her talent yet, but it was just a matter of patience and persistence, and Claudia had both in abundance.

"What is it?" Claudia set aside her glass and the papers and went over to Andie, who burst into tears the moment Claudia pulled her into her arms. It took a while until she could compose herself enough to tell her what happened.

"I'm so sorry." Claudia gave Andie another hug. "I know you love him, AB. The two of you belong together." Andie and Claudia had been best friends since they were two years old and got their tongues stuck to the same frozen flagpole. AB and CJ, their initials, became their nicknames in 1999 when Claudia persuaded Andie to play secret agents in the basement.

"How could he move on so quickly?" Andie dabbed her eyes with her sleeve.

"Don't worry, sweetie, he'll come crawling back to you in no time."

"I don't think so, CJ." Andie lay down on the sofa, propping her head on a silver-blue throw pillow. "Have you seen Johnny's interview with Helen?"

Claudia took her phone and searched for the YouTube video.

"I think he's in love with that woman, whoever she is." Kicking off her beige stilettos, Andie winced when one of them nearly knocked the white vase off the coffee table.

"When he came to see me, he didn't even let me touch him. And when he said he'd be there for me and the baby, he also said he wasn't going to leave her. I tried googling him to see who she is, but there are no recent photos of him and a girlfriend." No one seemed to know who that woman was or what she looked like, except for Helen and Jimmy.

Claudia watched Johnny's interview with a frown on her face. "What does 'she has a very special way of making sense of the world' even mean? Sounds like a fancy way of saying the woman is autistic. And he says she has a lot of scars. He must've lost his mind. I thought he was obsessed with perfection. I mean, look at the women he's dated." She got up to fix them both a cocktail.

Andie shrugged. "I think she sounds interesting. Maybe he was bored with 'perfection.'"

"Please. I'd bet my *Knight Rider* collection she's attractive despite the scars."

"*Knight Rider*? If we make the bet, you'd better offer me something more recent than an action crime series from the 80s. How about *Monk*? I like smart and odd."

"Apparently so does Johnny." Claudia rolled her eyes.

Andie grabbed another pillow, hugged it to her chest. "I don't know what to do. I want him back. We were supposed to be a family." She'd already envisioned it: the house, the dog, the picket fence. She really wanted a baby with him. "It's not fair." She massaged her temples. "What would you do if you were me?"

Claudia handed Andie a martini and sat in the armchair. If it weren't for her freckles and the long red curls, she would have looked like a mafia boss about to reveal plans for taking over the city: all self-assured and determined. "I'd start by talking to his mother. Maybe Eleanor will tell you more about that woman. And we also need to remind Johnny why he fell in love with you." She brought one finger to her lips. "Don't tell him yet that there is no baby."

"That sounds devious, CJ. Not telling him the truth, I mean. I'm okay with the rest."

"I'm not saying don't tell him, just that you hold off until we've figured out a plan. And honestly, AB, it took him over a week to decide if he wanted to be involved in raising the child, now you take some time to deal with your pain. There's nothing wrong with that."

***

The next day Andie went to see Johnny's mother. His childhood home hadn't changed since the last time she'd been there. Eleanor had been awarded the palatial house in the divorce and was fastidious about keeping the antique furniture and exquisite art in pristine condition.

"You look tired, sweetheart. Are you okay?" Eleanor led her into the living room, offering her a seat and coffee.

Andie waved her off. "It's okay, nothing to worry about."

"Let me know if there's anything I can do for you. Even if you and Johnny are no longer together, I still care about you."

"Thank you, Eleanor." Andie stared at her coffee. The cup looked like it was meant for a doll. "How is Johnny these days?"

"I haven't seen or heard much from him lately." Eleanor dropped three sugar cubes in her coffee and stirred it with a silver spoon. "He's been out of town a lot."

"He told me he's seeing someone. Have you met her?"

Eleanor nodded. She looked beautiful for her age, and elegant, like a queen surrounded by opulence. "I was hoping the two of you would get back together. I must say I was disappointed when I found out about that woman." She pulled down the sleeves of her fuchsia blouse. "I'm only saying 'that woman,' because I'm not allowed to reveal her name. She is a very private person. If you ask me, it will be the reason those two won't last. Johnny told me he has his doubts about it too. But you know him, he's stubborn and persistent. I have yet to meet someone who matches his resolve."

That was excellent news. Andie bit the inside of her cheek to keep from smiling. "What is she like?"

Eleanor took another sip of coffee. "I met her only once and it was quite awkward. I didn't know who she was or how Johnny felt about her, and she behaved rather oddly. I think it's safe to say we won't become friends anytime soon."

"Is she autistic?" it popped out of her.

Eleanor suspended her cup in midair.

"Um, sorry, not that it would be a bad thing. I'm asking because I saw Johnny's interview with Helen, and she said something that could be interpreted that way."

"I haven't seen the interview but I admit that was my first impression, and Johnny also mentioned something along those lines. She is socially challenged, I can tell you that much." Eleanor set her cup on the table. "I don't understand why he chose to be with her when he could be with someone as lovely as you."

Andie gave Eleanor's hand a squeeze. "Who knows, maybe we'll find our way back to each other."

"I'd love that." Andie knew she was the daughter-in-law Eleanor had been hoping for. The woman had told her so on numerous occasions.

"Do you think Johnny is serious about her?"

Eleanor fiddled with the little spoon. "I wish I could tell you no, but I've seen how his face lights up when he talks about her. And the way he looks at her, like she's a mystery box he can't wait to open. You know how men are," she added with a roll of her eyes, "they love a challenge. And that woman makes him work extra hard."

Andie fought to suppress her disappointment but Eleanor noticed it anyway.

"Don't worry, sweetheart, their relationship won't last. He'll be yours again in no time."

***

When Claudia came over later that day, Andie was still in low spirits. She lit a cigarette while she told her best friend that Eleanor wasn't a fan of Johnny's new girl.

"She wants him to be with me."

Claudia grabbed Andie's cigarette and stubbed it out before she returned to her favorite armchair. "Sounds like good news to me. So what's with the long face?"

Sagging against the sofa cushions, Andie

covered her face with her hands. "She thinks Johnny is serious about that woman."

"Not ideal, but really, how serious can their relationship be after, what, a month or two?" Claudia drummed her fingers on the armrest. "I take it you didn't find out her name?"

Andie pressed one of the silver pillows to her face, groaned, and then placed the pillow under her head. "It's hard to find out who she is because Johnny makes people keep it quiet."

"Interesting. I wonder why." Claudia thrived on drama and conspiracies.

Andie shrugged. "Eleanor thinks it's why they won't last."

"Great news for us, right?"

"Maybe." Andie put two sticks of peppermint gum in her mouth. "But how can we find out who she is?"

"Maybe she's famous and doesn't want people to find out she's dating Johnny because it could damage her reputation. Or she's really young and it would hurt his reputation."

"Maybe." Andie got up and made them both another martini, their signature drink. "Don't you think it's weird when someone who doesn't give a shit what the media says suddenly cloaks himself in secrecy?"

"You know what we could do..." Claudia took the glass Andie was holding out to her. "We could follow Johnny to see where she lives and what she looks like, and take it from there."

"You watch too many crime shows." Andie carved her hands through her hair. "You want me to stake out Johnny?"

Claudia smirked.

"No way, CJ. I don't want to get slapped with a restraining order for stalking my ex. That would seriously damage *my* reputation."

"Fine, then let me do it."

Andie thought for a moment, but couldn't come up with a better idea. "Just don't get caught."

***

Three days later, Claudia reported back that Johnny hadn't met with any women but that he'd stopped by a remote, gated community up north in Ventura County. Could be where his girlfriend lived or where they met so paparazzi couldn't get pictures, Andie thought as she paced her living room. Claudia suggested driving up there to see who she was, but how could they possibly do that without Johnny finding out?

"Maybe we need to draw her out," Claudia said, gazing into her martini glass as if it were a crystal ball. "We could make use of the little intel we have. I'm sure some reporters would appreciate a tip that helps them dig up who Johnny Graham is boning these days."

Andie shook her head. She'd hate it if someone did something like that to her. A former classmate once posted humiliating pictures of her on the Internet, which spread across the tabloids like a brush fire. For weeks reporters had pestered her with requests for comment.

"So you're going to sit there and let that woman steal your man?"

"I don't want them to be together, but—"

"No *but*, Andie. If you want him back, fight for him. There's no way of knowing when or if he's going to leave her. And that bitch thinks he's having a baby with his ex and is fine with standing between him and the mother of his child? That's not nice of her either. You and Johnny belong together, AB. Everyone thinks so. He just needs a little reminder."

"I'm fine with showing him why we should be together, but going after his girlfriend is too extreme." She pointed a warning finger at her friend. "I mean it, CJ."

"At least call him and try to set up a meeting. Tell him to bring her along."

"Fine." Andie took out her phone and texted Johnny. He wrote back he could be at her place in half an hour.

***

Right after he saw Andie, Johnny drove up to Jonata. He couldn't shake the feeling that telling Lumiana about Andie's request to meet her would lead to trouble. Just the thought of being in the same room with her and Lumiana made his eyelid twitch. But Andie was right. He couldn't involve Lumiana in the life of their baby without Andie knowing her.

When he and Lumiana were alone on the swing bed out in her backyard, Johnny told her about his meeting with Andie. "She'd like to get to know the woman who's going to be in her baby's life."

"I hope you are joking." Lumiana straightened. "Why would you think I'd agree to meet her? And why now, Johnny? The baby isn't even born yet. She isn't even past the first trimester. I can't believe you were expecting me to be fine with this."

He reached for her hand, but she got up and mumbled something foreign before she took off in a walk that accelerated into a sprint.

Johnny pounded his fist against the seat cushion. He couldn't blame her. Lumiana could've left him when she found out he'd gotten Andie pregnant, but she chose to stick with him. That was more than he could've hoped for. It was selfish to put her through all of this just because he didn't want to lose her.

He stalled for a while, telling himself it was because Lumiana needed some time to cool off, and not because he was a chicken.

Johnny trudged back to the house, then knocked on Ana's open door because Lumiana was nowhere to be found. The little girl was standing in front of an easel, painting the sunset.

"Hey, kiddo, have you seen your mom?"

"She said she was going out for a bit. Is everything okay?"

"Yes," he lied. "I'm going for a walk. Are you going to be all right alone in the house?" When she nodded, he said, "I'm taking my phone. Call me if you need anything."

Johnny strolled down the driveway toward the narrow gravel road. He found Lumiana huddled in the checkered picnic blanket under the big old oak tree where he'd told her about the baby.

"I thought I might find you here."

Lumiana blinked at him through long wet eyelashes.

He could kick himself for making her cry.

When Johnny sat next to her, he touched her cheek, but she turned her head. Seeing a tear roll down made his throat close up. "We should be enjoying the beginning of our relationship, but instead you're stuck paying for my mistake."

Lumiana sat up and wiped her face with her sleeve. "I don't know what you expect me to say. That you're having a baby with another woman bothers me more than I thought it would."

He tried to ignore the nausea spreading through his gut.

"I don't want to feel this way, Johnny. This situation makes me anxious."

"I understand," he murmured. "I'm sorry, Lu."

"I know you are. You have said that repeatedly. But it doesn't make this go away." Lumiana squeezed his hand. "I want to be with you, but I need some time to organize my thoughts. And I need to talk about it with someone other than you."

"Please don't tell your family. They'll hate me for this." He was pretty sure Shawn was going to use him as his personal punching bag.

"I only have my family," she reminded him. "Asking me to go through this alone is not fair."

He took both her hands in his. "Do you want me to go and you call me whenever you're ready?"

"Would that be okay with you?"

He didn't have much of a choice—anything else would be selfish. He blew out a long breath and nodded, wishing he could turn back time.

Lumiana got up, and so did he. They held hands as she walked him to his car.

"This is it then?"

His insides contracted when she said, "For today."

Johnny stepped closer, easing her chin up, so he could look at her. Seeing the pain in her eyes made him want to smash something.

She kissed him, then left without looking back.

When Johnny drove off, a car on the side of the road pulled out after him and followed him home.

***

That evening, when Ruby Kyle strode into the living room of the Santa Monica apartment she shared with Janice, her roommate was watching Johnny's concert special with their fellow bloggers Liz, Sondra, and Pauly.

How pathetic they all were, Ruby thought, and sat in the tufted lounge chair opposite them.

Janice lowered the volume. "How did it go?"

Flipping her hair back, Ruby smiled. She loved this part where they looked at her like she was the queen of the beehive. "I found out where his girlfriend lives," she sang. She also found out where he lived, not that she intended to share that valuable information.

"What's next?" asked Pauly, the only one of the four who wasn't easily fooled.

"What do you think we should do?" Ruby liked them to believe she was a team player, when in reality she thought of them as her minions.

She'd already set her own plan in motion more than a week ago. Each time Johnny stopped by Mansfield Park, she had continued her flirtation with him, and a few days ago he'd even joined her for her lunch break.

They were perfect for each other: she looked like a model but didn't have the busy schedule of one, which Johnny had said in an interview was why he and Andie Woodhull broke up.

When Johnny's new girlfriend, the frigid professor Dr. Lumiana Harding, had proven to be impossible to befriend no matter how charming Ruby acted toward her, she decided to give Lumiana an incentive to make her understand that being with Johnny wasn't in her best interests.

Now all she had to do was wait and see—and pretend there was merit in the other four bloggers' ideas. She went with Pauly's: follow Johnny and his girlfriend until they got a clear photo of them together, then sell it to the highest bidder.

***

After saying goodbye to Johnny, Lumiana could barely keep the tears at bay as she made her way back to her house. Did she want to be involved in his baby's life? Would she and Andie get along? She didn't know how to make friends, if her awkward conversations with that nurse Ruby were any indication. She needed to talk to someone in her family, but Johnny was right. If she told Shawn, he'd tell her to end things with him. Maybe Candela would be more supportive.

Two hours later, while Lumiana was scrubbing the kitchen floor, the doorbell rang. She took off her gloves and strode through the freshly cleaned living room to answer the door.

"Hi, Mike, is everything okay?" Lumiana attempted to smile, but didn't quite succeed.

"Are you okay? You don't look so good."

"I just had a rough day."

"Let me know if I can do anything for you."

"Thanks, Mike." She smiled at him. He was like a big, strong papa bear, taking care of all the cubs in their tiny community.

"There it is, that lovely smile." He grinned, and held up the envelopes in his hands. "A courier dropped this one off for you." He tapped a blank envelope. "And these came in the mail. I thought I'd save you a trip to the mailbox."

He stacked the letters, frowning at the one on top. "This one's from Johnny, according to the courier. I felt like there was something off about her though—strange accent, maybe Eastern European, blond hair, long legs, pale. I wasn't sure what to make of her, so to be safe I asked Uncle Sam to run a preliminary."

Uncle Sam was the Arendt-Garcías' security advisor. The former Navy SEAL had been working with her parents for as long as she could remember.

"Thanks for telling me, Mike." When Lumiana reached for the letters, Mike stepped back.

"We have her on camera. The thing is, she was wearing a baseball cap and tinted glasses. I don't know how well we can see her face. Linus is checking the video footage. But if you'd like to look at it, might be worth a shot. You know I'm required to report any suspicious activity, so you might get a call about that. Can I open this for you?"

"You don't think it contains a toxin, do you?"

"No, but better safe than sorry."

"Mike, I am not letting you do this." She yanked the envelopes from his hands, took a few steps back, and ripped the blank one open. She pulled the folded letter out of the envelope and waved it. "It's a normal piece of paper, see?"

Lumiana stuffed the letter back in its envelope. Then she handed it with the others to Ana, who'd just joined them but disappeared back into the house before Lumiana had a chance to remind her not to snoop. Ana read anything she could get her hands on. If the letter was from Johnny, she didn't want her to see it before she did—especially if it mentioned the baby.

"You're very stubborn," Mike scolded her. "We're going to tighten security for a while and I'll check the area more frequently. If this letter contains anything unusual, you need to tell me immediately. Your parents are strict about following protocol."

"I can take care of myself, Mike. And Johnny has written me a note before so it's probably from him. Please don't worry."

"I know you are a strong woman, Lumiana, but this is my job."

Mike adjusted his hat, then told her that he suspected someone might be stalking Johnny because a few days ago a car had stopped near the gate shortly after he arrived, but then the driver turned around and drove off. He'd dismissed it at the time because now and then people get lost and end up at Jonata by accident.

They said goodbye and Mike walked a few steps down the driveway before turning around. "I forgot. Did you hear about Pluto? That's messed up, right?"

"DiMarco's dog?"

"Yeah. Looks like a hit-and-run. He didn't make it."

Lumiana's eyes stung. "Oh…" Pluto belonged to Lumiana's sister's girlfriend DiMarco, a soldier who'd just returned from war. Pluto was her emotional support animal. She loved that dog.

"I told them they shouldn't let him wander past the gate. But all of you Arendt-Garcías are hardheads."

***

Meanwhile, Ana sat on the living room couch, eyeing the envelopes she'd put on the coffee table.

After a minute, she picked them up and put them next to her.

When curiosity outweighed her resolve to avoid another 'respect boundaries' lecture, she opened all the envelopes, took out the letters, including the one from the blank envelope that was already open, and stacked them in a neat pile.

She hesitated for another moment, checked that her mother wasn't coming, and then began reading them. The first was a maintenance bill, the second and third were royalty statements, but the fourth made her heart race. She dropped the rest of the mail, which scattered on the floor.

When Ana hopped off the sofa she slipped on the letters, sending them skittering under the couch and the coffee table.

***

Lumiana was returning to the living room when Ana came running out.

"What is it, *angelito*?"

"*Mamá*, I read your letters," she cried, waving the paper in her hand.

"Letters are private, Ana. If I wish for you to know what someone wrote me, I would tell you. Give it to me," she demanded, but Ana dashed past her and out the door, shouting after Mike, who was still within hearing. He turned and ran toward Ana, with Lumiana a few steps behind her. They both reached her daughter at the same time.

"Ana, give me the letter," Lumiana ordered.

"No, this is not a nice letter." Ana handed it to Mike.

"This is ridiculous. It's *my* letter."

"Shut it for a second, both of you," Mike barked, looking at the paper. Lumiana and Ana went silent at his hard tone, which brought out his Nigerian accent. Mike was as sweet as can be, but he was also seven feet tall and built like The Rock. People preferred to stay on his good side. "This is bad," he muttered. "Ana, you were right to show me this."

"You are upsetting me, Mike. May I please see the damn letter?" Lumiana held out her hand.

"Fine, but don't touch it with your bare hands. Maybe we'll be able to lift some prints."

Mike got a tissue from his pocket, and carefully passed the letter to Lumiana. A cold shiver ran down her spine as she read it.

I know who you are and where you live.
If you don't want this information to go public,
cut all ties with Johnny Graham.
You have until the end of the week.

"I don't care how strong you are, Lumiana. This is a serious threat to your safety and that of your family and our community. I'm going to put a guard on you 24/7 until we figure this out."

Mike gave her a stern look. "And I'm ordering you to contact Johnny right away. This might be a safety concern for him as well. I'm serious, Lumiana. Don't take matters into your own hands. You have a daughter too—remember that."

16

BAD

"Obstacles do not block the path,
they are the path."

—ZEN PROVERB

Had her prayers been answered, Andie wondered when Johnny showed up at her door that night. Two visits in one day. Seemed like CJ's plan was working.

Andie led him into the living room and turned down the radio.

Thankfully it wasn't one of Johnny's songs, which she'd been listening to all morning. *Wonder* really was his best album yet. But it hurt that the songs revealed so much not only about the woman who inspired his masterpiece, but also

about Johnny's relationship with that woman—
the kind of relationship Andie wished she had
with him.

Johnny stood in the middle of her glass-
walled penthouse, wringing his hands. "I talked
to my—" He shook his head mid-sentence. "The
three of us won't be meeting anytime soon. The
way it looks right now, I'd say probably never.
She's close to breaking it off." Johnny fell onto the
sofa.

"I'm sorry to hear that," she said but couldn't
contain her smile.

"No, you're not. You can't even keep a straight
face." He let out a frustrated sigh, then looked
around the room. "I need a drink."

She went and got him his favorite whiskey,
which he downed in one go.

Johnny dragged his hands through his hair
and cursed. "She asked me to give her time."

"I'm sorry, Johnny. What do you want me to
say?"

"Nothing. I'm not in a good place right now."

She patted his knee. "Maybe it's a sign that
you're meant to be with me."

He pinched his lips together, and got up from
the sofa. "I shouldn't have come here."

Andie grabbed his hand and pulled him back
down. "Don't leave, please. I didn't mean to pressure you." She got up and refilled his glass.

"Are you trying to get me drunk?" With a huff,
he pressed his palms to his eyes. "God, I could use

another drink. Just, please, stay away from me."

"You think you won't be able to resist?" She brought him a refill.

He took a sip, then set the glass on the table. "No funny business, Andie."

"I won't do anything you don't want me to do," she promised. "Besides, the last thing I want is to sleep with you because you're upset with your girlfriend. I want you to sleep with me because you want to be with me."

He didn't respond. His face was blank but his posture was open. She couldn't get a read on him. "You know what I find interesting?" she said, tapping his arm. "That you came here, even though you could've gone anywhere else."

"That's because I did something you asked me to do and it blew up in my face."

Andie leaned back against the sofa cushion. "To be fair, I didn't know how she'd react. And honestly, I expected her to break up with you right after you told her I was having your baby. But she stuck with you, so maybe she really just needs some time."

The last thing Andie wanted was to argue. She loved having Johnny around and would try to keep him with her for as long as she could. Even if that meant hiding her own feelings. "It's going to be okay," she said, linking her fingers with his.

Johnny's cell phone rang, and he pulled it out of his pocket.

Andie spied the caller ID—Jane Austen—figuring it was his girlfriend when his jaw tensed. She hoped he would let it run to voicemail, but he let go of her hand and went to open the door that led onto her balcony.

***

"Hey," Johnny said into the phone as he closed the glass door behind him. Goosebumps began to dot his skin. Although they hadn't been together for long, he knew Lumiana wouldn't change her mind that quickly.

"Johnny, it's me, Ana."

His stomach tightened. It was the first time the girl had called him. And today of all days? Something wasn't right. "Why are you whispering?" Johnny walked up to the glass railing to make sure he was out of earshot.

"Has my mom called you yet?"

"No, but I wasn't expecting her to call me tonight." His chest ached when he remembered how she looked earlier. He hated to be the reason for her tears.

"Um, something happened after you left."

When Ana didn't elaborate, he said, "You're worrying me, kid. Tell me."

"My mom got a bad letter, and Mike told her she should call you to make sure you're okay, because someone might be following you."

That can't be right.

Johnny balled his hand into a fist. "Can you put your mom on the phone, please?"

"No, then she'll know I called you. And she's already angry because I read the letter first and gave it to Mike."

"Ana!" Johnny heard Lumiana hiss in the background.

"Now she knows, so please put her on the phone."

"Ana wasn't supposed to call you," Lumiana said when she took over the phone.

"When were you going to tell me about this?"

"I don't know," she said, her tone distant. "I needed some time to think."

"Unbelievable," he muttered, pulling at the hem of his shirt. "Don't you think I should know about this, especially when it appears to be my fault?"

"Did you tell anyone about us who can't be trusted?"

"Not that I'm aware of. It's out there that I'm seeing someone, but except for my closest family, no one knows it's you. Are you sure it was because of me?"

"Your name was mentioned in the letter."

His muscles tensed. "Is there anything I can do?"

"Yes. Stay away from me and my house until the security team has figured out who sent this. And…"

"And what?" he snapped, irritated by her harsh tone.

"And perhaps take extra precautions. Be careful that no one is following you or enters your house. I don't want you to get hurt."

"Thanks for your concern," he said, softening. "I'll be careful. I'm going to make a few calls right after we hang up. Can you tell me what the letter said? Maybe I can help identify who sent it."

"Don't worry about it."

He growled. "It's not okay that you're shutting me out. We're supposed to be a team."

There was a long pause before she answered. "It said, 'I know who you are and where you live,' and the person threatened to make that information public."

She told him a woman had delivered the letter, but because there were no fingerprints on the letter other than Ana's and Mike's, the security team was working on getting her a picture, which Lumiana promised to send him as soon as she received it.

"What do they want?"

After a moment's hesitation, she said, "Just, let's not see each other until this is over."

"Whoever sent this wants us to break up, is that it?"

"Yes."

Not a chance in hell. "Okay, maybe then it's not a stranger."

"Why do you say that?"

"Did Mike say anything to you about what the woman looked like?"

"He said she was white, blond, and had long

legs."

"Great, that narrows it down," he scoffed. "Real blond or fake blond?"

"I don't know. Mike said she disguised her face."

"There are a few people I can think of who aren't too happy I'm with you." His mother, Andie, Adam, Shawn...

"Like your mom?"

"Or your brother," he shot back. "My mom wouldn't do something like this. I don't know who would. It's crazy..." The thought that someone he knew would want to hurt him like that was nauseating. "Let me ask around. But until we know more, I want you to have someone with you at all times. Can you give me Mike's number? I want to make sure someone keeps an eye on your house."

"Already taken care of," Lumiana told him. "As for the letter writer, perhaps it's one of your many admirers."

He snorted. "Like who?"

"Half the hospital and rehab staff. There were quite a few blond women there who expressed interest in you."

"I didn't think you'd noticed."

"I'd have to be blind and deaf to miss it. And since I am neither..."

"Right." He wondered if she was a little jealous, but knowing Lumiana, it might as well have been an objective observation. "It's all speculation anyway. It's just as likely someone hired her." He scratched his cheek. "Look, I know you need your space and I respect that, but could you send me a text now and then, so I know you're okay? Or when there's an update?"

"Okay." She sighed. "I miss having you here. I wish things were different."

"Me too. I'm sorry I made your life so complicated. That wasn't my intention."

"I know that." There were voices in the background. "I have to go. Shawn and the security team are here. Be safe, Johnny," she said and hung up without giving him the chance to say anything else.

***

Andie was sitting on the couch leafing through a fashion magazine when Johnny returned to the living room. She craved a martini and a cigarette, but remembered that it might adversely affect her pretend baby.

"You're dating Jane Austen? I thought she died in 1817." At least that's what she'd read on Wikipedia. Andie smiled, but corrected her facial expression when she saw Johnny's.

Without saying a word, he sat next to her, closed his eyes, and groaned.

"What is it, Johnny?" She touched his leg.

"Someone threatened my girlfriend. It's not you, is it?"

What the hell? "No, of course not. I don't know

who your girlfriend is. How would I get in touch with her?"

"I don't know. This whole thing doesn't make sense. I was careful not to reveal who she is." He tapped a fist against his lips. "Apparently someone followed me."

Andie knew that wasn't easy to do. Where Johnny lived and where he spent his days wasn't public knowledge. She knew he was careful. He took different routes and cars, and Mag had even taught him how to shake a tail.

"I think it's either someone we know or someone from the hospital or the rehab facility where my dad is staying... Whoever it is, hopefully we'll know soon, because she got caught on camera."

"I swear it wasn't me, Johnny. Is she all right?" The thought that it may have been Claudia made Andie's stomach turn. She reflexively touched a hand to it.

Johnny put his hand over the one she'd placed on her belly. "Sorry. I didn't mean to upset you."

Right, the nonexistent baby.

"She'll be fine," he said as if it were a given. "She knows how to defend herself, which I've never found more reassuring than today." He ran his hands over his thighs. "I have to go, it's getting late. Thanks for being there for me." He gave her a kiss on the cheek and got up.

"I'll always be there for you. We are family now. You can count on me. And I hope you find the person responsible. Even though I wish you were with me instead of her, I don't want her to get hurt," she told him, and meant it.

***

That night, Johnny tossed and turned in his bed. He was confident that no one would get onto his property because a high fence with security cameras surrounded the community he lived in, but Lumiana's house was vulnerable. The fence that ran around the vast Jonata land parcel was more symbolic than functional, and the only security they had was two guards at the entrance gate.

He'd talked to Mag earlier to make sure they upped his security but decided against telling his family for now. If it really was one of them, he needed to go in with a clear head and a plan.

***

At the same time, Lumiana was lying in her bed, more angry than scared that someone was threatening to expose her. She hoped the culprit would try to get onto her property, so she could see them punished.

As a precaution, she had sent Ana off to stay with her parents at Casa de Esperanza, and Shawn, who was Special Ops, insisted on keeping her company for the night. If anyone knew how to fight, it was her brother.

There was no way Shawn was involved. He may not like Johnny, but he'd never do anything to hurt her. Besides, Shawn would tell her to her face that she should cut ties with Johnny instead of playing games. Especially when those games affected the whole family.

Her sister Ayana got a 24-hour guard too at the off chance that this was related to Abeto Alazar, the man who wanted her dead. Uncle Sam had posted guards along the fence that ran around Jonata, but the area was so large they'd need a small army to secure it entirely.

***

Early the next morning, Claudia came to Andie's for breakfast. They sat at the kitchen island, sipping coffee, while Andie told Claudia about Johnny's visits the day before.

"Get this, CJ, he accused me of blackmailing his girlfriend." Andie watched Claudia cough up part of her croissant. "Quite the coincidence, don't you think?"

Claudia spilled her coffee.

"Oh, come on, please tell me you didn't have anything to do with this." Andie grabbed a pack of cigarettes from the counter, lighting one.

"I did it for you," Claudia stammered. "You were going to lose him. When I saw his interview with Helen, I didn't say anything because I didn't want to hurt your feelings. But Johnny loves that homewrecker. Did you listen to his new album? Because I don't think he'll leave her, not voluntarily. All I did was write her a note telling her to stay away from Johnny. He belongs with you,

AB."

"Are you insane?" Andie yelled, throwing her hands in the air. "They got you on camera! You could get arrested. What were you thinking?"

"I just wanted to help." Claudia wrung her hands. "Also—on the way back I... I hit something... or someone..."

"Dammit, CJ. I told you to be careful." Andie paced the kitchen wishing she could smash something. "God, if Johnny finds out, he's never going to speak to me again." Then she went dead quiet. "What do you mean you hit something or someone?"

"I... When I left the envelope, the guard... he looked at me like he knew something was up, so I hurried back to the car. My heart was racing. I wanted to call you. I took my eyes off the road, just for a second to grab my phone. There was a loud thump. It startled me so much, the car spun. I was scared out of my mind... I... I didn't know what to do. So I drove off..." Claudia tucked her arms around herself.

"He was right," Andie said, once she got over the initial shock. "Johnny said it's probably someone he knows. Goddammit, CJ. Who knows how long it'll be before he gets his hands on the picture from that security camera? We have to think of something, fast." If it wasn't too late already. Maybe the police would come knocking on her door any minute.

Claudia stared back at her mutely.

Andie was in no mood to be sympathetic. "If you can't get it together, give me the damn address. I'm going to drive over there and apologize to the woman—maybe she'll understand."

Claudia grabbed her by the arm. "Are you sure? There's a gate and security. I don't want you to get in trouble for something I did."

"It's too late for half measures." Andie got her keys. "It's either that or it ends badly for both of us. I know you were trying to help, but dammit, CJ, your ideas have gotten us in trouble ever since we were little girls. I hope you'll learn from this."

"At least let me come with you. I used a disguise when I went there. Blond wig, prosthetic nose, accent, the whole shebang. Even rented a van with fake plates. And I wore gloves to make sure I didn't leave any fingerprints."

Andie could see a gleam of pride in Claudia's eyes. "At least you learned something from those damn TV shows."

***

Andie and Claudia arrived at the Jonata community gate two hours later. The winding road had made her nauseated as though she were actually pregnant. This place couldn't be more hidden. Trees, shrubs, and rocks flanked the narrow road. And the tan brick building next to the red steel gate blended in with the landscape.

They smiled at the young security guard who gaped at them and waved to the other man approaching the car.

"Oh my God, Mike, look, it's Andie Woodhull! She's Johnny's ex."

At least now they knew they were in the right place.

Mike gave the young man a warning glare. To her, he said, "How can we help you, Ms. Woodhull?" His gruff tone turned Andie's hands wet with sweat.

"As your colleague pointed out, Johnny was my boyfriend." Andie rolled back her shoulders. "I know this must look strange, but I'm here to talk to his girlfriend. I have something important to tell her."

"I don't know what you're talking about," Mike said, his expression unreadable.

"I know she isn't expecting me, but it's about the letter she received yesterday. I think I might know who sent it. Can you call her and let her know I'm here?" Andie smiled politely, but it did nothing to soften Mike's stern face.

"Please step out of the car and come with me."

"Are you arresting me?" Andie joked, tightening her grip on the steering wheel.

"This is a serious matter, Ms. Woodhull. A resident received a credible threat, and you just became my number one suspect. You have motive."

"I assure you it wasn't me." Andie slid her palms up and down the steering wheel. "Johnny and I left things on good terms. I'm here to help."

"Please take a seat in my office while I make a few calls. I'll be right back." Before he left, Mike asked to see their IDs. Andie prayed to God that Johnny wasn't one of the people he was going to call.

The other security guard led them into the small brick building and asked them to have a seat in a dark, cold office that looked suspiciously like an interrogation room. There were three plastic chairs around a sharp-edged metal table and a black desk in the back of the room that held nothing but a few pens and papers. The walls were bare. They sat in the two uncomfortable chairs facing the door and looked out the only window, which gave them a view of the road.

***

While Mike was pacing in front of the gatehouse, trying to get a hold of Lumiana, he saw another car pull up to the gate. Emma Arendt's by the look of it. Ana climbed out of the SUV and waved goodbye to her grandmother as she drove off.

"I need you to stay close until I reach your mom," Mike said to the little girl when she joined him.

"Is something wrong, Mike?"

"It's nothing to worry about, sweetie. This won't take long." He tried again to reach Lumiana on his cell phone.

Ana peeked through the office window, pressing her nose against the glass. "Mike, oh my gosh, look, it's Andie Woodhull! Does Peyton know she's here? Can we get her autograph?"

Peyton, Mike's daughter and Ana's best friend, was at soccer practice, otherwise he could've won the Father of the Year Award. His daughter was Andie Woodhull's biggest fan. He'd recognized that woman instantly because Peyton had a large poster of her in her bedroom.

"Get back here! She can't know who you are. Please keep quiet for a moment," Mike said, wiping his forehead.

The girl stepped away from the window.

"Lumiana, finally," Mike said into the phone.

"Is everything okay with Ana?"

"She's fine. She's here with me. Listen, there's someone else here who wants to talk to you. I didn't tell her anything, but it's one Andie Woodhull, um, Johnny's ex. She said she might know who sent you the letter. I can have her questioned. My gut says she's involved." After prolonged silence, Mike said, "Are you there?"

"Yes, sorry. Let me think for a second... Is Johnny with her?"

"No, she's with a friend, Claudia Jean McAllister. What do you want to do?"

"Please, Mike, no one can tell her who I am," Lumiana reminded him.

"Of course not. But I need to know how you want to proceed, otherwise I'm calling it in."

After a pause, she said, "I'm coming over."

***

Andie knew the instant she saw her that the young woman standing in the door was the mystery girl Johnny was seeing. Her hands and legs were covered in scars of various sizes. And her eyes were striking, with one eye noticeably darker than the other. There was something about her that gave Andie goosebumps on her arms and butterflies in her stomach.

"I like your dress, and I love the necklace, it's gorgeous." Andie pointed at the white pencil dress and the golden heart-shaped locket, which looked like folded angel wings.

Johnny's girlfriend didn't speak, but covered the locket with her hand.

Andie raked a hand through her hair. "Sorry, I'm a little nervous."

"Why are you here?" the young woman said, her voice firm and clipped.

"Can you sit down, please? I'm just here to have a friendly chat, woman to woman."

"Why are you here?" she repeated and remained standing.

"You're not going to make this easy on us, huh?" Andie smiled warmly, but her opponent kept a stony face. 'Socially challenged' was a mild way to put it. "I came here because it was brought to my attention that someone is trying to blackmail you, and I know who it is."

'Blackmail' was such a strong word for what

Claudia had done, Andie thought. Then she recalled what CJ had said about 'hitting something' and prayed to God there wasn't an actual tragedy involved in all this.

"Is it you?" the woman asked. There was something intense about her, like her energy could blast you to smithereens.

"No, it's not." Andie shifted in her seat, and so did Claudia.

"How did you get here then?"

Shit. She couldn't have known where Johnny's girlfriend lived unless she was the one who was stalking him. "This is why I'm here," Andie sputtered. "I... I confronted the person who did it, and she gave me your address."

"Why would I believe you?"

"You have to trust me," Andie pleaded. "I'm here because I want to apologize on behalf of that person, and appeal to you, so you won't press charges. It's someone I really care about."

"Blackmailing is a criminal offense. Do you know how much it cost my family to increase security? Or what it's like to lie in bed at night, unable to sleep because someone threatens to hurt you and your family? You are seriously asking me to forget all about it just because you asked nicely?"

"I'm so sorry. I'll pay for it. But I'm begging you, please let this go."

"No!" The woman slapped her fists on the table. They all flinched at the bang.

"Then you leave us no choice." Taking out her phone, Andie snapped a picture of the woman.

"What did you do that for?"

Claudia also shot her a questioning look, but caught on quickly. "Insurance," Claudia said, giving Andie a reassuring nod.

"You leave us no choice," Andie added, her hands shaking. "I have to protect my friend. She made a stupid mistake, but she's a good person. And I can't let you tell Johnny about this either. It would destroy everything for me."

"So your solution is to blackmail me yourself?" the woman asked.

"What would you do to protect the people you love?"

Blinking rapidly, the woman opened and closed her mouth. As beautiful as she was, Johnny's girlfriend looked nothing like what Andie had imagined. She also wasn't from the U.S. Andie could tell because of her slight but distinct accent.

"I don't like that I have to do this to you," Andie said, clasping her hands together in her lap. "But I can't let you take my friend and the man I love from me." Her voice cracked. "I have your picture and your address and I'll give it to one of those bloodthirsty paparazzi unless we come to an agreement. And don't bother calling security. I've already sent your picture to my friend. She's going to use it unless you sit down and work this out with me."

"What do you want?" The young woman's chin trembled—maybe she wasn't as tough as she appeared.

"You'll give me an agreement in writing that you won't press charges, because this whole thing was a misunderstanding. And you can't tell Johnny or anyone else about this." Andie's pulse thrummed in her ears as she listed her demands.

"We also want you to stop seeing him," Claudia said, squeezing Andie's hand under the table. "He belongs with Andie. They're having a baby. And..." Claudia leaned forward in her chair. "I want you to give her your necklace."

The woman pressed her fingers against her breastbone before she clasped the locket.

"Claudia." Andie shook her head. "That won't be necessary."

"No, Andie. It is necessary," Claudia insisted. "That way she'll learn what it's like when someone takes away something of value to her, just like she has done to you."

Andie tried to take a calming breath and peered at the woman, who looked wild with shock. "Um, in turn, we won't tell anyone anything about you or ever bother you again in any way. I swear to God. I promise you'll get your locket back when we're sure you're holding up your end of the deal."

***

Her pulse hammering in her ears, Lumiana

stalked over to the corner desk. She got a pen and wrote the statement Andie requested on a blank piece of paper, signing it as illegibly as possible, so they couldn't read her name in case they hadn't found it out already. The letter only said 'I know who are' and not what exactly they knew about her, aside from where she lived. Then she returned to the table and pushed the paper toward Andie.

"You're not going to fight this?" Andie asked as she glanced at the written statement. "You're fine with giving up Johnny?"

"You asked me what I would do to protect the people I love. The answer is: whatever it takes. I don't want to be with him anymore." Her eyes watered, and she turned away, so she could wipe them without those awful women seeing it. "I want my old life back." She couldn't be with someone who put her family at risk, as unintentional as it had been. Her happiness wasn't more important than her siblings' safety.

Lumiana opened the door and signaled Mike to join them.

"Mike, Ms. Woodhull explained everything to me. It was a misunderstanding and I don't wish to pursue this matter any further. Please tell Uncle Sam to shut down the investigation. I will cover the costs incurred."

"Are you sure?" The way Mike looked at her, she knew he didn't believe her.

"I am. One last thing, Mike. Johnny and I are

over, he just doesn't know it yet and neither does…" She didn't want to say her daughter's name, and she didn't have to. Mike gave a slight nod. "Please don't let him past the gate without calling me first." She tried her best to keep the emotion out of her voice.

"I'm sorry to hear that. I really liked the guy. Thought the two of you were meant to last." Mike fixed Andie and Claudia with a hostile stare.

"No, Mike. It's time things get back to normal." Lumiana bit back tears. "Can you send…" she gestured toward the door to indicate Ana, "Can you send her home? I need a moment."

"I'll let everyone know. Call me if you need anything."

Lumiana forced a smile before Mike left the room, closing the door behind him.

The women stood.

"The necklace," Claudia demanded. When Lumiana hesitated, and Andie tugged at Claudia's arm, Claudia barked, "Did you hear what I said? Your address is all those bloodsuckers need to make your life a living hell."

Lumiana inhaled deeply, and then carefully removed her locket. She pressed it against her heart for a moment. *Whatever it takes*. Her chest hitched when Claudia held out her hand.

"Leave," she almost shouted when Andie and Claudia didn't move.

Andie touched a shaky hand to her stomach. "I… I'm sorry, I feel—"

"Don't." Lumiana cut her off, fighting the urge to rip their hearts out and stomp on them with her bare feet. "I gave you everything you asked for, now leave!"

***

Claudia took her trembling friend by the hand and led her to the car. Because Andie just stood there, staring into the distance, Claudia decided to drive.

As soon as they were on the road, Andie let out a sob and covered her face with her hands.

Reaching over, Claudia patted her arm. "I'm sorry, AB. It was the only way. She wouldn't let this go." Claudia hoped her own stomach would settle soon. She did feel remorseful, but she couldn't deny the whole thing had given her a thrill—not to mention that it was great practice for her audition next week.

"I can't believe you took her necklace. Was it necessary to humiliate her like that?"

"I may have gotten a little carried away."

"You think?" Andie pushed her hair back with both hands.

"Okay, it was mean. But it's just a necklace." She reached into the pocket of her jeans to retrieve the long thin gold chain and handed it to Andie. "We can return it when this is over."

"I swear, if I didn't know you so well, I'd think you're evil." Andie slumped in her seat. "You're going to make a great actress one day."

"Thank you." Smiling, Claudia turned up the music. Nothing like "No Diggity" to help you get your groove back.

17

LAST REQUEST

*"Love does not claim possession,
but gives freedom."*

—RABINDRANATH TAGORE

When Lumiana got back to the house, her daughter was standing in the hallway, her arms crossed below her chest.

"Where is your locket, *mamá*?"

Reflexively, Lumiana touched the spot where the folded angel wings used to sit. The locket had been an extension of her, one of the few things she had left of her parents. And now that was gone too. The price she had to pay for letting Johnny into their lives.

Her heart thumped wildly in her chest as rage

coursed through her veins like lava. She hurried past Ana into the living room and grabbed the nearest pillow.

Pressing her face into it, she let out a muffled scream. She wanted to run after those women, scratch their eyes out, hurt them like they'd hurt her. It had taken every ounce of self-control to resist the violent urge.

Ana, who'd followed her into the room, began to cry.

Lumiana swallowed her own tears. "I apologize, *angelito*. I didn't mean to frighten you." She reached for her daughter and hefted her into her arms.

"This will all be over soon," she promised, picking up her phone to send Johnny a text to say she needed to see him.

He replied moments later, assuring her he'd come over as soon as he could.

***

An hour and a half later, Johnny arrived at Jonata's entrance gate. Lumiana's message had surprised him, and not in a good way, because she never summoned him like this. So when he saw Mike's lips pressed together in a grimace, he knew something was wrong.

"Can you wait here?" the guard said, scratching his neck. "I have to call her."

"I've got a bad feeling about this." A very bad feeling, like he was hiking through the woods and was about to step into one of those traps that would catapult him into the air, leaving him dangling from a tree.

"I'm sorry, man." Mike couldn't even look him in the eyes.

Lumiana got to the gatehouse a few minutes later. She must've been nearby to get there so quickly.

She climbed into his Porsche and without looking at him, told him to head down the road away from the gate.

When they'd driven half a mile or so, Lumiana told him to pull over. They both got out and stood by the front of his car, an arm's length apart, surrounded by shrubs and trees.

"Please don't—" he said as heat rose behind his eyelids.

She tugged her arms around herself. "You don't know what I'm going to say."

"Don't insult my intelligence, Lumiana. I know you're breaking up with me. You look like you've been crying all day, you didn't let me come to your house, and you didn't give me a kiss either. You can't even look at me."

Tears choked her voice. "I'm so sorry, Johnny."

"Yeah, me too." He pressed his fingers to his eyes.

"I can't do this anymore. It's just too much—"

"Lu, please." He reached for her, needing to bridge the distance between them.

She hugged him. "Thank you for taking a

chance on me."

"Please, you didn't take much time to think this through. Is this because of the threat?" It fucking kept him up at night too. That he'd made it to Jonata without driving his car into a ditch was remarkable. He couldn't say what was worse, to think someone they knew wanted to hurt them or that he had a stalker.

Holding on to Lumiana, Johnny blew out a long breath. It wasn't supposed to go like this— not this time, not with her. But no matter how much he wanted to stick this out with her, he understood she had to protect her family. They would always come first for her.

"There is no threat," Lumiana mumbled against his neck, her hand clenching in his shirt.

He wasn't sure he'd heard her right. "What are you talking about?"

If he thought she'd clear that up for him, he was wrong.

Leaning back, she placed her warm hands on either side of his face. Her hands were always warm, always soft. "I need you to hear me," she said. "I took all the time I need. I hate feeling like this. You belong with Andie. You are going to be a dad. I cannot be the reason a child doesn't get the family it deserves. You need to make it work with her."

It wasn't what he wanted. And he needed her to see that.

Nudging her against the car, Johnny kissed

her roughly. The longing for her took him over like a fever. Gripping her hips, he lifted her onto the hood, and when he pushed into her, her breath released on a moan.

They held on tight as pleasure and pain ripped them apart.

***

Afraid she might break down on the way home, Lumiana kept taking shallow breaths. When she walked past Mike, he mumbled how sorry he was, but she barely noticed him. Nor did she feel the long walk back to her house. She opened the front door as quietly as she could and hurried upstairs before Ana could intercept her. With a heavy breath that ended on a sob, she fell onto her bed and into a long, deep sleep.

***

When Johnny arrived home, he went straight for the liquor cabinet and drowned his pain in scotch. Once his brain was sufficiently numb, he sent his mother a text, which prompted her to call him.

"What's going on, Johnny? I didn't understand your message."

"Lu broke up with me," he slurred into the phone.

"Oh, honey. I'm sorry."

He gave a half-laugh. "No, you're not. You don't like her."

"You're drunk. I'm coming over," she said and hung up.

***

Eleanor arrived at her son's home forty minutes later and found him lying on the floor with his guitar, belting out a heart-wrenching rendition of "Hey Jude."

Johnny was right, she didn't like his girlfriend, but she didn't like seeing her son like this either. And as much as she hated to admit it, Lumiana had been a good influence on Johnny, encouraging him to bring his family closer.

Eleanor sat next to her son and stroked his arm.

"Andie is pregnant with my baby," he blurted out.

"Andie?" she uttered. "You cheated on Lumiana? Oh, Johnny—"

"No, ma, I didn't cheat on her. Contrary to what everyone believes, I'm a one-woman-at-a-time kind of guy. It happened before we got together. Andie just kept it from me." His face looked distorted. Alcohol probably wasn't the only drug he was on. "Lu said she can't be the reason a child doesn't get the family it deserves."

"I'm sorry, honey. But considering what she's been through and how important family is to her, I can understand her point of view."

"I know, but it hurts. I love her and Ana so much. I want to be with them." He drooped on

344

the floor like a pile of wet rags.

"I'm sure they feel the same about you." Eleanor took his hand. "Do you remember what you told me the other day, that one of the things you like about Lumiana is that she's committed to doing the right thing? Sometimes the right thing feels like the wrong thing, and you still have to do it."

She spoke from experience. Divorcing her husband went against everything she believed in, but they had to stop making each other miserable. "I can't believe you're going to be a dad…" She hoped he'd have a girl. She loved her sons and grandsons, even her ex-husband, but it would be nice to have someone she could relate to with a little more ease.

"Something else happened too, and I think it's why she broke up with me. She said that she was trying to find a way to be okay with me having a baby with Andie, that she just needed some time. But then she didn't take the time and broke up with me instead."

"What are you talking about?"

He rolled over on his side. "Someone threatened to expose her if she didn't break up with me. And I'm sure it was someone I know, I just don't know who—" It came out with a yawn. "It wasn't you, ma, right?"

"No, of course it wasn't me, Johnny. I know I wasn't supportive of your relationship, but I'd never do anything that would endanger a child."

"Andie said the same thing when I asked her if it was her, minus the endangering a child part. She doesn't know Lu has a kid. I was convinced it was one of you, but now I don't know what to think." Johnny grabbed the bottle and polished off the rest of the scotch.

Eleanor got up, straightened her pantsuit. "I hope this binge drinking is a one-time thing. I don't want you to become a cliché."

"Ma, I'm not an addict."

"Isn't that what they all say?" she countered. "Please be careful, Johnny. I'd hate it if you made that kind of news in addition to all the stuff that is already being said about you. I know you want to live your life on your own terms, but these things reflect poorly on our family—please keep that in mind as well."

"I know what I'm doing. I'm not driving, I'm not going out, and this was the exception."

"Imagine what Lumiana would think if she saw you. Let her be your voice of reason."

"She'd probably ask me if I would care for a cup of tea," he said, trying to imitate Lumiana's accent. "I wonder if she has one that goes with post-breakup depression."

***

When Lumiana woke up after her binge sleeping, Ana was sitting next to her reading *Diary of a Wimpy Kid*. She cuddled up to her daughter. Nothing mattered more than her family, and she would always do what was needed to protect them. Even if it meant losing Johnny.

Her chest constricted when she remembered that she could no longer speak to him or touch him. He wouldn't be there when she needed him. Just like Jayjay. The realization stole her breath.

Ana gave her a kiss. "Are you okay, *mamá*? You didn't say goodnight and you slept for a very long time."

Lumiana brushed the hair from Ana's face. "I apologize, *angelito*. I am not okay, but I promise I will be."

"Johnny is not coming back, is he?"

Lumiana shook her head.

"*Mamá…*" Ana sniffed. "That makes me so sad."

Lumiana touched her lips to her daughter's head and held her close.

Ana clenched her hand on the sleeve of Lumiana's dress. "I will miss him so much."

"I'm so sorry, Ana, I really am. I wish I could do something to make this better for you." She swallowed against the dull ache in her throat. "I wish none of this ever happened."

"I don't believe you!" Ana scooted away from her. "You were happy with Johnny. I saw it with my eyes."

"That doesn't mean we were meant to be. It didn't work out for us—that's how life is sometimes." Lumiana reached for Ana's hands but her daughter crossed her arms.

"Life sucks."

"I know life is not fair sometimes. But we'll get through this. Losing Johnny is not the worst thing that ever happened to me. I will be okay in no time, I promise."

Ana slapped her hands onto the mattress. "But it's the worst thing that ever happened to me. I want Johnny to be my dad. It's not fair. I hate that he is gone." Ana turned around and cried into the pillow, her little body shaking with sobs.

Lumiana gasped at the pain she felt. "You need to forget about Johnny. He is not your dad. Jayjay is your father." It broke her heart that Ana had been so young when he died she hardly remembered him. "You were not supposed to have this kind of relationship with Johnny," she said, but her words intensified Ana's crying. "It's all my fault. Your father would be so disappointed in me."

When they went downstairs a while later, Lumiana tried to cheer her daughter up with her favorite lunch, but Ana refused to eat and stomped back to her room, slamming the door behind her.

"Take your time," Lumiana said through the closed door. "But not eating is unacceptable."

All day Ana sulked and left her room only to get food. She ignored Lumiana completely—something she had never done before.

***

Monday was Ruby's day off. At breakfast with Janice, they sketched out their agenda for the next few days. Then she spent the rest of the morning updating the blog with photos of Johnny at various promotional events. Both his single and the new album had hit the top of the charts the week before, giving her a lot to write about.

Sunday night she and Janice had gone to his concert in L.A., and she needed to select the best photos from that as well.

Ruby couldn't believe they still hadn't been able to get a picture of Johnny and Lumiana together. Maybe today would be her lucky day.

In the afternoon, Ruby drove up to Jonata, parking her Honda out of sight of the gate. She'd seen the guards, and the last thing she needed was getting caught loitering. Fortunately, the area was forested and the dead-end road curved and sloped, making it easy to stay hidden.

Ruby had been tailing Johnny since the weekend she found out that Lumiana was his new girlfriend, and she'd even managed to follow him home. But Lumiana was the one who'd led her to Jonata and the institute where Lumiana worked.

Figuring out the woman's routine had been child's play because Lumiana was visiting Jerold Graham several times a week. On Mondays, she usually got home around three, so Ruby knew there was a good chance the professor would show up here soon.

With a bit of luck, Lumiana might go out again to meet Johnny. There was a lot of buzz about who his secret girlfriend might be and getting a candid shot of the two of them was guaranteed to bring in some money. And she could use it. She still needed to pay off her nursing school loans.

An hour and a half passed and there was still no sight of Lumiana. Ruby was getting ready to drive away when a silver van with tinted windows and a schoolchildren sign drove past her toward the Jonata gate. The van passed her again a few minutes later. She peered up the road and saw a little girl heading her way.

Curious, Ruby got out of her car. She pretended to be searching for a cell phone signal when the girl walked up to her, seemingly surprised to see someone out here in the middle of nowhere.

"Hi," the girl said. "Are you lost?" She was tiny and adorable, maybe four or five years old, and of East Asian descent.

"Hi there," Ruby said with a warm smile. What was the closest town called again? "Yes, I was supposed to go to Las—something, but I must've taken a wrong turn and I can't get a phone signal out here."

"Las Espitas? I can show you the way," the little girl offered.

"Yes, Las Espitas. Thanks." She'd gotten bored

anyway, maybe Lumiana had after work plans. "Where are you going?"

"Calabasas."

"Calabasas? In Los Angeles County?" That was where Johnny lived, about an hour away. Did the little girl know him? "How are you getting there?"

"Um, I'm going to take a bus." The girl didn't sound convinced.

Ruby had no idea what bus service was like out here, but she doubted there were many of them—if any. "I tell you what. Since I missed my meeting, I might as well drive home. Calabasas is on my way if you want a ride."

"Really?" The girl smiled.

"Yeah, sure, my car's over there."

***

That evening, Lumiana came home late from a staff meeting at work, hoping to find Ana in a better mood. Instead, she couldn't find her at all. She searched in and around the house, shouting her daughter's name, but got no response. As panic began to spread through her gut, she called Mike to see if Ana had gone over there for a play date. But she wasn't there either.

Mike and his wife helped Lumiana do another search of the house and property, which proved fruitless. So Mike alerted Uncle Sam who sent out a team to scour the area and the school grounds.

By seven o'clock they'd confirmed that Ana

had been dropped off at the gate, but they failed to find any trace of her.

"Have you called Johnny?" Shawn asked Lumiana, his hands squeezing her shoulders, holding her upright. "Maybe she's with him."

Crying and hyperventilating, Lumiana clung to her brother as if he were a lifebuoy. "We broke up."

"Shit. Why didn't you tell me, Lumi?" When she didn't respond, he said, "Call him. Maybe he's heard from her. I'm sure he'd want to know."

**

Johnny was in the middle of a dinner with family and friends at his Calabasas home when his phone rang. One look at the caller ID, and his breath caught in his throat.

"Sorry, I have to get this," he said, excusing himself.

Once out of earshot, he answered. "Lu?"

All he heard was heavy breathing.

"Hey, what's going on?" He went upstairs to his bedroom and closed the door.

"Ana... She's missing," Lumiana cried into the phone.

"What? Are you sure?" He leaned against his bedroom wall, covering his mouth.

"We've been looking for her all evening. I was hoping she might be with you."

"She isn't here, Lu. I wish she were. Have you contacted the school?"

"She left school at the usual time. The shuttle dropped her off, but the guard at the gate didn't see her walk by. Now it's getting dark—"

"I'm sure she's okay." He staggered over to his bed and sat down. She had to be okay.

"You don't know that."

"But I have faith, and so should you. Does she know we broke up?" he asked, bracing himself.

"Yes."

"How did she take it? Do you think that might have something to do with it?"

"She was very upset. She…"

He could hear her rapid breathing and cursed. "Lu, please, you need to be strong now."

He heard her blow out a shaky breath. "She refused to eat. And she wouldn't talk or look at me. It was so unlike her. I cannot live with myself if anything happens to her."

"I never meant for any of this to happen." He wouldn't forgive himself if Ana got hurt.

"I know that. This is not your fault. It's mine. I shouldn't have brought you into her life in the first place."

He hung his head. "Please, don't say that."

"Do you know what the last thing she said to me was?" Lumiana blew her nose. "She wishes for you to be her dad. After such a short time, how can that be?"

He couldn't think of an acceptable response. Because the truth was, he wished for the same. He wanted the three of them to be a family.

"I have to hang up now," she said, her breath hitching. "Please call me if you hear from her or if you can think of where she might be."

"I will. You do the same. I still care about you and Ana. I need to know she's safe." When she didn't reply, he pressed further, "Promise me, Lumiana."

"I promise," she murmured and hung up.

When Johnny rejoined his guests a few minutes later, they looked at him like they were waiting for a sermon. He had no words. All he wanted was to send everyone home and drive up to Jonata to be with Lumiana, to help find Ana.

God, how much worse can this get? And why did he finally find his person but loving her was wreaking havoc on her life? He couldn't blame Lumiana that she thought bringing him into their lives had been a mistake.

"You've been gone... for a while, son," his father said. "Everything okay?"

His dad's recovery had been going so well they were allowed to take him out for dinner. It had been a fun evening—until this. He needed Ana to be safe.

"You don't look so good, bro," said Jason.

Without a word, Johnny sat at the table, finished his wine, and forced a smile. "Please, enjoy your meal. Everything is fine."

Conversation resumed, but he could only stare at the plate in front of him.

Come on, Ana, I need you to come home. Please

don't do this to your mom.

It was the worst feeling. A clawing fear that made him feel like he was going to throw up.

He'd only felt it once before. When he was at the park with Jack and the twins a couple of months ago, one of the boys had disappeared in the split-second they were distracted by his toddler brother throwing a tantrum. Thankfully they found the missing twin hiding under the slide in less than a minute.

But this was so much worse because Ana had gone missing hours ago. He had to do something. He couldn't just sit here having dinner while the little girl was somewhere out there.

Johnny didn't even notice when his guests stopped talking.

"Something is obviously wrong," his mother said, snapping his mind back to the present. "Can I talk to you outside?"

He didn't respond.

"His ex called," said Andie, who was sitting next to him.

"That's none of your business," he said, pressing his palms to his eyes for a second. He just wanted to wake up from this nightmare.

"Johnny!" his mother chided him.

He laid a hand over Andie's. "Sorry."

"Excuse me, Johnny," his household manager interrupted.

"Not now," his mother barked.

"Ma!" Johnny turned to face the man. "What is

it, James?"

"There is someone here to see you."

Johnny got up from the table and followed James down the hallway. Sitting in the armchair by the door was Ana.

"Oh, thank God." Johnny rushed over to her. He wrapped her in his arms, needing a minute to find his voice.

"Have you lost your mind?" he said finally. "Your mom is worried sick. Everyone's been looking for you."

Tears spurted from her eyes. "I miss you *so* much. My mom said I have to forget about you. But I can't."

Johnny hugged her closer. Her arms came around him as she cried against his neck. "I miss you too." *So fucking much.* He stroked her head. "How did you get here?"

Ana told him she was going to take the bus, but then she met a woman who offered to drive her. The woman had taken her out for frozen yogurt before she dropped her off.

"You hitchhiked?" Johnny croaked. "That's so dangerous, Ana. Never do that again, you hear me." He scrubbed a hand over his mouth. "God, I have to call your mom, she's going to be so relieved. And then she's going to kill me."

He got the phone from his pocket and dialed Lumiana. She picked up after one ring.

"Please tell me you found her."

"Hang on." Johnny put the phone to Ana's ear.

"Talk to your mom."

"*Mamá…*"

He could hear Lumiana's loud sob when she heard her daughter's voice.

"Please don't cry, *mamá*." Ana rubbed her eye with her fist. Johnny hugged her to his chest.

"Stay where you are," Lumiana ordered. "Do you hear me? Do not move," she said before she hung up.

Johnny gave Ana a kiss, then got up and led her into the living room. "Everyone, this is Sophie."

Ana tugged at his hand. "My name isn't Sophie," she whispered.

"Tonight it is. Don't say a word until your mom gets here. Can you do that for me?" He didn't know whom he could trust anymore. And he didn't want to give Lumiana another reason to be upset with him.

Ana clung to his leg like a marmoset.

"What's going on, Johnny?" his mother asked, putting down her fork.

"Sorry for the interruption to this otherwise lovely evening. Unfortunately, I need you all to do me a favor. It's imperative for the safety of this little girl that whatever happens here tonight stays between us." The last thing he wanted was to make this situation any worse for Lumiana.

***

At the same time, Lumiana rummaged through

her nightstand drawer until she found the letter Johnny had left after their first weekend together, because his address was on it. Then she ran downstairs, told all the family members who'd gathered that Ana had shown up at Johnny's, and rushed out to her SUV.

As she drove toward Johnny's house, a sickening mix of emotions—anxiety, relief, anger, exhaustion—forced her to pull over, so she could throw up in the bushes.

She hadn't expected to see Johnny again, much less see where he lived. But all she wanted was to have her daughter safely back. If that meant seeing him again, so be it.

Lumiana scrubbed her hands over her face before she knocked on Johnny's door. When an old white man who looked like he'd stepped out of a film noir answered and asked her to wait at the door, she was taken aback, but recovered quickly. There was no way she'd wait a minute longer.

Shaking her head, she pushed by him.

"Miss, you can't just storm in here!" the man called. But by then Lumiana was standing in the entrance of Johnny's living room, paralyzed by all the people looking at her. The first person she noticed was Andie. They stared at each other in mortification.

Her daughter was on Johnny's lap. Ana jumped down and rushed over to her.

Lumiana held her tight, both of them struggling with their tears.

"I was worried sick about you." Her words were muffled against Ana's hair.

"I'm so sorry, *mamá*."

***

Like his guests, Johnny watched Lumiana and Ana cling to each other. He let out a huge breath. But after a closer look at Lumiana he had a hard time sitting still. She looked like an addict going through withdrawal. Her eyes were red and swollen, and she was shivering uncontrollably. Her hair was a tangled mess, surely from raking her hands through it repeatedly. She wore a pair of beat-up boots and the large UCLA sweatshirt over her white dress.

Seeing her like this, all he wanted was to scoop her up and wrap her in blankets.

Cautiously, he approached them.

"You could have told me you had company," Lumiana hissed, yanking at her hair.

"You didn't give me a chance," he said, his voice equally low. "But you have nothing to worry about. They're all sworn to secrecy."

She glared at him, then faced her daughter. "Why did you come here? How did you even get here?"

"I missed Johnny. He said he'd be there for me whenever I need him, and that I could come see him anytime—"

He coughed, "But I didn't mean without telling your mom and all by yourself!"

Lumiana shot him a murderous look, and then put her hands on Ana's shoulders. "Your father would be heartbroken if he knew you're trying to replace him. It is bad enough that I couldn't resist—"

"No, *mamá*." Ana cupped Lumiana's face. "You need to let him go. Shawn said *papá* would want you to be happy and move on with your life. And he would want the same for me," she said with calm determination. "I'm sorry I ran away, but it hurt me that you broke up and I didn't get to say goodbye to Johnny. It's not fair. I don't understand. We were happy, and now I'm not even allowed to see him."

No one dared to make a sound.

Lumiana scrubbed her face like she wanted to peel off her skin. "I'm glad everyone here gets to witness what a clear failure I am as a mother—"

"*Lumiana*," Johnny's dad interrupted her. "Can I talk to you?" He got up, using a cane, and ushered her out of the room.

***

Andie felt her face turn red the second Jerry spoke the name Lumiana. Hearing Johnny's girlfriend's name made her somehow more real. She wished she could undo what she had done to that woman. Her actions weighed so heavily on her conscience she'd been to church nearly every day to pray for forgiveness. If it weren't for protecting her best friend, she'd confess it all.

"She's not a bad mother," the little girl said, loud enough for everyone to hear.

"I know, kiddo," Johnny said, stroking his hand over the girl's shiny black hair. "Your mom is just very tired. She didn't mean what she said." He wiped away her tears. "I'm so sorry I didn't say goodbye to you. I wish things had gone differently."

Andie's hands trembled as she saw the love between Johnny and the girl. He would've been a great dad.

She needed to tell him there was no baby.

18

SOMEWHERE ONLY WE KNOW

*"The only way to make sense out of
change is to plunge into it,
move with it, and join the dance."*

—ALAN WATTS

Lumiana followed Jerry upstairs to Johnny's bed-room. It was strange being in Johnny's home. The modern rustic interior with Japanese influences suited him, but it wasn't the place where they were together. This felt all wrong. She shouldn't be here.

Lumiana hesitated before she walked into the bedroom as though the doorway led into a par-allel universe... and maybe it did. She couldn't believe her eyes. It looked so much like her own bedroom with the shoji screens and the beige and green accents over contemporary bamboo furniture. Had they unknowingly hired the same interior designer?

Jerry took a seat on the sofa, gesturing for her to do the same.

She sat next to him, hugging one of the embroidered throw pillows to her chest.

Jerry put a hand over hers. "Angel. You're not a bad mother... This wasn't about you. Johnny disappeared from Ana's life... without saying goodbye." Jerry still had trouble speaking, but after spending so much time with him she hardly noticed. "Ana is mature for her age, but she's still a child... She doesn't understand."

Lumiana made an effort to smile when Jerry tried to convince her to give her relationship with Johnny another chance. But she couldn't. It wasn't about what she wanted.

Jerry patted her hand. "He told me you think you're destroying a family... But you, more than anyone, should know that modern families come in all shapes and colors. Just look at your own family... and how well you all turned out."

She squeezed his hand. "I appreciate what you're attempting to do, but the situation is far more complicated than you know. I have to do what I believe is best for my family."

He sighed but nodded. "And you can't blame me for trying to do... what I think is best for mine. And that is having you and Ana be part of it. I hope you're going to change your mind... Johnny is better off for having known you. I hope you'll come to feel the same about him."

She did feel the same about him. As much as it hurt now, meeting Johnny had revived parts of her that she'd buried a long time ago. "I appreciate that, Jerry. Please know you and Eleanor have raised your son well. Johnny is a good man and I'm grateful for the time I got to spend with him."

"Really? Despite the mess I've left behind?"

Lumiana jerked at the sound of Johnny's voice, feeling a flush of heat when she saw him standing in the room, a gentle smile curving his lips.

"Sorry to interrupt," he said, rubbing the back of his neck. "I wanted to let you know I've sent everyone home. Also, Ana fell asleep on the couch downstairs. I covered her with a blanket, and she didn't even stir, so I think she's out for the night. Dad, James is going to drive you back to Mansfield Park, if that's okay with you."

Jerry got up. "No worries, son. You two should talk... Find a way to leave things on good terms... for Ana's sake." He gave them each a hug, and then closed the door behind him on his way out.

Lumiana sat on the bed, crossing her arms. Then she realized it was *his* bed and jumped to her feet.

Grinning, he took a step toward her. "It's weird seeing you in my bedroom."

"What is weird is that your bedroom looks

a lot like my bedroom." She squirmed when Johnny took her hands.

His lips twitched. "I guess that's why I've slept so well at your house. It instantly felt like home. Well, that, and because I got to sleep next to you."

She let go of his hands, and sat on the sofa, staring at the floor. She couldn't do this with him. Seeing him, hearing his voice, it was too much.

He joined her. "Can you look at me, please?" When she didn't, he touched her bare knee, giving her goosebumps. "I know it's been a hard day for you. I just want to have a conversation and that's easier when you're not talking to your feet."

She inched farther away from him because all she wanted was to climb into his lap and cry on his shoulder. This day had been a nightmare—she'd felt scared, humiliated, and lectured—and she knew he'd comfort her if she let him. But she clung to what little was left of her pride. "What do you want, Johnny?"

"What I want is for us to be together—"

She pulled at her hair. "I can't be with you. And that's not what I meant. I mean, what do you want to do that makes things easier on Ana?"

He exhaled sharply. "I want to have a proper goodbye. And I want you to tell her she can keep in touch with me if she wants. Of course, she has to tell you about it so something like today won't happen again."

"You can have a proper goodbye. But how are we supposed to move on if you stay in our lives?"

"Why does moving on require that I'm completely out of your lives?"

Her throat closed up and she lowered her head. "Because seeing you hurts so much. All I can think of is that I want to be close to you. How can I move on like that?" He tried to take her hand. "Please don't touch me. I'm barely keeping it together as it is."

He slapped his hand on his thigh and then got up to pace. "Why are you fighting this so much? If you want to be close to me, you can. You know I love you. Why are you pushing me away?" He sat on the bed, pressing his hands to his temples. "I feel like there's something you're not telling me, because this whole thing makes no fucking sense."

She stared at him open-mouthed. Her voice broke when she said, "You love me."

"I love you." The way he looked at her, so impossibly sad, she wanted to curl up in his arms and cry.

She was so close to telling him about Andie and her devious friend. But instead she summoned the last ounce of strength she had and said, "I told you, I have to do what is best for my family, and I'm not willing to be the reason a child grows up without one."

"Fine, don't tell me!" He cursed at the ceiling, one hand on his hip, the other sliding across his jaw. "I know it's not the real reason you broke up with me. You're a terrible liar, Lumiana."

"Please, Johnny, let it be." She blinked away the tears.

He answered with a small nod. "I hope one day you can be honest with me."

Lumiana pressed her fingers to her forehead. She was so tired, her eyelids felt like lead.

"You should stay the night." Johnny touched her shoulder. "You're too exhausted to drive."

Reaching for his hand, she let him haul her to her feet. She hoped for a hug, but instead he got her a toothbrush and one of his t-shirts. At least she'd have his scent to keep her company.

Lumiana shuffled over to the adjacent bathroom. "Why do you have a butler? Is your family American royalty?"

"James is my household manager. He isn't here all the time, and he doesn't live here either. It was my mother's idea. James used to work for my grandfather before he vanished into thin air. My family isn't American royalty, but I come from a long line of successful lawyers and businessmen. Imagine their disappointment when I became the first to break their tradition."

Lumiana smiled at him. "Shame on you for being merely a critically acclaimed, award-winning musician." She patted him on the cheek, then closed the bathroom door behind her.

When she came out a few minutes later, Johnny went in.

Lumiana dove onto his California king bed and curled up under the cool, soft sheets. She was half-asleep by the time Johnny was done.

"You know I'm going to sleep here too, right?"

She opened one eye and saw him leaning against the door jamb, watching her.

He came up to the bed. "Move over. You're on my side."

"Do you mind putting on a shirt?" And perhaps a ski mask? The more of him was covered, the better.

"I do mind, actually." He crossed his arms in front of his chest, which only accentuated his muscles. "It's my house, my rules. Be grateful I let you sleep in my bed."

She threw a pillow at him.

"I tell you what, I'm going to sleep the way I always sleep, which is shirtless, but because you had a rough day, I'll let you sleep on my side of the bed."

She pulled the blanket over her face.

Her whole body sprang to attention when she felt Johnny's warm skin on hers. "Fine, you can hug me, but don't kiss me and don't move your hands," she said as a matter of principle.

"Yeah, sorry, I can't promise you that."

He brushed his lips over hers, deepening the kiss when she didn't retreat. His touch, comforting and feather-light, sent ripples of pleasure down her spine. She was aching with need—for him, for inner calm, for a lifetime together that wasn't meant to be.

He stroked her tears away, his hand cupping her cheek. He loved her. That beautiful, exasperating man.

Between gentle kisses, they slid off the few clothes that separated them. As she curled her arms around his strong shoulders, he trailed his lips across her neck and collarbone. They fit together so well it wasn't fair.

In another life, maybe.

When his hand cupped her butt, she hooked her leg over his, that sweet ache building as she burrowed into him.

"Are you sure you want this?" he murmured, his thumb tracing her bottom lip.

Reaching between them, she eased him inside her.

She wasn't sure of anything but her need for him. And so she let him take her to a place where —at least for a little while—they could be one.

***

When Lumiana woke up the next morning, Johnny's arm was possessively wrapped around her. His soft breath against her neck made her smile. She tried to disentangle herself, but he tightened his grip.

"Good morning, Doc." His voice had a sexy rasp that resonated in her core. He chuckled when she glanced under the blanket. "I'm happy to confirm it wasn't a dream, in case that's what you're checking." He cupped her breast with one hand while his other slid between her thighs, his fingers stroking her exquisitely.

"Stop it, Johnny."

"Are you sure? Last night you were singing a different tune."

She let him continue for another moment before she nudged him in the ribs with her elbow.

Releasing her, he stretched across the bed, giving her a magnificent view of his naked body. He grinned complacently when he caught her checking him out. "Go ahead."

She leaned in, but stopped just short of touching him. Before she had time to think or retreat, he pulled her onto him. She buried her face in his chest and sighed when he caressed her back. "Johnny, we shouldn't be doing this."

"Why not?" Fondling her behind, he pressed her against the hard length of him. "It feels so good, and we're both consenting adults."

"That's not it." She slid against him, relishing the friction. "I'm worried Ana is going to walk in on us."

"Good thinking." He pushed her off him, causing her to fall onto her back.

"You couldn't have done that more gently?" She shoved him lightly.

He pulled her close, giving her a kiss that left her breathless. "Please get out of my bed," he growled. "I'm trying not to go down on you, so unless it's what you want—"

She cut him off with a firm kiss on the mouth, then quickly slipped into her UCLA sweatshirt and padded into the bathroom. The last thing she wanted was to give Ana the impression they were reconciling.

***

Johnny stayed on the bed a while longer, sighing at the ceiling. He didn't want Lumiana to leave but didn't know how to change her mind.

He wished he knew why she was really doing this, because the reason sure wasn't the bullshit story she was trying to feed him.

Seriously, what were the odds the threat just disappeared and she broke up with him anyway? He was almost sure Shawn was behind it. Lumiana would protect her brother, *her best friend*. And she would believe Shawn if he gave her a good reason.

Johnny shoved his hands in his hair, huffing in frustration.

Whatever the reason for their breakup, it must be pretty bad, because he could tell Lumiana loved him too, even if she didn't have the courage to say those words out loud. It was in the way she clung to him when they made love, and all throughout the night when she slept wrapped around him, in the way she traced the scar on his arm.

Fuck. This was killing him.

"Damn it, Johnny," he heard Lumiana say

from the bathroom.

He grabbed his pants, put them on, and went to check on her. "What is it?"

He grinned when he saw her sitting on the vanity, all hot and bothered.

"You got me fired up, you might as well finish what you started."

He snorted out a laugh. "You act all sensible and coy one moment and the next you're ordering me to do you on my bathroom counter. How am I supposed to keep up?"

"So?" she said as she took off her shirt, a sly smile gracing her beautiful face.

Johnny locked the door behind him and stripped, grateful for another intimate moment with the woman he adored.

***

Lumiana went downstairs half an hour later. Ana lay sprawled across the three-seater in Johnny's living room, solving his crossword puzzles. It was funny in a sad way that she herself felt so out of place whereas her daughter looked like she belonged here, as if she were home.

Guilt hit her. Again she was taking Johnny away from Ana, and worse, from her daughter's perspective she had no valid reason to do so.

Exhaling slowly, Lumiana hoped that one day, when Ana learned the truth, she'd understand why it had to be this way.

"*Mamá!*" Her daughter beamed, a sight that

never failed to fill Lumiana with love and pride. She looked so much like Jayjay, especially when she smiled.

Lumiana pressed a hand to her heart, and with wobbly legs, walked over to join Ana on the sofa. Reaching for her daughter's hands, she drew her into her arms.

Ana nuzzled Lumiana's cheek. "I'm so sorry, *mamá*. Are you still mad at me?"

"A bit, yes. But I love you anyway. Just, please never do this to me again, okay?" She felt like she'd aged ten years since yesterday.

Ana nodded. "Where is Johnny?"

"He is upstairs getting dressed." Ana opened her mouth, but Lumiana spoke first. "We are not getting back together, but we agreed the two of you deserve a proper goodbye."

"Okay," Ana said in a somber voice that cut into Lumiana's defenses.

Whatever it takes, Lumiana reminded herself and pushed back her shoulders. She liked to think that Johnny would soon be nothing more than a memory, but the pressure in her chest told her it would be awhile before she could let him go.

***

"How are you ladies doing this morning?" Johnny asked Lumiana and Ana when they joined him in the kitchen. He'd seen them huddled together on the sofa earlier and decided to keep his distance, so they had time to restore their rhythm.

"Much better." Lumiana smiled at him from across the kitchen island. Like her, he had an open-plan kitchen with state-of-the art appliances. "It's nice to have you cook for a change."

"Well, you've never been to my place before. And I thought you wouldn't like it if I messed with your stuff when I was at yours." He took the sizzling vegetables from the stove, heated another pan for the eggs. "I don't mind cooking, but I'm not as good at it as you are." He actually liked cooking. He just rarely got around to it because he spent half of the year on the road.

"Let us be the judge." Lumiana covered Ana's hand with hers. The little girl's face lit up.

To think he'd been the reason the two of them were in tears last night gnawed at his conscience. It was hard to fathom that Lumiana was no longer his woman, that he'd lost the chance to become Ana's dad. How the hell had he managed to screw this up?

Becoming aware of the downward spiral, he snapped the black elastic on his wrist. Beating himself up wasn't going to change anything. All he could do now was pray for a miracle, give Ana a proper goodbye, and feed them what he hoped was his best omelet yet.

Once the first omelet was done, Johnny cut it in half and handed each of them a plate.

"What do you think?" he asked Lumiana after

she savored the first bite.

Her eyes closed with pleasure. "It's delicious. So much for you not being as good a cook as me." She took another bite, looking genuinely happy. He'd give everything to keep her that way.

"How do you like it, kid?"

Ana gave him two thumbs up, making his heart sing.

Once they were done eating, Lumiana sent Ana to the bathroom to wash up. When Johnny turned around after closing the dishwasher, Lumiana caught him in a rousing kiss.

"I hate you," he said, hugging her closer. She smelled of his spa-scented body wash. "I don't want you to leave."

"It has to be this way, Johnny. I'm doing you a favor."

"That's bullshit and you know it." He kissed her roughly before he released her.

Lumiana held on to his shirt. "I won't forget you," she said, making his chest ache. "Your dad said you were better off for knowing me. I want you to know that I feel the same about you."

He huffed. "This isn't fair. It took me a lifetime to find you—how am I supposed to let you go?"

Lumiana folded her arms around his neck just as Ana joined them.

"See, you love each other," the little girl said, jutting her chin. "Why can't you be together?"

"It takes more than love to make a relationship work," Lumiana told her, stepping out of his embrace. "This is a complicated matter—"

"So complicated even I don't understand it," Johnny muttered, and winced when Lumiana poked him with her elbow. "Can you turn around for a moment?" he asked Ana.

"Do you want to kiss my mom?"

"Just do it, please," he insisted, and Ana did as she was told.

Johnny gave Lumiana a thorough kiss. It didn't taste of goodbye. "Now go, and if you ever change your mind, you know where to find me."

Lumiana hugged him, then left to wait for Ana in the car.

Once they were alone, Johnny boosted Ana onto the kitchen counter. The girl's eyes glimmered.

Johnny forced a smile even though his chest felt like it was on fire. "I'm sorry it didn't work out with your mom and me. I wanted us to be a family just as much as you." Tears rolled down the girl's face. He took her in his arms. "I need you to be strong and I need you to look out for your mom. No more running away."

"I don't want this to be goodbye," Ana sobbed, tightening her grip.

"Me either, Ana, but it has to be for now. Maybe after some time passes we'll see each other again, you never know." Johnny held her for a while, then carried her out the front door where he set her down and kissed her goodbye.

"I love you, Johnny."

"I love you too, kiddo."

Losing Lumiana was tough enough, but letting go of Ana felt like too much.

After he'd closed the door behind him, Johnny sank into the club chair in the entrance hall. Hunched over, he sighed long and low, hoping to relieve the painful lump in his throat.

***

For five days in a row Andie had woken up with a black cloud looming over her head. As much as she enjoyed martinis, she wasn't known for holding her liquor.

Life sucks.

She needed to figure out a way to tell Johnny there was no baby, but she hadn't even heard from him since that evening at his house a week ago.

Had Lumiana broken their agreement?

There was something intriguing about that woman. Maybe it was her unusual eyes, or the fervent energy she exuded that affected everything within a thirty-foot radius.

Or maybe it was the way Johnny had looked at her, as though she truly was his one in seven billion. Andie couldn't remember Johnny ever looking at her that way.

Her thoughts were interrupted when Claudia showed up.

"You're still in bed?" she asked, her look both disapproving and concerned.

CJ never had a problem holding her liquor. *Lucky bitch.*

Andie covered her face with the blanket. "I have to tell Johnny the truth. I can't live like this. I hate what we did to his girlfriend." She felt the mattress dip when her best friend joined her on the bed.

Claudia pulled the blanket down. "You can't tell him, AB. Nothing good would come from it."

Andie collapsed against the tufted headboard. "We should've thought of that before we messed with the lives of innocent people. She has a little daughter, CJ. The girl ran away to Johnny's because she missed him and couldn't understand why he and her mom broke up. They looked for her for hours.

You should've seen her—Lumiana, that's her name. I've never seen anyone so scared and exhausted. Imagine if something had happened to her daughter because of what we did. I wouldn't be able to live with myself." Andie gave in to the tears.

Claudia hugged her. "I didn't mean for any of this to happen, and especially not that you're the one to suffer for it."

Andie linked her fingers with Claudia's. She needed to fix this.

***

Johnny was finishing up his morning workout session with Magnum when his phone rang. Ever since Lumiana broke up with him, he'd been exercising like he was training for the Ironman race: weights, running, swimming, cycling, and for good measure, kickboxing. Mag had told him to ease up, but it was either this or drowning his pain in scotch. Well, that and therapy.

James had slipped him a note earlier saying he scheduled an appointment for him with Dr. Sobel. 'You can cancel it, but I think you need someone to talk to, son,' his household manager had said.

"You're gonna get that?" Mag asked, bringing Johnny's attention back to the ringing phone.

Right. He reached for his phone and tapped the 'accept call' button.

"Andie, what's up?" Johnny signaled Mag to turn down the music.

"This is Claudia. I'm sorry to bother you, but you should come see Andie right away. I'm sorry to tell you this, but she lost the baby, and she's not taking it well."

She lost the baby…

Gripping the edge of the bench with his free hand, he lowered the phone and stared at it.

"Damn, boy, you're white as a sheet. I told you to take it easy." Magnum came over and put a hand on Johnny's shoulder, concern etched on his face.

"Did you hear me?" Claudia's voice sounded through the phone. "She needs you. *Now.*"

"Yes, of course. I'm on my way," he said and

hung up.

On his way out, he told Mag he'd catch him up later.

As Johnny drove over to Andie's he wasn't sure what to feel–disappointment, relief, sorrow? Unable to think straight, he nearly rear-ended a black sedan. Should've taken Mag up on his offer to drive him.

When Johnny got to Andie's, Claudia was waiting for him at the front door. She led him into the bedroom, where Andie was huddled on the bed, crying into a pillow.

Sitting next to her, Johnny gathered her in his arms. "I'm so sorry."

"Now you have no reason to be in my life anymore," she sobbed, clenching her hand in his shirt.

"I'm not going anywhere," he mumbled against the top of her head.

She hugged him tighter. "Please don't leave me."

"I'm not leaving."

Johnny sat with her until they fell asleep.

***

Andie woke up late in the afternoon, her head throbbing from all the crying. She needed a different kind of comfort, so she slipped her hand under Johnny's shirt. He stirred when she kissed his neck.

"Lu," he said as he woke up, a slow smile

spreading across his face. He jerked when he opened his eyes.

"Unbelievable." Andie moved away from him.

"Sorry, I can't. It's too soon."

"You're still hung up on her?" she asked, her voice wavering with suppressed tears.

"It's only been two weeks. And it's not just her. I miss her daughter too. We were close. It's not something you can shake off and be done with."

Would he try to get Lumiana back now that he knew there was no baby? The thought made her stomach shrink into a tight ball.

Johnny lowered his head, shaking it. "I hate that I'm the reason someone tried to hurt her, that her relationship with her daughter was jeopardized because of me. I hate that I made her cry. She deserves better—they both do."

It hurt to see him so desolate, but Andie felt relieved she still had a chance to win him back. She reached for his hand. "I love you, Johnny. And I hope you'll give us another chance. But I understand you need time and I'm willing to give you as much as you need."

Taking her in his arms, Johnny pressed a kiss to her forehead.

***

As the weeks progressed, Lumiana began burying herself in so much work it left her drained and moody. But with each new day there was also a little less tightness in her chest whenever she thought of her time with Johnny. She hadn't heard from him or Andie, which told her ending things had been the right decision.

"Are you all right, Lumi?" Shawn, dressed in nothing but red swimming trunks that showed off his warrior physique, eyed her from the chaise lounge when she joined him and Ana by the lake.

Slipping off her sandals, Lumiana lowered herself onto the dock and let her legs dangle over the edge of the warm bamboo panels.

"Yes, *mamá*, you don't look so good." Ana pushed her hexagon-shaped sunglasses up her petite nose. Her daughter's style was nothing if not eclectic. Today she wore a floral headscarf, a checkered crop top, and a linen skirt the color of watermelon.

Lumiana dipped her feet into the water, sighing with pleasure. Maybe it was the sweltering heat that made her lethargic.

"You're not pregnant, are you?" Shawn gave her one of his what-aren't-you-telling-me looks. It was hard to keep anything from him, and his Special Ops training didn't help either. Shawn could read people like an open book.

"Of course not." Lumiana pinched his toe. "That would imply I had intercourse." With Johnny gone, she no longer felt the need to brush up on her colloquial vocabulary. She kept reading *Fifty Shades* though. Purely to satisfy her anthropological curiosity, of course.

"Are you telling me you and Johnny didn't have that kind of relationship?"

Lumiana stirred her legs, the water gently lapping with the movement. "I'd rather not have this conversation in front of my daughter."

"*Mamá*, I saw you kiss. And Johnny slept in your bed when he stayed with us."

Turning to Shawn, Ana whispered, "He didn't wear a shirt. Peyton said they hugged in the nude because they were in love."

Ana smiled when she looked at Lumiana. "I think he could have put a baby in you. I hope he did."

Shawn grinned and Lumiana considered pushing him into the lake. "See, even Ana agrees with me. So, do you think Johnny might have put a baby in you?"

"He did not, and I don't wish to discuss any of this. I'm tired because I work hard."

Shawn and Ana frowned at her.

Okay, perhaps she was a bit irritable lately, but it had nothing to do with pregnancy hormones.

"I think you should see a doctor, Lumi. Just to make sure it's only because you've been working so hard."

To put an end to the conversation, she promised Shawn she would consult Gus if she didn't feel better after the weekend.

Her brother scooted toward the edge of the chaise lounge and began to braid her hair, something she knew he did whenever he wanted her to talk. That way she couldn't escape. Or at least not without getting scalped.

"On a different note," he said, expertly twisting her hair between his fingers. "Are you going to do the epilepsy fundraiser?"

"Helen and I have talked about it."

"If you're not up to it, everyone will understand." Shawn tugged on her hair.

Sneaky bastard.

"I want to do it." She rubbed her palms over her thighs. "I just hope I'll have the time and energy to do it well."

"I'm no psychologist, but I think it's quite the coincidence that all this 'not feeling well' started when you and Johnny broke up."

She gripped Shawn's wrist in warning. "Can we please not talk about him anymore? I'm trying to get him out of my mind."

"I know you are. But forcing it isn't going to work. It takes time, Lumi. Remember how you tried to force yourself not to have feelings for him? How did that work out for you? And you haven't talked to anyone about why you decided to end things. You looked all lovey-dovey the last time I saw you two together. Your breakup seemed sudden, that's all."

He made her turn, so he could braid the other side. "I don't know, but with the breakup, the threatening letter, and Ana running away, I'm worried that trying to pretend that none of this ever happened is slowly eating away at you."

Her family devoured psychology books with the same enthusiasm that most people reserved for suspense and romance novels. Unsolicited advice wasn't uncommon.

Shawn gave her hair another tug. "I want you to be yourself again, Lumi. Seeing you like this breaks my heart."

***

Johnny met his band mates in the studio that week to prepare for their next gig. With *Wonder* peaking at number one on the album charts, they had to keep the momentum going. And as grueling as it was, being so busy he barely had time to think couldn't have come at a better time. Lumiana still invaded his dreams but at least during waking hours he could pretend his heart was on the mend.

While making a fresh pot of coffee, Johnny overheard Adam on the phone.

"All right, Shawn. I hope she feels better soon... Yeah, I think there's more to the story, but I guess we'll never know... Sorry about how things turned out. I kind of feel at fault here..."

Johnny frowned at the coffee dripping into the pot, wishing he hadn't overheard Adam's conversation.

Was Lumiana not feeling well because of him? Did she miss him as much as he missed her? And why didn't she ever have a weak moment and call him in the middle of the night?

He snapped the elastic on his wrist twice. He needed to let it be.

After their session, when Earl and Toni were heading out the door, Johnny asked Adam to stick around. *Why?*

Because he was weak and liked torturing himself.

"Were you talking to Lumiana's brother earlier?" He handed Adam a cup of Colombian Supremo coffee—their favorite.

Adam sipped it, moaning in a mocked orgasm. "Yeah. Shawn's still my friend." Adam gave him a pointed look. "Thankfully."

Johnny could only imagine what Shawn wanted to do to him. A broken jaw came to mind... splintered kneecap maybe? Cement shoes? "Did you guys talk about Lumiana? Is she okay?"

"Are you sure you want to talk about her? I thought you were getting back together with Andie?"

There was that too. They weren't officially dating, but they'd been leaning on each other as friends, with the possibility of more. It was convenient and familiar, and just about what he could handle at the moment. But he still cared about Lumiana and there was nothing he could do about it except give it time. "I really loved her, you know. I think I still do."

"Don't repeat that in front of Andie." Adam

took another sip, then told him Lumiana hadn't been acting like herself. Apparently ever since their breakup, she'd turned into a tired, grumpy workaholic. "Shawn's theory is that she's either pretending the two of you never happened, or else you knocked her up." Adam grinned. "You didn't, did you?"

"Not that I know of." The odds that he'd gotten two women pregnant within a few months were pretty slim. The thought, however, made his chest flutter.

Crossing his arms, he propped his feet on the coffee table. "I'm sorry to hear she's not feeling well. If I had to guess, it's the former. And I think there's more to our breakup. She insisted it had to be this way, but then she kissed me like she didn't want me to let her go."

"It's kind of what we all think." Adam refilled their cups, handed him one.

"Did you know she received a threatening letter that told her to break up with me or else?"

"Yeah, it was a pretty big deal for the family. It scared the shit out of everyone. They amped up security and all."

"Right, so don't you think it's odd that all of a sudden she says, 'Oh, there is no threat,' and then breaks up with me like, what, a day later?"

Adam's phone vibrated, and he got up to go. "It sounds like there's more to it than she told you, but it might also be your hurt pride. Lumiana is the first girl who really got to you and then just left. If you want my advice, let her be and focus on Andie. The two of you are a much better fit."

Adam was probably right. Lumiana had suffered enough because of him, and things were going well with Andie. Maybe it was time to start a new chapter.

PART 3

19

NEVER LET YOU GO

"Your heart knows the way. Run in that direction."

—RUMI

Eight weeks after his breakup with Lumiana, Johnny felt ready to take his budding relationship with Andie to the next level.

The two of them had spent some time together as friends, but the last time they went out Andie was wearing a revealing black dress; it reminded him how long it had been since he'd had the pleasure of touching a woman.

Andie had been beyond happy when he asked her to be his date for a fundraiser on Helen Green's estate, and he was determined to make that evening special.

When they arrived at the entrance, dapper from head to toe and ready for an evening of exquisite food and entertainment, they ran into Helen, who not only stopped mid-stride, but also raised her eyebrows so high it looked almost comical.

"What are you doing here?" she hissed, her gaze darting around like she was trying to catch a fly.

Johnny put an arm around Andie. "Johnny Graham plus one. We're on the list."

"There must be a mistake... Excuse me."

Okay...

Helen turned to the greeter next to her. They both scanned the guest list and found that Johnny was indeed on it.

"What's going on, Helen?" he asked, a strange tingle in his gut.

But before Helen could answer, her assistant came and whisked her away, muttering something about missing canapés.

Johnny and Andie strolled into the elegant *Great Gatsby* themed ballroom. Tall, feathered centerpieces towered over stately gold and black place settings, giving the tables a dramatic look.

Andie was buzzing with excitement when they managed to snag seats with a good view of the stage. She loved Art Deco and there was plenty of it here: from the chevron place mats to the stage with its sunburst backsplash and a golden replica of New York's Chrysler Building.

The waiter had just brought them two glasses of champagne when Lumiana's brother walked by their table, doing a double take.

"Johnny?" Shawn stared at him with the same mortified expression they'd seen on Helen's face. But there was something else there too that simmered below the surface, like Shawn wanted to wring his neck.

Go ahead, try me.

Johnny gave him a saccharine smile, but it did nothing to ease the awkward tension. "Shawn. I didn't think I'd see you here. How's it going?"

"Are you kidding me?" Shawn pushed up his sleeves. "What are *you* doing here?"

Johnny bared his teeth. "How about someone tell me what the hell is going on?"

Shawn's expression softened ever so slightly. "Hm. You honestly have no idea?"

"I don't. So please, *enlighten me.*" This was one of Lumiana's favorite expressions and the irony didn't escape either of them.

"If you want my advice, *leave.*"

Andie put a hand on his arm. "What's going on?"

Johnny was losing patience with Shawn. "Tell me."

Shawn sighed dramatically, like answering them was beneath him. "Most of my family is here because it's our annual epilepsy fundraiser. And you're not exactly our favorite person."

Johnny shook his head, wondering if Lumiana was nearby. The thought prickled his skin. "Why did I get invited to this thing then?"

"I have no idea, but that must've been a mistake."

They probably sent out the invitations while he and Lumiana were still together. "Well, I came here to have a nice evening, and I intend to enjoy myself and my lovely date, so deal with it."

"I can't force you to leave, but consider yourself warned." Shawn glared at him before he left.

Johnny massaged the space between his brows.

It only went downhill from there. Whenever someone from Lumiana's family passed their table, they shot him a hostile look. He could understand why they weren't happy to see him, but it wasn't entirely fair. The breakup had been Lumiana's doing, and he'd kept his distance like she'd asked.

Maybe it was about Ana running away? Or the threat?

"You didn't answer my question." Andie laced her fingers with his. "I'd like to know what's going on."

Johnny took a sip of champagne, then frowned into his glass.

Andie traced her finger over the tattoo on his wrist. "I think we'll have a better chance of enjoying this evening if you tell me what makes these people so uneasy about your presence."

With a sigh, he explained that Shawn was

the brother of an ex (better to keep it vague if he wanted this evening to have a happy ending) and that the people glaring at him were part of Shawn's family.

And there's Adam, of course. He waved his friend over.

"What are you doing here, man?" Adam gave him and Andie a quick hug.

"Apparently I was invited by mistake."

Adam tapped one of the empty shell-back chairs at their table. "Do you mind?"

Johnny gestured for him to sit. "Do you think we should leave?"

Adam gave the waiter a nod of gratitude when he handed him a glass of champagne.

"Up to you. But if you choose to stay, you might want to keep a low profile."

A few minutes later, the three of them were so engrossed in conversation they were surprised when the lights dimmed and the show began.

Seemingly out of nowhere, Lumiana's powerful voice pierced the air, raising the hair on Johnny's skin. She was singing "Feeling Good," which he knew was one of her favorite songs from the sixties.

"What an incredible voice," marveled Andie, her hand clasping his wrist. "Do you know who this is?"

The stage was still dark as the song began, so they couldn't see the singer. He didn't need to see her. He'd recognize her voice anywhere.

"That would be my ex," he mumbled, finally understanding why Lumiana's inner circle was surprised to see him.

"I didn't know you dated a singer. Who is she?" Andie's grip tightened.

The question soon answered itself.

Johnny swallowed hard when the spotlight came on.

There she was, the reincarnation of soul queens past, all her gorgeous curves accentuated in a long, elegant dress.

"I-is that Lumiana?" Andie sputtered. "I didn't know she could sing."

Adam touched his shoulder. "Sorry, man. I tried to warn you."

Didn't do a very good job now, did you? Johnny took a gulp of champagne. Then he shrugged his shoulders and rolled his head from side to side.

Adam clapped him on the back. "You're going to be okay?"

I guess we'll have to find out.

***

Andie couldn't believe her eyes. There she was, up on stage—Lumiana—the woman who could so easily ruin her life.

Andie stared at her, her hand clenching on Johnny's sleeve.

Lumiana was a vision of elegance and sensuality in a fitted 1920s inspired gown. Her voice, smoky and seductive, would do Aretha Franklin proud.

It can't be.

"Life sure has a wry sense of humor," Andie said under her breath.

It was hard to reconcile this Lumiana with the woman she and Johnny had seen last: instead of red-eyed, hysterical, and dressed in an old UCLA sweatshirt, she now looked fresh-faced and confident, the cream-colored dress luminous against her dark skin. A white flower pinned to the side of her head sparkled in the spotlight.

"Is it okay if we stay?" Johnny's question broke the spell they were under.

Andie grabbed the champagne glass and guzzled it in one go. "As long as you stay close to me. I'd rather not run into her." She pressed a quick kiss to his lips but it did nothing to calm her nerves. It actually made it worse because she could feel the nervous tension emanating from him.

They both wanted to avoid a face-off with his ex, but part of her hoped Lumiana would see that she and Johnny were back together, that the pain they'd all suffered hadn't been for nothing.

After "Feeling Good," Lumiana and her brothers and sisters sang a soulful rendition of James Morrison's "Beautiful Life," The Heavy's "What Makes A Good Man?" and finished the set with "Seasons of Love."

"She's looking great," Adam said with a nod toward the stage.

"Yeah," Johnny agreed, his expression softening.

Andie gave an automatic smile to the waiter who refilled her glass, and then emptied it in a few gulps. "I agree, she looks great. Didn't think you were into plus-sized women though," she teased Johnny, "or exotic ones for that matter. At least none of your previous girlfriends looked like her." It wasn't fair that the guys were ogling Lumiana like the woman was some sort of retro bombshell while she had to work extra hard to maintain her supermodel slenderness.

Andie gestured to the waiter to top up her champagne flute.

"Better make sure Lumiana doesn't hear you call her *exotic*," Adam said to her. "And there's something seriously wrong with our society if bodies like hers are considered 'plus-sized.'"

To Johnny, he said, "But Andie is right, man. Lumiana is quite the deviation from the women you normally date, not just in terms of looks, but also personality."

They must have struck a nerve, because Johnny was having none of it. "I don't want to talk about this."

"And why is that?" Andie took another gulp of champagne. "Are you still hung up on her?"

"No," he replied without looking up. "But I don't want to talk about her where someone close to her might overhear."

"Spoilsport," Adam coughed. "Hey, would you

mind if I asked her out?"

Johnny rolled up his sleeves. "I swear I'm over her, but I hope you're kidding."

"I don't see why he can't ask her out if you're truly over her," Andie reasoned, downing the rest of her champagne. "Adam is a good man."

"That has nothing to do with it." Johnny angled his head, the gesture both disbelief and challenge. "Would you have liked it if I'd dated Claudia after we broke up?"

She would've had his balls if he'd done that.

"Relax, guys." Adam chuckled. "I'm messing with you. Shawn would break my neck if I touched his little sister. Which reminds me, the person you should really avoid this evening is him. I'm serious, Johnny. Shawn is short-tempered and you're currently number one on his shit list."

***

After her performance, Lumiana noticed that members of her family were encircling her wherever she went in the ballroom. She knew they were watching out for her because it was the first time she helped organize the fundraiser, but when Shawn and Gus tugged her away from the buffet, she'd had enough.

"What are you doing?" she asked her brothers, hands on hips. "I swear I am fine. We have practiced this a million times. I know what I have to say and when to smile. I remember my safe word and where I can go if I get over-whelmed. There is no need for you to follow me around like babysitters and bodyguards."

Putting an arm around her, Gus guided her to a table at the opposite side of the room. "We should just tell her what's going on, and then she can decide for herself if she wants us to stay close."

Shawn shook his head.

"Please," she said, coming to a halt.

"Johnny is here, and he brought a date," Gus blurted. "His ex, the one he knocked up. I don't think she's pregnant though. She's skinny as a stick considering she's supposed to be, what, five months along?"

If Gus didn't know, who would—her brother delivered babies for a living.

"Way to go, Gus!" Shawn said because Lumi-ana couldn't hide her mortification. "That's why I didn't want to say anything."

Lumiana drank the rest of her champagne in gulps, pressing a hand to her chest as the alcohol burned its way down her throat.

Shawn told her that Johnny had gotten in-vited by mistake and seemed to have no idea she'd be here.

Well, he knew now seeing how she'd been standing center stage the past twenty minutes. So she straightened her posture and decided to woman up. Johnny was entitled to move on with his life, and although it would be uncomfortable facing him again, she couldn't leave the party. It was her job to make things run smoothly.

Lumiana got herself another glass of champagne and breathed a little easier when her brothers promised to keep an eye on Johnny so their paths wouldn't cross.

"Milo?" Lumiana beamed at the mountain of a man as he was sauntering toward her. He looked gorgeous in a snug vintage suit that brought out the natural glow of his russet brown complexion. "I didn't know you were coming. I'm so happy to see you!"

"Everyone's so proud of you for doing the fundraiser," he said in his deep, velvety voice. It was the only voice she loved hearing as much as Johnny's. Both men were made to sing the blues, and she wished she could just go and find Johnny, so she could introduce them. He and Milo would love each other, she was sure of it.

Milo gave her a peck on the lips and wrapped her in a bear hug. "I missed you, Wild Child." Milo was a successful jazz musician who had been spending most of the past decade touring the world with his band. He was also the only one allowed to call her that. "I saw you perform earlier. You were amazing. Promise me we'll do a duet later."

"Of course. I'd love to." She'd had an innocent crush on him since she was sixteen and admired him as a musician.

Taking her hand, Milo swiveled her around.

"Look at you, all grown up and glamorous."

Lumiana felt her cheeks burning. She'd been complimented on her look all evening, which was a novelty for her because she never got dressed up like this. "It certainly is a deviation from my usual attire, but I wanted to fit in."

He swiveled her around once more. "That's too bad," he said, grinning, "because you, Lumiana Harding, were born to stand out."

***

Adam, Johnny and Andie were still chatting at the table when Lumiana and a really tall guy appeared in their line of sight. He knew the man from somewhere, Adam thought, trying to recall if he was one of Lumiana and Shawn's brothers. It was hard to keep track of all the Arendt-Garcías and the many foster kids that had come and gone over the years.

"Oh, look, she brought her boyfriend." Andie gave a catty smile. "He looks like a real man," she added with a purr as they watched the guy tuck his arm around Lumiana's waist. "No wonder she's so giggly."

"What's that supposed to mean?" Johnny straightened and looked sullenly at Adam, who merely shrugged. As far as Adam knew, Lumiana didn't have a boyfriend.

"I'm just saying he looks very masculine with those big hands and broad shoulders. What is he, seven feet tall?"

She probably wasn't that far off with her assessment, Adam thought, biting back a laugh when he saw Johnny's glare. The guy looked like he worked out with The Rock. And Andie was right about one thing, he'd never seen Lumiana so perky.

"It's Milo Sy," Johnny said, smoothing his hands over his tie. "He's an incredible musician."

That rang a bell. Milo was one of the foster boys who used to hang out with him and Shawn back in the day. Didn't recognize him without the Afro and the retro Steve Urkel glasses.

"Do you know him?" Andie asked, her gaze still glued to the man.

"No, but I'm a fan of his music," said Johnny. "He's worked with the greatest musicians in the world."

Adam nodded. "I met him years ago. He's one of the good guys."

"Did you know Lu was seeing someone?" Johnny so obviously tried to play it cool but Adam knew him too well to miss the flicker of dread in his eyes.

"Nope, but good for her. She seems happy."

***

A while later, Milo appeared on stage and took a seat at the antique Mason & Hamlin baby grand piano. Seeing Milo Sy perform was going to be a treat, Johnny thought, as he polished off his scotch. The liquor burned his throat, a welcome distraction from the dull ache in his chest.

"Ladies and gentlemen, sorry to interrupt," Milo's voice sounded through the state-of-the-art sound system. "I'd like to ask the lovely woman who sang for us earlier back on stage. She owes me a duet."

As the crowd applauded, Milo gave a microphone to one of the service staff who hurried over to Lumiana and handed it to her.

Johnny scrubbed his hands over his face, agonizing over whether he should step outside. He'd barely made it through her first performance, and now she was going to sing with a man he idolized.

When Milo began belting out Herbie Hancock's version of the U2 & B.B. King duet "When Love Comes To Town" in his raspy blues voice, the audience whistled and cheered.

Meanwhile, Lumiana slowly made her way toward the stage and Milo, dazzling the crowd with her equally powerful voice.

Johnny pressed a fist to the throbbing in his chest. He should've been the one up on stage singing with her.

"Yeah man, that's what I'm talking about!" Adam clapped. "Too bad you didn't get her to do the album with us."

Johnny felt tempted to deck his best friend for being a smartass.

As the evening wore on, Johnny noticed that one

or more of Lumiana's brothers seemed to be close by wherever he went. Sadly, it made him want to revert to his reckless ways. At some point he'd even fantasized about grabbing Lumiana and pulling her behind that freaking replica of the Chrysler Building. It sucked that she still affected him that way.

Did she feel the same? Was that why her brothers kept watch over him?

Fuck it. He'd had enough of this shit. So he went to confront Shawn and Gus, who were standing by the buffet.

"Are you guys keeping an eye on me so Lumiana and I don't run into each other?" Even though he'd asked the same of Adam earlier, it pissed him off that Lumiana seemed to have had the same idea.

"This is an important evening for us," Gus said, putting a hand on Shawn's arm, presumably to keep him in check. "So yeah, we're trying to avoid any disturbances."

"Why would I cause a disturbance? Our breakup was amicable. Does she know I'm here?"

"She knows you're here with your ex," Shawn growled. "And she's cool with it."

Ha, we'll see about that. "If she's cool with it, then it shouldn't be a problem if I talked to her, right?" It was petty, but it gave him satisfaction to see Shawn's jaw twitch.

"You've got to be kidding," Shawn snapped, and Gus had to use visible force to hold him back.

"You're on a date, remember? I don't think your recycled girlfriend would appreciate you chatting up your ex. By the way, how's the baby daddy thing working out for you?"

Nostrils flaring, Johnny jabbed a finger at Shawn. "That's none of your fucking business. And what are you giving me such a hard time for? I wasn't the one who broke things off."

"Just so we're clear," Shawn stepped closer, invading his personal space, "Lumiana is our fucking business. We're family. If you mess with one of us, you mess with all of us."

"And you're a liar, Johnny," said Gus, wedging himself between Shawn and Johnny. "We know you got your ex pregnant. You're the one who messed things up."

He had enough sense to own his mistakes, and this one in particular he'd live to regret for the rest of his days.

"Stop this, all of you," Lumiana's voice sounded from behind him, making Johnny realize he'd vastly underestimated how it would feel to stand next to her again. "I told you I didn't want a scene. This is neither the time nor the place. And Johnny is right. I was the one who broke things off. He is free to be with the mother of his child. Now let it go and enjoy the evening."

Shawn and Gus shot Johnny a glare that could have cut through bedrock before they left Lumiana and him standing there, looking at their feet.

His pulse thrummed in his ears.

"My brothers mean well," she stammered, "but they can be overprotective sometimes."

She was about to leave, so Johnny clasped her arm.

"Hey, wait. You don't have to run. We can have a friendly conversation for a minute."

Lumiana turned and finally looked up at him, her intense gaze hitting him like a punch. "That is not a good idea, Johnny." She glanced down at where his hand touched her arm.

"A damn minute won't kill you," he muttered, noticing the satisfying goosebumps on her skin. Because she still made his stomach dance, he'd been hoping seeing him did the same to her.

Lumiana straightened to try to match his stature, just like she had done when he confronted her in her office the day they met. He didn't realize it at the time, but that act of defiance, the wild spark in her eye when her gaze bored into him, was the moment he fell for her.

He smiled at the memory as he let go of her arm. "You look stunning. I've never seen you all dressed up."

Lumiana ran her fingers over the sequined bodice of her delicate dress. "I feel like I'm wearing a costume."

He met her piercing gaze. "It's weird... being here with you, but not as close as we used to be..." He raked a hand through his hair. "Sorry," he murmured when she gave a slight headshake. "Your performances were incredible. I'm glad to see you putting yourself out there."

For a moment he considered telling her he wasn't going to be a dad after all, but she seemed happy, and he'd already wreaked enough havoc on her life.

"Thank you," she said, touching his hand.

His fingers tingled in response, which made the urge to hug her almost impossible to withstand.

That moment, Andie and Milo joined them.

Lumiana let go of Johnny's hand but her gaze remained locked with his until Milo hugged her from behind and gave her a kiss on the cheek.

"You must be the infamous Johnny Graham. Heard a lot about you." Milo extended his hand.

Johnny shook it. "Milo Sy. Nice to meet you, sir. Big fan of your music. And I'm sorry my bad reputation precedes me." He winced when Andie nudged him with a little more force than necessary. "Um, and this is Andie, my..."

He didn't want to say 'girlfriend,' and he didn't have to, because Andie slid her hand in his and said, "I'm Johnny's girlfriend. It's an honor to meet you, Milo. I'm sure not all you've heard about him is true."

Johnny kept his gaze trained on Lumiana, who stared back at him with a stony expression. What gave her feelings away was the motion she always did when she felt vulnerable: reaching up, she closed her hand around her locket. Except, she wasn't wearing it. She noticed it too, and quickly put her hand behind her back as she lowered her gaze to the glossy floor.

Milo smiled at him. "How are you guys enjoying the evening? Lumi did a great job putting it all together, didn't she?"

The effortless intimacy between Lumiana and Milo made Johnny's blood boil. "I didn't know you organized it," he said to Lumiana.

She told them that every year one of her brothers and sisters helped their mother who'd suffered from childhood epilepsy put together this fundraiser. This year it was her turn.

"Well, it has been my turn for a while, but my anxieties have prevented me from doing it in previous years." The genuine affection that brightened her eyes made Johnny's stomach flutter. "Since I met you I've been working hard to overcome my fears."

Johnny's chest swelled with pride. "I think you did an outstanding job." He felt a little less guilty now, knowing there was at least one positive thing for her that came out of their relationship.

"How long have you known each other?" Andie asked Milo and Lumiana.

"I've known her for over a decade. You're in your late twenties, right?"

"I am, yes," Lumiana confirmed.

"Really?" Andie said, tilting her body toward Lumiana. "You don't look that old."

Johnny bit his lip, knowing how much Lumiana disliked people commenting on her youthful looks.

"You should've seen her at sixteen, she looked twelve at most." Milo grinned when Lumiana scowled at him. "She's come a long way since then."

"How long have you two been dating?" Johnny and Andie asked them almost in unison.

Lumiana and Milo frowned at each other, and Andie wrapped her arm around Johnny's waist.

Lumiana's face twisted with humor. "First Shawn, now Milo?"

"No way!" Milo exclaimed. "You think Lumiana and I are a couple? And you thought Lumiana and Shawn?" He shook his head, visibly trying not to laugh. "She's my baby sister," Milo clarified. "And even if she wasn't, I'm not into women that way."

"Wait, you have two gay brothers?" Johnny asked, a flush creeping up his neck. Milo didn't fit the gay stereotype, and neither did Shawn.

Lumiana shrugged. "Do you have a problem with that?"

Johnny scratched his forehead. "Not at all. I'm just surprised, and quite frankly embarrassed that I made the same mistake twice."

"What mistake are we talking about?" Adam said when he and Shawn joined them. "*Lumiana.*" He mockingly saluted her.

"*Adam.*" She snarled at him.

Shawn put an arm around Lumiana and

Adam. "It touches my shriveled little heart how much the two of you have warmed up to each other after all these years." He gave Lumiana a kiss on the cheek. "What did we miss?"

Lumiana told her brother about the misunderstanding, which amused everyone but Johnny, whose mind was hung up on a more important revelation: Lumiana's unchanged relationship status.

"So, you're not seeing anyone?" He felt about ten pounds lighter when Lumiana looked at him like he should know the answer.

"I wasn't looking for a partner when I met you. And now everything is back to normal. Why would I mess it up again?"

"Wait," Andie said to her. "Are you saying you never want to be with another man again until the day you die?"

"Don't get her started," Adam said, too late.

"I already met the love of my life, but then he died. I don't wish for a replacement. It took a while, but I am content with my life. And I don't need a man to make me happy."

"But you're not even thirty. You have more than half your life ahead of you." Andie said, looking at the men in their group, shout-whispering, "Does this make any sense to you?"

For the record, it didn't.

"So, what you're saying is, if you hadn't met Johnny, you would've stayed alone forever?"

"I am not alone," Lumiana assured her. "I have

a big family."

Andie wasn't satisfied with that answer. "Don't you miss having sex, or even just feeling close to someone?"

Johnny couldn't help the smirk tugging at his lips.

"What are you smiling about?" said Lumiana, taking a step toward him.

He'd missed that fire in her eyes.

Without thinking, he took a step forward. But just as he was reaching out to close the distance between them, Helen came over to introduce Lumiana to a few important guests.

"I have to go." Lumiana grabbed a glass of champagne from a nearby table and drank it all at once. "I hope you enjoy your evening. I'd say it was nice seeing you again, but then I'd be lying."

Helen pulled her away before she could say anything else.

***

Because Lumiana wasn't much of a drinker, the alcohol quickly went to her head. She was shaking when Helen led her out of the ballroom.

"Why are you doing this to yourself?" Helen said as she walked Lumiana down the hallway. "You said we should make sure you wouldn't run into them. How is it then that you end up talking to them, and about such personal stuff?"

Lumiana's jaw hurt from clenching her teeth so much. "I thought I could handle it." She wiped away a stray tear, grateful that Helen had gotten her out of there because seeing Johnny with Andie was too much.

With Jayjay, Lumiana had never felt this ugly burning in her chest because they'd always been each other's one and only. But Johnny wasn't hers anymore, and that realization constricted her chest and broke her heart all over again.

Helen stopped in front of the restroom. "I didn't want you to get hurt, but it looks like you already did."

Spots flashed in her vision. "I'm still in love with him, Helen."

"I know, sweetie." Helen gave her a hug. "But you have to pull yourself together now. This is a special evening. A lot of people—big donors—are hoping to meet you." Helen's assistant waved at her from the other end of the hallway. "Go to the restroom and freshen up. I'll be right back."

All Lumiana could think of as she splashed her face with water was going home and getting out of that dress. This evening had been a mistake. Why did she have to intervene when Shawn and Gus could have handled Johnny?

Leaning against the cool wall for a moment, she wiped her eyes. When she opened them, Andie was standing in front of her.

Lumiana recoiled. "What else do you want?" she said through gritted teeth. "I did everything you asked. He is yours. Please, just leave me alone."

With surprising force, Andie pushed her. Lumiana's head hit the textured wood and metal frame of a large wall mirror. For an instant, twinkling lights flickered rhythmically to the buzzing in her ears. It was like the day she ate fermented fruit, tripped over a tree root, and hit her head on a low-hanging branch.

When the fog began to dissipate from her mind, Lumiana couldn't breathe. Andie's mouth was covering hers.

She tasted of strawberries and champagne.

Then Andie let go of her and sank to the floor.

In shock from the unexpected assault and still dizzy from the alcohol, Lumiana slid down the wall and sat leaning against it. Once she was able to grasp one of the thoughts floating in her head, she yelled at Andie, "Are you out of your mind?" She touched the back of her head and felt the swelling.

Andie began to hyperventilate, her shoulders jerking like a broken jumping jack. Lumiana crawled into one of the stalls to get her a sanitary napkin bag she could breathe into.

"I'm... so... sorry," Andie said between hitching breaths.

"Keep breathing into the bag," Lumiana ordered.

When Andie calmed down, Lumiana confronted her again. "Why did you push me?"

"I had too much to drink. I didn't mean to

hurt you."

"And why did you kiss me?" Lumiana still saw everything, including Andie, a little blurry.

"I... I'm not a closeted lesbian, I swear."

"Kissing a woman doesn't make you a lesbian. It irks me that people have this innate need to label everything, especially something as fluid as sexuality." Lumiana inhaled deeply and regretted it instantly because nausea struck her with such force she had to throw up into Andie's paper bag.

Andie got her a wet towel. "I wish you were a bad person, that I could hate you and not feel so guilty. But the more I learn about you, the more I like you. You're odd, but in the best way. Under different circumstances we probably would've been friends."

Andie sat on the floor and put her head on her knees. "I wish Johnny would look at me the way he looks at you. You have no idea what it feels like when the man you love leaves you and immediately finds the woman of his dreams—like you were nothing, like you're the consolation prize or some amusement to pass the time before the real thing comes along."

"I never meant to fall in love with Johnny." Lumiana rubbed her cheeks. "I tried so hard not to. I'm very sorry this happened to you, but it doesn't excuse you for threatening everything I have built over the years. You really hurt me. It has to stop, Andie. I can't take much more of this."

She reached for the sink, but didn't manage to get a hold of it. Andie helped her up. Lumiana stood over the sink and washed her face. Andie was holding her steady when dizziness made her sway.

"I'll leave you alone, I swear. Please don't tell anyone about this."

"I need to go back out there. Helen is waiting for me. Just, please stay away from me."

"I promise," Andie said, wiping her cheeks with a paper towel.

Lumiana staggered out of the restroom with one hand on the wall for support. Her vision was so blurry she could hardly see where she was going.

Helen was waiting for her at the door. "You've been in there quite a while—"

"I'm not well, Helen," Lumiana said, trying hard not to vomit again. "Please don't be alarmed, but would you mind calling me an ambulance? I hit my head. I think I might have a concussion."

Helen took a closer look at her, feeling the lump on the back of her head. "You are bleeding, Lumi... Wait here." She made Lumiana sit on a cushion-covered windowsill in the hallway, out of sight from the guests, then she ran off to get help.

20

TRUTH

*"However disorienting, difficult, or humbling
our mistakes might be,
it is ultimately wrongness, not rightness,
that can teach us who we are."*

—KATHRYN SCHULZ

Andie and Johnny arrived at her place late that night. She poured them a nightcap, hoping to erase the restroom confrontation with Lumiana from her memory. "Here is to a weird evening and many more to come."

Andie touched her glass to Johnny's. More alcohol probably wasn't a good idea, because it loosened her tongue. *Oh, by the way, I kissed your ex—no biggie, right? God.*

"Sorry about that." Johnny took both their glasses and set them on the table. "I thought it would be more romantic, and without the ex factor."

"The night's still young." Andie toed off her stilettos.

The worst part was she could still see Lumiana's shocked face, hear her incredible voice, feel her soft lips against hers. She understood why Johnny had fallen in love with that woman. Hell, she was half in love with her herself.

And then there was the undeniable truth that was growing impossible to ignore: Johnny and Lumiana still loved each other. Anyone with half a mind could see that.

Johnny gave Andie a kiss that continued all the way to her bedroom. There was something off about it though.

Andie tried her best to ignore the sinking sensation in her stomach, and told herself it was just her nerves that were jittery, because it was their first night together since the pregnancy scare. Except Johnny's movements lacked their usual finesse too. And he didn't look at her.

Going through with this would be a repeat of the last time they had sex. He'd take her doggie style so it was less intimate, and maybe so he could pretend it was Lumiana instead of her.

Just as she was about to tell him to stop, Johnny scooted out of reach because something on the nightstand caught his eye.

"Where did you get that locket?" He motioned toward the golden heart-shaped angel wings on a small decorative plate next to her bedside lamp.

Andie touched a hand to her throat, feeling like it was full of sand. "Um, this old thing? My assistant found it at a thrift shop." Her words came out shaky. Why was this damn necklace still here? Hadn't she told her housekeeper to send it back to Lumiana?

Johnny inspected the locket, then stared at her like she was the incarnation of Judas, betrayer of Jesus Christ. "Andie, what have you done?"

"I don't know what you're talking about—"

"The locket." He held it up. "How did you get it?"

"I told you, my assistant got it from—"

"There's no way you got it from a thrift shop," he said, his voice raised. "This is Lumiana's locket."

"How do you know? And even if it were hers, maybe she didn't want it anymore."

"I've seen her wear it a gazillion times—except tonight." He slapped his palm against his forehead. "I saw her reach for it. Like phantom pain." He rubbed his thumb over the heart-shaped angel wings. "You have no idea how much this locket means to her. There's a picture of her birth parents in here." He opened the locket and handed it to her. "She'd never give this away. It's a family heirloom and this is the only picture she has of her parents... Fuck, Andie." He pulled at his hair. "You're the one who black-mailed her."

"It's not what it looks like." She tried to take his hand, but he held it up in protest. "I had no choice," she said, her voice cracking.

"You had no choice?" He scrubbed a hand over his mouth and turned away for a second. "Tell me everything, and you better not lie to me any-more."

"I can't—"

"You have to," he said, violent energy eman-ating from him. He'd never raise his hand to her, she knew that, but he also wasn't going to let this go.

"No, please, Johnny." Andie reached for him, but he got off the bed.

"Don't touch me," he warned. "The truth. *Now*."

She tried to run out of the room, but he blocked her.

"This ends now, Andie. Tell me what the fuck is going on."

She sank to the floor in front of him, sobbing uncontrollably.

He sat next to her, patting her back. "Please."

She brushed the hair off her face, and then told him how she and Claudia had forced Lumi-ana to break up with him.

"God, Andie," his gaze darted around the room, "I can't believe you did this."

Thinking back, neither could she. She tilted her chin toward the ceiling to keep the tears from falling. "Lumiana still loves you though."

He shook his head, laughing dismissively. "She broke up with me."

Andie touched his shoulder. "Only because she had no other choice." She would fix this. It was likely her only shot at redemption if she didn't want to fry in hell.

"You always have a choice."

"In theory, yes. But people make unreasonable choices when they face dire circumstances. And in her case it wasn't unreasonable, it was rational. She sacrificed your relationship, her own happiness, to ensure the safety of her family." Andie sat up straighter. "I may go to hell for this anyway, so let me confess to everything."

Johnny touched a hand to his stomach. "There's more?"

"I'm the reason she's in the hospital right now." When Andie came out of the restroom at the fundraiser earlier, there were flashing lights outside the hallway windows. She'd peered through the glass and saw the paramedics loading Lumiana into the back of an ambulance—a sight she'd been trying to deny all night.

"You've got to be kidding."

Andie told him about their restroom run-in. "I could tell she thought I was waiting for her, but I swear, I wasn't." She covered her eyes with her hands. "It all happened so fast... I... I kissed her." Her cheeks burning, she pressed her face against her knees.

"I'm sorry, what?" Johnny poked her in the shoulder so she glanced up. "Did you say you kissed her?" When she nodded, he muttered, "That must've been one hell of a kiss."

She was a bit fuzzy on the details. Alcohol didn't mix well with overpowering emotions. "I don't know what came over me. I must have pushed her so hard her head hit the wall mirror."

Johnny let out a long, resigned sigh. "I don't even care about what I've been going through, but Lumiana, she didn't deserve any of this."

"I'm deeply sorry, Johnny. You can hate me all you want, I deserve that. I made a bad choice, but I was trying to protect my friend."

Johnny shook his head. "It's my fault."

"It's not. I could've chosen to handle this differently. There is no one but me to blame."

He smoothed his hands over the linen fabric of his light blue suit pants. "It's not as simple as that. And I do blame myself. I shouldn't have shown up at your doorstep that night and then left you like that, much less sleep with you without protection. I know you're not a bad person, Andie. I'm angry and disappointed, but I don't hate you."

They stared at the silvery carpet for a while.

"Do you still love her?" Andie asked, knowing the answer. But Johnny needed to admit this to himself too. "Because if you do, you should go after her. You deserve to find out if your relationship would've worked out if it wasn't for me."

"What makes you think she'd take me back after this?"

"She loves you, Johnny. Didn't you see how she looked at you when we were talking with her and her brother?" Thinking, Andie tapped her lips with her finger. "Make a grand gesture. Propose to her or something—women really like that."

"She isn't most women." Johnny got up. "Maybe it's best to respect her wishes and leave her alone."

"Come on, Johnny. Lumiana also said she wishes to be celibate for the rest of her life. Clearly she doesn't know what she really wants."

***

The next morning Lumiana woke up in the hospital with a headache the size of Finland. Because the room spun, she lifted her hands to her head, but her right hand wouldn't come up. When she opened her eyes, and saw the reason why, she blinked a few times. "I'm not dead, am I?"

Sitting by her bedside holding her hand was Johnny. "Why would you say that?"

"You're not supposed to be here." Her skin prickled where it touched his.

He shrugged. "Guess what, I found out why you broke up with me."

What? How? Oh my God, was she imagining

him being here? Maybe the trauma to her brain was more severe than the doctors thought.

Right then, someone came into the room to bring her breakfast.

"Do you see that man sitting next to me?" she said to the aide.

"Um, yes. Are you all right, Dr. Harding?"

Johnny stroked her hand with his thumb. "You think you're hallucinating? I'm holding your hand, Lu. Don't you feel that?"

The aide eyed her expectantly.

"I do. I'm fine. I was just making sure my head is fine too."

The aide gave her a quick smile and left.

"How are Andie and the baby?" Lumiana asked, beginning to remember some details from the night before.

"There is no baby."

Her jaw dropped. Maybe she was hallucinating after all.

"Andie's not pregnant. It was a false positive. She just kept it from me after she found out."

That can't be true.

Snatching her hand from his, she tried to roll over to face away from him, but the movement made her dizzy.

When Johnny touched her leg, she squirmed at the contact even though there was a blanket between her skin and his. "Can you please let me explain? I'm not here to upset you. I just want to talk."

"Fine, talk." She pulled the blanket up to her chin. "Can you please let go of my leg?"

"Why?"

"Because..." The truth was he was making her nervous—the good kind—and she worried he would once again wear her down with his kindness. She'd never met a person who could get her to do things she had no intention of doing as successfully as Johnny did.

"That's not a convincing argument, so tough luck." He left his hand on her leg and gave it a light squeeze. "I know Andie and Claudia paid you a visit and blackmailed you into breaking up with me. And I also know she pushed you into a wall and kissed you."

Lumiana sat up like a puppet on a string.

"Hey, easy!" Johnny reached out to hold her steady. "You need to keep still, remember?" He sat next to her on the mattress and cupped her cheek. "Are you okay?"

She leaned into him, closing her eyes at the warmth of his touch. "I don't understand."

"Andie admitted everything to me last night." With his free hand, Johnny propped a pillow behind his back. "You should eat." He pointed with his chin at the breakfast tray.

"I don't feel like eating right now." In fact, she felt like she might throw up again.

Johnny carefully pushed her down onto the pillow and slid his hand back into hers.

She must be dreaming.

After all that Andie and Claudia had put her through, Andie just told Johnny the truth, setting her free?

Lumiana put her other hand on her fluttering stomach. "Andie isn't going to tell everyone who I am now, is she?"

"No. Besides, you held up your end of the deal," Johnny said in an accusatory tone.

"Does she know you're here and telling me all this?"

"It was her idea. Andie feels terrible for what she's done." Johnny tightened his grip on her hand for a second when she attempted to pull it away. He knew her so well he could gauge when something she did was an act of defiance rather than a need.

"They took my locket."

"I know. That's how I found out." He leaned closer, and because his scent began to cloud her mind, she allowed herself to rest her head on his shoulder.

"Do you think I can have it back?" She snuggled up to him, placing her hand on his chest. Because she could feel his heartbeat quicken, she hugged him tighter.

He was here. He was real.

Johnny covered her hand with his. "I'll see what I can do. Andie's confession came as such a big shock, I just wanted to get away from her. I forgot to take it." He nuzzled her forehead, his lips nearly brushing against hers. "Does that mean I can see you again?"

She tilted her head a little, so close she could feel his breath. Tiny zips of pleasure shot through her core. Hooking her finger into the collar of his shirt, she closed the distance—

"*Mamá!*" Ana shouted from the door, making them jerk apart. "Johnny!" Her daughter ran over to him and hugged him so enthusiastically he fell back against the pillow.

Lumiana smiled at them.

Ana wrapped her arms around Johnny's neck, giving him a kiss just as Candela and Milo came into the room.

"Are you and my mom back together?" Ana asked, hope filling her eyes.

They all looked at her. She hated to disappoint her daughter again, so all she said was, "Can you come here and give me a hug?"

Ana cuddled up to her.

Johnny gave both of them a kiss on the head before he got up.

"Are you leaving?" Ana's voice was laced with disappointment.

"You don't have to go on our account," Candela assured him.

"It's okay. I need to get going. I just wanted to tell Lumiana something, which I did, so..." He stuffed his hands in his pockets.

She wished she could read his mind. It felt awkward now with her family here.

Ana stood on the bed and gave Johnny another hug.

"It was great seeing you, kiddo." Then he said goodbye to Candela and Milo, and left.

Lumiana put up a brave front for her family, but all she wanted was to curl up under the blanket and cry.

***

After a week without a word from Lumiana, Johnny felt almost sure she no longer wanted him to be part of her life.

The performances his band had lined up kept him busy, but when he had Friday off, he felt tempted to spend the day getting cozy with a bottle of scotch, so he went to visit his father.

It was amazing to see the progress his dad had made. His speech was almost as fluent as it used to be.

"Have you talked to Lumiana yet?" His dad was sitting on a light gray three-seater between white-gray throw pillows. He pushed his stylish glasses back up his nose and gestured for Johnny to sit in the tufted armchair opposite him.

Johnny put his feet up on the matching ottoman. "Nope. I think she's done with me. And I can't blame her. I messed up her life so bad, I think she's just glad this nightmare is over."

"She still comes to visit me."

Great, Lumiana managed to keep in touch with his dad but didn't send him even one lousy text message.

"She's a sweetheart. And she's strong-minded too, like your mother."

Johnny slouched in the chair. "I thought you hated that about Ma."

It's actually one of the reasons I fell in love with your mother, and I believe it's also why she fell for me. It's only a problem if neither is willing to compromise."

Johnny tapped a finger to his temple. "I'll keep that in mind. Did Lumiana say anything?"

When Ruby came into the room to bring his father his medication, Johnny gave her a smile. Then he watched her leave. The way those white pants clung to her tight butt got the "Thong Song" stuck in his head.

"She doesn't talk about you or what happened." His dad's words had the same effect as if he'd dumped a bucket of cold water over his head. "What she did tell me though when I repeatedly asked her about her missing locket is that Andie has it. So, get it back and go see her. I'd hate it if you gave up this easily."

It wasn't about giving up but about doing what's right.

Sighing, Johnny sat up straighter. "How did she seem to you when you saw her?"

"She was very quiet at first, but the last few days she's been her normal delightful self."

"You really think showing up at her place is a good idea?" Johnny fiddled with a petal that had fallen off the bouquet on the small side table.

"Come on, son. You didn't hurt her on purpose, and she knows that. Go and get her locket. It means a lot to her and it's something she can't replace."

With any luck, Andie still had it. He'd been putting this off only because he'd have to confront Andie again to get it, and he was still mad at her.

Johnny got up and gave his father a hug. On his way out the door, he turned to face him once more. "What did you say to Lumiana when you met her for the first time? She never told me."

His dad gave him a crooked grin. "I told her how much she means to you and asked her to take good care of you."

Johnny smiled. "What was her reaction?"

"She promised me she would try her best to honor my wish."

**

Ruby pushed her cart with such force, it banged against the door frame of Mr. Bennett's room.

How was Lumiana still in the picture?

Maybe she needed to make good on her threat after all and send a few reporters her way. She thought the letter she'd sent had worked perfectly. Lumiana broke up with Johnny and now he was a bigger flirt than ever. So why was he still hung up on her after all this time?

Ruby gave the cart another hard shove. She'd rather eat her own toenails than let that prickly professor get her hands on him again.

The problem was that Lumiana wasn't an easy target. Security was tight at both her home and her office. The fan club hadn't managed to get a picture of Johnny and Lumiana that proved they ever were a couple. And no matter how many times they filtered the photo that Janice had taken, it was useless.

She needed a new plan that would get rid of Lumiana permanently. Then Johnny could finally be hers. They were destined to be together. She'd known it from the moment she first laid eyes on him. And soon he would realize it too.

***

After visiting his father, Johnny dropped by Andie's. Much to his relief, she gave him Lumiana's locket, expressing both her regrets and the hope there would come a time when they could be friends again. *Unlikely*, he thought, but he wanted to be civil, so he told her *maybe*.

In the afternoon, Johnny drove up to Jonata. He was surprised when Mike let him through the gate without calling Lumiana first.

As he approached her house, he felt a flutter in his stomach. With Lumiana he never knew quite what to expect, but that was a big part of why he loved being with her.

He rang the doorbell.

No one answered, so he walked around to the

patio, where he found her stretched out on one of the large sofas, reading a book.

Johnny sat next to her.

"*Warrior of the Light*," he read the title aloud.

"It's one of my mom's favorites. She likes telling us the lessons from the book and often quotes from it. I'm reading it again to use the lessons during story time with Ana."

Johnny smiled at her. "Speaking of Ana, is she around?"

"She is out playing with Peyton. Are you here to see her?"

"I was hoping to, but it's not why I'm here."

"Why are you here then?" Lumiana put her book down, looking at him with wary eyes.

Johnny got a small red box from the pocket of his jacket and handed it to her.

Lumiana opened it and teared up. Warmth radiated through his chest when she caught him in a fierce embrace. "Thank you so much for getting my locket back."

"You're getting me all wet, Lu," Johnny laughed as he wiped away her tears.

She stared at him when he lay down on the cushion next to her. "You are going to stay?"

"I didn't come all the way up here for five minutes. I'm tired, so if you don't mind, I'd like to relax for a bit. Go read or something."

When Johnny woke up a while later, Lumiana was still next to him reading. She held the book in one hand while absently running her fingers across the scar on his arm with the other. For a moment he just lay there, savoring the shivers that her touch sent across his skin.

God, he'd missed her.

Sorry, babe.

Without preamble, he pulled her on top of him, knowing it would startle her.

Lumiana was warm and soft and smelled of jasmine. But more than anything she felt like home. Her mouth came down on his, reminding him that this was where he belonged.

Johnny slid a hand in her hair, drawing her closer as his lips parted hers hungrily. He swept his tongue over hers, again and again, until—

"Johnny!" Ana's voice brought the moment to an end.

You gotta be kidding me.

Breathing heavily, Lumiana moved away from him, whereas he sat up and thought of road kill—an instant erection deflator.

The girl came running toward them and jumped into his arms. He'd missed Ana like crazy and seeing the pure joy on her face at the sight of him meant the world to him.

"Are you going to stay for dinner?" Ana said, her eyes sparking with hope.

"I don't want to make your mom uncomfortable." Johnny glanced at Lumiana, who looked adorably flushed.

"If it doesn't make her uncomfortable that

you kiss her, I'm sure she will be fine if we have dinner together."

Little Miss Smartypants. Johnny tickled her. "Is dinner okay with you?" he asked Lumiana.

When Lumiana agreed, Ana thrust a fist into the air and shouted "yes!"

21

TRY

"Dripping water hollows out stone,
not through force
but through persistence."

—OVID

While Lumiana prepared a strawberry salad in the kitchen, she listened to Johnny and Ana playing *Connect Four* at the dining table. It warmed her heart to see how much the two of them adored each other, but it also angered her that she was the one preventing them from sharing more moments like this.

She knew Ana still wanted Johnny to be her dad. Just last week Mike had shown her a drawing that Ana made when she was playing with

Peyton. It told the story of how the two girls and their dads went camping in Canada where they befriended a bear cub. Despite her young age, Ana was an exceptional artist, so there was no denying that the tattooed man Ana depicted as her dad looked like Johnny.

After dinner, Lumiana and Johnny cleared the dishes while Ana changed into her pajamas. Both of them stayed quiet, but the tension crackling between them made her palms sweaty.

Johnny flinched when Lumiana reached for a towel and accidentally brushed against him.

"Sorry," she murmured. "Am I making you nervous?"

"Isn't that usually the other way round?"

"I am nervous," Lumiana admitted, fiddling with the tag on the dishcloth. "I know you are going to want to talk about us, and I'm thinking of what I'm going to say."

"So you haven't made up your mind yet?"

She pinned her arms against her stomach. "Do you still want this?"

"I wouldn't be here if I didn't."

She shrugged. "You could just be here to return my locket."

"Yeah, right. You know damn well that I want to be with you."

She raised herself on tiptoes and kissed him, but he lowered his forehead to hers and sighed.

"I'd appreciate it if you could refrain from kissing me until you're sure what you want. It's not fair to give me false hope or get me turned on when you don't plan on seeing it all the way through."

"That wasn't my intention."

He leaned against the counter, pinched the bridge of his nose. "I know it wasn't. But I think you sometimes underestimate the effect you have on me."

Lumiana crumpled the dishcloth into a ball. "I wanted to express my gratitude."

"Forget I said anything."

"Fine." She tossed the towel on the counter and crossed her arms. "I apologize that I kissed you. It won't happen again."

Johnny laughed at her. She shoved him, which amused him even more.

"Stop laughing," she ordered, swatting at him.

He caught her wrists and held her at a safe distance. "Stop acting like a little girl."

"What's going on?" asked Ana, interrupting their tiff.

Johnny leaned against the counter and ran a hand over his jaw in that devastatingly sexy way of his. She wanted to launch herself at him.

Maybe Johnny could read her thoughts, because he smirked.

Turning her back to him, she said to her daughter, "It's nothing, *angelito*. Are you ready to go to bed?"

"No. I want to play with Johnny. I never get to see him anymore."

Lumiana crouched, taking her daughter's hands. "It's late, Ana. Maybe you can spend some time with him tomorrow."

"Is Johnny going to stay with us tonight?"

"Do you have somewhere to be tomorrow morning?" Lumiana asked him, unsure whether she wanted him to answer yes or no.

His smile was blinding. "You're asking me to stay?"

Before she knew it, her ovaries made the decision for her. "You let us stay at your place last time, and we have plenty of room if you'd like to spend the night."

"Sure."

"See, he is going to be here when you wake up, so you can go to bed now." Lumiana gave Ana a goodnight kiss.

"What about the story?" Ana protested.

Lumiana looked at Johnny. "Would you like to do it?"

"Absolutely." He scooped a delighted Ana over his shoulder and carried her to her bedroom.

***

When Johnny returned to the living room, Lumiana was on the sofa reading again. She lay on her back, her legs dangling over the edge, while the dog snoozed on her stomach.

Johnny crossed to her. "That doesn't look comfortable." He gave her a kiss on the forehead, then settled next to her to pet Monroe.

"Ana loves you," Lumiana said, her brows knitted in thought.

"I feel the same about her."

"She wishes for you to be her dad. Is that something you want too?"

After their last conversation about his relationship with Ana, honesty didn't seem like a smart idea. "I know you're scared she'll forget about Jayjay and I don't want to interfere—"

"No, Johnny," Lumiana put her hand on his arm, "I want to know how you feel. Please don't tell me what you think I wish to hear."

He loved that little girl, it was as simple as that. The joy and pride he felt whenever Ana hugged him, or smiled at him, made him wish she could be his. "It's something I've been thinking about a lot."

"Does that mean yes?"

He shifted so their gazes met. "It does, yes."

She regarded him for a moment. "Even if the two of us aren't together?"

"Where are you going with this, Lu?"

"Please, answer me."

Sighing, he stretched his arms out over his head, then let them drop. "Ideally, I'd like for the three of us to be a family, but if you're asking whether I'd want to be there for her in general, the answer is still yes. I think it would be good for her to have a father figure in her life. Does that answer your question?"

"Yes, thank you." Lumiana smiled at the ceiling.

Pulling her close, he gave her a heartfelt kiss. It meant a lot that she would even consider him to fill such an important role in her daughter's life.

"Wait." She pressed a hand to his chest. "So I'm not allowed to kiss you, but you are allowed to kiss me?"

"Life ain't fair, Doc."

With one quick move that had her squealing, Johnny flipped her over his shoulder and carried her upstairs to her bedroom.

"Just so you have time to wrap your head around it, I won't be sleeping in the guest room." Johnny put her down on her bed.

Lumiana pulled him onto her, bringing her mouth to his.

"Whoa, wait! You can't kiss me, remember?" He stood back up.

As she moved toward the edge of the bed, she straightened in front of him, slipping her hands under his shirt. With her fingers splayed across his chest, she rubbed her palms over his pecs.

Johnny frowned at her, but Lumiana merely shrugged and touched her lips to his neck, cruising up to his earlobe, nibbling. Her hot breath made his erection strain against his pants. *Traitor*.

He angled his head, but otherwise remained rigid.

"You said I can't kiss you unless I'm planning

to see it through to the end." Her hand sneaked under the waistband of his pants.

Fuck it. It's been too damn long.

His breath caught when Lumiana wrapped her fingers around his shaft and stroked him. His eyes drifted shut. He'd missed her touch, the mindfulness with which she gave pleasure.

Freeing him, her luscious mouth took him in, his muscles tensing and trembling as her tongue and hands skimmed over him. His breath grew more and more ragged and when he felt he couldn't take more, he pulled her up.

"Feeling frisky much?" he rasped when she tugged at their clothes between heated kisses.

Her breathing as labored as his, she held up her hands. "Would you like me to stop?"

"Never." Johnny drew her against him and scattered licks and kisses down her throat. God, he loved her silky skin. As he lowered his mouth to one of her nipples and pulled it into his mouth, he slid his hand between her legs.

When Johnny touched the heat of her core, Lumiana clenched her hand in his hair and called out his name as his tongue mirrored the circling motion of his thumb.

Then Johnny grabbed a condom from the nightstand. Once he had it in place, he gripped her hips and buried himself deep inside her. Holding still for a moment, he gazed at her. Lumiana was fervent and wonderful and turned his whole damn world upside down.

We could have it all, Johnny thought as they linked their hands and moved together until their bodies shuddered, *why can't you see that?*

***

Lumiana reached for Johnny when she woke up, but the sheets next to her were cold; his clothes were gone too. Squinting, she peered at the clock on her nightstand. It was early—4:30.

Where did he go?

Lumiana stretched to relieve the stiffness in her neck, but it tightened again when she thought of Ana's reaction. Her daughter would be upset that Johnny left without saying goodbye again. She couldn't keep doing this to Ana, giving her hope, only to take it away.

Lumiana put on her shirt and went downstairs. Maybe Ana was awake. Her daughter was an early riser, though half past four was early even for her.

Lumiana opened the door to Ana's room a crack, then fully when her chest hitched. Ana wasn't in her room.

Please don't do this to me. Lumiana inhaled sharply. Ana wouldn't run away again, she reminded herself, sucking in another breath.

Stay calm. Check the house.

Lumiana rushed into the living room and huffed when she heard laughter coming from the kitchen. She stood still with her hands clutched to her chest until her nerves settled.

Then she padded into the kitchen, where Ana was sitting atop the island. Johnny stood next to her, drinking a glass of water. Both of them smiled as Lumiana took a seat at the counter.

"You look like you got up on the wrong side. Everything okay?" Johnny asked her.

Lumiana grunted in response. She considered throwing the dish towel at him when he grinned, but because her daughter was sitting right there she decided to be mature. "It's still very early," she said, rubbing her eyes.

"See you later, kid." Johnny ruffled Ana's hair before he went over to Lumiana, took her by the hand, and led her back upstairs. "Why are you so grumpy?"

Sighing, Lumiana lay down on the bed and drew the blanket over her head.

Johnny rolled on top of her and pulled the blanket down. "Talk to me," he said, caressing her cheek.

"It's embarrassing."

His thumb grazed her lips. "You know you can tell me anything."

She hesitated, but then admitted that she thought he'd left without saying goodbye.

"I went downstairs to get water." His features softened. "That's why you're upset? Because I wasn't there when you woke up?"

"I told you it's embarrassing. I love waking up next to you. You are so warm and soft." Lumiana dragged the blanket back over her head.

He pulled the blanket back down, stroked her arm. "You can still have that if you want."

She moved closer to him. "But without the shirt—for authenticity," she added when he raised his brows.

Johnny took off his shirt, and caught her admiring him. He took good care of his body and that in itself was a trait she found exceedingly attractive.

"You like what you see?"

Lumiana cuddled up to him, settling her head on his chest. "I'm physiologically programmed to like it."

"So love has nothing to do with it?" He ran his fingers up and down her spine. She purred at the blissful sensation.

"There is that too." In a universe where he wasn't famous, and she didn't have a family that needed protecting, she would have allowed herself to dream of the fairy tale ending.

But this was real life: she had a daughter she needed to think of, a past that kept haunting her, and a love of her life who left a cleft in her heart so profound she doubted it would ever heal. Johnny deserved to be with someone who could give as much as he gave.

"Comfortable?"

Lumiana placed a kiss on his chest, then trailed her finger across the scar on his arm.

But what about Ana? Her daughter and Johnny had a relationship of mutual affection where both of them got as much as they gave.

"You can spend more time with Ana," she decided, "if the two of you would like that."

He stopped stroking her back. "Um, really? Are you sure?"

She straddled him. "You are very good with her, and she adores you. There is hardly a day she doesn't talk about you, and she is overjoyed whenever she sees you. I wish for her to be happy, Johnny. Having you be part of her life makes her happy."

She brushed her hands over his chest. Johnny might be the only chance Ana had at having a dad because there wouldn't be another man in her near to distant future.

Johnny pulled her so close, she gasped. "If that's what Ana wants, then I'd love to spend more time with her."

"Just promise me to keep her out of the tabloids and out of harm's way."

"I'll do my best, I promise." Johnny kissed the top of her head.

A few minutes later, Ana appeared at the door. She shuffled over in her fuzzy bunny slippers and climbed onto the bed, squeezing in between them. "*Mamá*, can I stay here with you and Johnny?"

"Of course, *angelito*."

"Can I tell her?" Johnny asked, and Lumiana gestured for him to go ahead.

Ana's eyes widened when he took her hand.

No matter how tough Johnny looked and acted, he had a soft spot for her daughter that was visible to anyone who saw them together. Even Shawn said so.

"You've said before that you wished I could be your dad. Do you still feel that way? And if you do, is it because you want me to be with your mom, or do you think you'd want that even if your mom and I aren't together?"

"I want you to be my dad because you are cool and I love you."

His face lit up. "Good, because that's how I feel about you too. Your mom said you and I can spend more time together if you want."

"Really, *mamá*? You're okay with it?" Ana's eyes were glimmering.

"I wish for you to be happy, *angelito*, and Jayjay would want that too."

Ana pressed her cheek to Lumiana's, then reached for Johnny to pull him closer.

As much as Lumiana enjoyed this illusion of family, she felt it was time to take a step back to give Ana and Johnny a chance to develop their relationship without her getting in the way.

The three of them lay there for a while cuddling, until Ana's stomach growled.

***

Throughout the next two weeks, Johnny spent lots of quality time with Ana. They went hiking, swimming, paddle boarding, and his personal favorite: kart-racing. Who would've thought hanging out with a seven-year-old could be so much fun?

He enjoyed teaching Ana new stuff, especially how to play the guitar. She was a curious child and there wasn't much she wouldn't try. Except for American fast food, apparently.

Ana informed him that she didn't eat food that wasn't 'certified humane' and lectured him in great detail about factory farming until he lost his appetite. Surely Lumiana was to blame for that. And he would've exchanged passionate words with his favorite professor, but he barely got to see her. And when he did, Lumiana made sure there was so much space between them he'd have to grow longer arms to be able to touch her.

He didn't know what to do. Whenever he asked Lumiana to hang out with Ana and him, or be alone with him, she was too busy with work or found some other excuse.

Did she really need to trim the rug on a Sunday afternoon?

He didn't even know that was a thing. Maybe it was a euphemism, Johnny thought when Adam strolled into the studio with a big grin on his face.

Ana was in the apartment above the studio doing her homework, so Johnny wanted to use the time to go over the set list for their upcoming gig.

Adam plopped onto the sofa and helped himself to Johnny's fresh cup of coffee. "I see you've been spending time with Ana. Does that mean you and Lumiana are back on?"

"See?" Johnny repeated, prying his cup from Adam's hands.

"I saw a picture of you and Ana in one of those tabloid magazines at the dentist's office. You were playing together in some park."

"Shit." He'd promised Lumiana this wouldn't happen. "And no, we're not back together. She agreed to let me spend more time with Ana, or at least she did until she finds out about this. Did they figure out who Ana is?"

"Relax, man. You've got nothing to worry about. You were smart enough to bring Jack and the twins along. They wrote something harmless like 'Johnny Graham had an adorable family outing in the park.'"

Great. He shot his friend a hostile look when Adam reached for the cup that Johnny had just set down. "How about you get your own coffee? And maybe some help while you're at it, you're a goddamn addict."

"Fuck you." Adam took Johnny's mug and ran his tongue along the rim. "What crawled up your ass this morning?"

Johnny refused to take back his cup when Adam handed it to him. "No thank you, not after what you've done to that mug."

"When was the last time you got laid?"

Johnny rubbed his brow with his middle finger.

"That long, huh?"

"Shut up, Adam." Johnny slouched against the cushion. "I have to tell Lumiana that Ana's face ended up in the tabloids. It'll probably give her the last push she needed to tell me we're never getting back together."

"How come you're so pessimistic all of a sudden?"

"It's just that I've hardly spent any time with her since the fundraiser, and she's avoiding me. So forgive me if I'm a little low on optimism these days."

"Ah, women," Adam leaned back and misquoted Erasmus's *Adagia*, "Can't live with 'em, can't live without 'em."

Johnny poured two fresh cups of coffee, handing one to Adam. "I'll drink to that."

***

Friday evening, Adam joined Shawn for a small gathering at Casa de Esperanza to finish planning their upcoming fundraiser. Once a year they held a charity concert, so they could continue to support CDE's many foster children.

Adam had convinced Johnny and his band to perform at the event, because he wanted to give back to the Arendt-Garcías for all they had done for him. Plus, it might help reconcile Johnny and Lumiana. Adam couldn't stand seeing his buddy moping around the studio any longer. Something had to give.

After a pleasant dinner that involved jazz and homemade stone-oven pizza, Adam, Lumiana, Candela, and Shawn lounged outside on the patio with two bottles of Argentinian Malbec.

"How's life treating you, Lumi?" Candela asked as she topped off their glasses.

"*Bien.*"

Again with the one-word answers? Exhibit A why he and Lumiana weren't friends. Adam was used to Johnny and Shawn talking his ear off. He didn't know how to deal with someone so quiet and intense.

Candela poked Lumiana with her foot. "Good? That's all you have to say?"

"What would you like me to say?" Lumiana glanced at Adam, then lowered her gaze to her glass.

To be fair, she probably didn't want to talk about her personal life in front of him, knowing he was Johnny's best friend and might blab to him.

"What's going on with you and Johnny?" Candela asked her the one question Adam really wanted to hear the answer to. But her answer never came. No surprise there.

"Not much, apparently," Adam muttered, taking a sip of Malbec when the others eyed him curiously. To Lumiana, he said, "I saw him yesterday, and he told me you're avoiding him."

"Is that true?" Candela shot her a disapproving look.

Lumiana didn't respond, and instead stared at the colorful lanterns swaying in the breeze.

The woman was the most closed-off person Adam had ever met. But Johnny and Shawn adored her, so he had to make an effort to find a way to love her too. "I don't know what your deal is, Lumiana," Adam gestured with his glass, "and it's none of my business, but I thought you should know he's close to giving up on you."

There, maybe scaring her into action might do the trick.

He could practically see her insides tighten, but she remained silent.

What's it going to be, Lumiana?

Adam put down his glass, scratched at his temple, and then administered the final blow. "You know, one of the things Johnny loves about you is that you have strong morals and are committed to doing what's right and fair. But you keep stringing him along, which is neither right nor fair. You need to tell him what you want. And if you don't want to be with him, that's fine too. Just tell him. That's all I ask."

***

After two fun-packed days, Johnny drove up to Jonata Saturday evening with Ana asleep in the backseat. Jack Johnson's "Bubble Toes" played on the radio, reminding Johnny of his own Queen of the Hearts.

Just the thought of telling Lumiana about Ana's tabloid debut made him shrivel in his seat. He also needed to tell her he couldn't wait for her to come around anymore. That she hadn't figured out by now whether she wanted to be with him made it fairly obvious that she didn't really want this.

Lumiana met them at the door. "How was the sleepover?"

"It was awesome!" Lumiana boosted Ana into her arms and gave her a kiss. He didn't get one.

Better talk to her now before he lost the nerve. "Ana, could you give your mom and me a moment alone?"

She nodded, and when Lumiana set her down, Ana ran off to greet the animals.

Johnny and Lumiana remained standing in the entrance, glancing at each other like teenagers about to go on their first date. He hated the distance between them. It was only an arm's length but it felt like miles.

"There's something I need to tell you," he said finally, his voice firm, a little firmer than intended. "When I took Ana to the park the other day—"

"Oh, this is about the picture?" Lumiana pressed a hand to her throat.

What did she think he was going to say? "I'm truly sorry about that. I swear I've been careful about where I take her, but there was a high-profile celebrity at the park that same day, and someone must've recognized me and thought, 'why not get the two-for-one special.'"

"It's actually a very cute picture."

"So, you're not mad?" He fiddled with the black elastic on his wrist.

"I'm not happy about it, but I know you're doing your best to protect her. Let's just not have this be the norm, okay?"

Johnny nodded.

Just say it.

"Is there anything else?" Her wary eyes searched his face.

Yes.

No.

C'mon, say something.

Johnny opened and closed his mouth, pulling at his ear.

"So we will see you Saturday at CDE then?" Lumiana said.

"Yeah, about that…" He wished he could sit down.

"You're not canceling at the last minute, are you?" Concern spread across her face. "They are counting on you, Johnny."

"I'll be there. Relax." What was another week, right? It wasn't the foster children's fault that his love life was in shambles. He could tell her after the concert.

Lumiana smiled, and part of him wanted to pull her close and kiss her, make her see that she was *it* for him. But she already knew that, didn't she? And still, it wasn't enough. "Can I give you a hug, or are we not doing that anymore either?"

At last, she stepped closer and wrapped her arms around him. Inhaling her flowery scent, Johnny stroked a hand over her hair before she eased back.

"We'll see you Saturday," she said and remained standing there as he walked away.

***

Lumiana pressed her palm against her chest as she watched Johnny trudge down the driveway. He'd been twisting the elastic on his wrist again. And then his comment: 'Can I give you a hug, or are we not doing that anymore either?' She would have preferred it if he yelled at her. But not this, not resignation. *Is Adam right?* Was Johnny done with her?

Lumiana went back into the house and closed the door. Leaning against it, she tipped her head back and stared at the ceiling. But the answer didn't come, so she shuffled into the living room, frowning at the mess in front of her.

Ana's drawing papers, and the folder with the picture of Johnny and Ana in the park that Uncle Sam had given her, had been knocked off the table and lay scattered on the floor.

She crouched to pick it all up and spotted a few papers lodged under the couch: Ana's drawing of Kirk, the maintenance bill and royalty statements she'd been looking for, and a plain piece of paper folded in half. She opened it and froze.

Better stay away from Johnny Graham.

She pounded her fist against the sofa. "Are you kidding me?"

22

ONE LIFE

*"And the day came when the risk to remain
tight in a bud was more painful than
the risk it took to blossom."*

—ANAÏS NIN

Three hours later, after Lumiana had dropped off Ana at Mike's, she banged on Andie Woodhull's penthouse door. *Unbelievable, that woman.*

"Lumiana?" Andie said when she opened the door. Claudia came up to stand next to her.

"Did you write this?" Lumiana shoved the note into Andie's face.

Andie looked at it. "I didn't," she said and passed it on to Claudia.

"It... it's the note I sent you," Claudia said,

studying the paper.

"Why?" Lumiana barked. "I thought we sorted this out. Johnny and I aren't together. What is the point in sending me this?"

Claudia opened and clothed her mouth a few times. "Um... I don't understand... It's the note I dropped off like, what, three or four months ago," she reminded Lumiana.

"This is not the letter you sent me." Lumiana yanked the paper from Claudia's hand and pointed at it. "It only says, 'Better stay away from Johnny Graham.'"

"I... I don't know what you want me to say. It's the note I wrote you, *the only one*." Claudia looked questioningly at Andie.

"It's not exactly a threat," said Andie. "Sounds more like you're telling her to be cautious. Please tell me we didn't do all we did to her because of this." She took the paper from Lumiana's hand and waved it in front of Claudia, whose head flinched back slightly.

"I told you I didn't threaten her life or anything. I thought we did it because of the hit-and-run, because I got caught on camera."

Lumiana shook her head. "He died because of you."

The blood drained from Andie and Claudia's faces. Claudia hurried down the hallway and puked into an empty decorative vase before she disappeared into what Lumiana presumed was a bathroom.

Motioning her inside, Andie closed the door behind her. They walked over to the kitchen, which had a panoramic 180-degree view of Los Angeles.

Lumiana sat at the ebony table, staring at the paper in her hands. There must be something she was missing.

Andie lit a cigarette, her hand a bit unsteady. "Who was 'he?'"

Lumiana lifted her gaze. "Pluto. My sister's girlfriend's Labrador retriever."

Andie got to her feet, stubbed out her cigarette, and rushed out of the room. She returned a minute later with Claudia.

"I'm so sorry about the dog," Claudia offered, sinking into one of the dark green mohair chairs.

Lumiana got up to leave. "I still don't understand. If this note is yours, who sent the threatening letter?"

***

Late Monday afternoon, Lumiana sat in her office, putting the finishing touches on the material she planned to hand out to her students. Work helped her cope. And she needed it. She missed Johnny, missed his alluring smirk, the gentleness in his touch, the slide of his strong body against hers. And she missed hearing his voice.

In a moment of weakness, she'd listened to his new single, "Wonder." It was a lovely, upbeat song that put a smile on her face.

She still couldn't believe he'd dedicated his work to her, or that she'd touched him so deeply it manifested in art.

Lumiana felt the tears pushing at her eyes, so she got up and walked over to the bookshelf. Taking out a book on indigenous cultures, she opened it on the windowsill and started taking notes. Eventually, she became so absorbed in the task that she forgot her surroundings...

her feelings...

her worries...

Until she felt a painful prick on her upper back and flinched, crying out as the pain began to spread. Black spots clouded her vision, her rapid heartbeat thrashed in her ears. She fought the urge to spin around.

'Muscle memory, Lumi,' she heard Shawn's voice inside her head, 'it's all in your mind.'

"Don't move!" a shaky voice said from behind her. "Don't you dare turn around."

Lumiana acted on autopilot, just as she and Shawn had practiced hundreds of times over the years. In one quick motion she picked up the heavy book she'd been reading and slammed it back against her attacker's head. She heard a knife clatter onto the terracotta tiles and turned to see her assailant lurch into the desk and then slide to the floor.

Lumiana's breath came out in short bursts, her pulse racing. She gripped the windowsill for support.

At that moment Candela came in to pick her up for after work drinks. "Holy shit!" she cried, staggering back a couple of steps. "*Estás bien?*"

Lumiana knelt next to the unconscious woman and brushed the blond hair from her face. "*Sí*," Lumiana said, still trembling. "We need to call Gus, Big G, and Uncle Sam. I want this handled quietly." Stumbling to her feet, she reached a hand around to her throbbing back.

"*Esa perra got you good, Lumi*. You're bleeding pretty bad." Candela made her sit on a stool, then carefully pulled up her shirt to examine the cut on her back.

Lumiana said a silent prayer, thankful that her white dress and Jayjay's UCLA sweatshirt were safe at home—she couldn't take another loss.

Lumiana cast a glance at her attacker, who remained on the floor, unmoving. She bit back the mounting pain, angry with herself that she'd been so oblivious to the woman sneaking up on her.

"I think this is Jerry's nurse. Why would she do this?" Lumiana tried to take calming breaths. "Can you close the door, but not completely, and not with your bare hands? And don't touch the knife."

"*Sí, señora*." Candela mockingly saluted her.

Her sister was a kick-ass lawyer who knew a lot more about securing evidence than she did.

***

Friday afternoon, Johnny and Adam were hanging out in Johnny's kitchen when his household manager came in to give him the week's mail. Fortunately, James threw out the junk, so Johnny only had to look at what was necessary.

Taking a seat at the counter, Johnny leafed through the letters while Ella Fitzgerald's rendition of "Bewitched, Bothered, and Bewildered" played in the background.

He smiled at the colorful invitation from Casa de Esperanza. The private concert would be held tomorrow at four pm on the athletic field adjacent to CDE's spacious backyard.

They expected at least a thousand people, Adam had told him, making it their biggest event yet. For security reasons, CDE's property would be closed off to attendees, but would serve as a hub for staff and performers.

"What are you smiling about?" Adam eyed him over the rim of his coffee mug.

Johnny handed him the invitation.

"We're still playing there, right?" Adam asked, taking a bite from his sandwich. He'd reminded Johnny about the gig a hundred times since the band had unanimously agreed to do it.

"God, yes. Please stop asking." Johnny took another look at the invitation. "Do you think Lumiana will perform?"

"In front of a thousand people?" Adam looked at him like he'd suggested she'd get on stage naked. "I doubt it. I'd be surprised if she showed up at all. This benefit concert is annual and I've never seen her attend, not even once."

"I haven't talked to her since Saturday, but she said she'd be there."

"Maybe to drop off Ana." Adam gave him a narrow look. "Wait, if you haven't talked to her since Saturday, do you know what happened Monday at the institute?"

Adam went on to tell him about Ruby Kyle's attack on Lumiana and her subsequent arrest. Johnny struggled to keep his food down.

"That crazy bitch was obsessed with you."

Ruby had tried to bribe one of the institute's guards to help her get to Lumiana, and when the guard refused, the nurse took matters into her own hands.

"When Uncle Sam went through the nurse's apartment, he found a shrine and an explicit diary in her closet. Just thinking about it makes my skin crawl."

"That's some messed up shit." Johnny pinned his arms to his stomach, wondering if he'd led Ruby on. Sure she'd flirted with him, and he may have flirted back, but he knew where the line was. There had been no sexual innuendo, just fun conversations. And she knew he had a girl-friend.

Crazy. She'd seemed so sweet and normal. It was hard to believe she was that deranged. Or that he'd been so clueless. "Why is this the first time I'm hearing about it?"

"The Arendt-Garcías decided to keep it quiet. The diary also revealed that Ruby was the woman who took Ana to your place the day she ran away. We're lucky that's all the nurse did. She was a real psycho."

Johnny pushed the rest of his sandwich out of sight. "God, I can't believe that this happened on top of Claudia and Andie's stunt."

"So I guess you also haven't heard that the letter threatening to expose Lumiana's identity was from Ruby, not Andie and Claudia." Adam gave him a brief account of Lumiana's discovery Saturday night and her visit to Andie's apartment.

"Isn't that the mother of all ironies?" Johnny gave a dejected sigh. "I wanted nothing more than to make Lumiana happy and all I did was screw up her life and put her and Ana in danger."

Adam put a hand on his arm. "These were circumstances beyond your control. You didn't hurt her on purpose. She'd kick your sorry ass if she heard you blaming yourself for this."

"How is Lumiana?" Johnny wondered if he should call her, even though it stung that she hadn't told him about this.

"Aside from basically getting stabbed in the back, she's fine. She whacked that nurse over the head with a 900-page whopper on indigenous cultures," Adam said, grinning.

Johnny held his churning stomach. As much as he wanted to see Lumiana and make sure she was okay, he decided she really would be better off without him.

***

The next day at three pm, an hour before the first guests were due to arrive, Johnny, Adam, Earl and Toni pulled up in front of Casa de Esperanza. The house was already abuzz with helping hands of all ages and nationalities. It was almost like the *Fiesta de las Culturas*, but with an air of urgency.

Johnny was hoping to spot Lumiana and at least see for himself that she was all right, but he doubted he'd find her here. Too many people rushing around making noise—it would set her brain on fire.

The people he did find, to his amazement, were his parents and his brothers. They were sitting out on the patio sipping watermelon Herbie Hancocks while Ana and Peyton entertained them with a hula-hoop show.

Adam took Earl and Toni on a tour of the grounds and Johnny went over to greet his family.

"What are you guys doing here?" he asked, smiling when Ana jumped into his arms.

His father, who looked dashing in dark-wash

jeans and a button-down with rolled up sleeves, told him that Lumiana had invited them the last time she'd visited him at Mansfield Park.

"We haven't seen you perform in years," his mother said, placing a hand over his dad's. She looked pretty in white jeans and a sunny blouse.

It still felt strange to see his parents so civil with each other. *What a diff'rence a stroke makes.*

"We thought it would be nice to see you in your element," his dad added.

Seriously? He needed to get himself one of those Watermelon Man cocktails.

"Plus, it's for a good cause," Jason said, unbuttoning the jacket of his tailored suit. He must've come here straight from the office. "I convinced the other partners in my firm to help sponsor the event."

"Oh, wow, great," was all Johnny managed at his family's unusual outpouring of support. "Has anyone seen Lumiana? I was hoping to talk to her before things get started. She's here, right?"

Ana confirmed her mother's presence but hadn't seen Lumiana since they helped spread picnic blankets across the field.

Johnny walked over to the side of the house and called Lumiana, but she didn't pick up. So he left a voicemail. "Hey. I heard about what happened with Ruby. I'm so sorry, Lu." He scrubbed a hand over his face. "...Anyway, I was hoping to talk to you to make sure you're okay. Call me, please."

Lumiana was headed upstairs to take a break in her old room when she ran into Adam and two men she'd never seen before in the hallway.

"Isn't she the girl from the video?" the guy in the baseball cap and horn-rimmed glasses said to Adam, who nodded. He thrust a hand out to Lumiana. "Hey, I'm Earl, and this is Toni," he said, pointing to the sturdy Italian man.

Earl reminded her a little of Jayjay, especially in the way he dressed—half intellectual, half athletic, with a hint of rascal. "We're in Johnny's band. Adam showed us a video of you a while ago. Damn, girl, you've got some pipes!"

She froze, and Adam picked up on it. "That means he likes your voice," he told her in Japanese. "They don't know about you and Johnny, or Ana, so relax."

Lumiana gave a sigh of relief and thanked Earl for his oddly worded compliment.

"Are you going to perform this evening?" Toni asked, leaning against the door jamb of her old room, effectively blocking her escape route.

Earl rubbed the palms of his hands together, grinning. "You should jam with us!"

"Me?" Lumiana shook her head repeatedly.

Toni and Earl looked at Adam, who shrugged. "She's shy. Come on, guys, let's see what Johnny's up to." Adam winked at her before he escorted the men downstairs.

Lumiana took a few deliberate breaths, willing away the butterflies in her stomach. Then she went to take a nap to recover from the sensory overload of all the people bustling about. Or at least that had been her intention.

The moment she'd made herself comfortable, there was a knock on the door. She covered her face with a pillow and groaned.

"Lumiana?"

No, go away.

"Adam." She threw her pillow at him, which he managed to catch. "What do you want?"

"God, it eludes me what Johnny sees in you." He sat at the end of her bed. "You need to talk to him."

"Why?" She grabbed another pillow and clutched it to her chest because those unwelcome butterflies flared up again.

Adam tossed her phone across the mattress. She must have left it downstairs. There was a voicemail from Johnny.

"I told him what happened with Ruby Kyle. Which is something you should've done yourself, by the way. He's gotten it into his head that he's the one to blame for everything. I want you to put him out of his misery."

"I never said it was his fault." Lumiana sat up. "Why would he think that?" She'd considered telling Johnny about his dad's nurse, but there was an unspoken tension between them that she didn't know how to handle. Or quite possibly she was just too much of a coward to address the state of their relationship. Everything with Johnny felt intense. If they started over, he'd want marriage and children and living together, and she didn't know if she could give him any of it.

Adam brushed a hand over his boyish chin. "He thinks it's his fault because he loves you and sees it as his job to keep you safe."

"I don't need to be protected."

Adam growled. "That's beside the point, Lumiana. He's just making up reasons that help him explain why you don't want him."

"I never said I don't want him." She jabbed a finger at Adam. "I love him." She touched a hand to her mouth. "I love him."

Adam thrust his hands in the air. "Then what the hell is the matter with you?" He got up to leave, but stopped in the doorway. "Show him!" he said before he left.

***

Johnny and his band were sitting by the left side of the stage, watching Lumiana's brothers Milo and Gus perform The Black Eyed Peas' "Where Is The Love?" Ana was next to them singing along to the chorus.

There was a slight change in the lyrics, where they asked for heavenly guidance from father and mother rather than just Father. Johnny wondered if it was a religious, political, or foster family thing—whatever, he liked it.

Milo and Gus were amazing performers, and the crowd loved them. Maybe they'd be open to a collaboration.

Johnny rolled his shoulders. They were up next, the last act of the evening. The sun set, and with the flick of a switch, the vast field transformed into a sea of lanterns and tiny outdoor lights.

Johnny quickly checked his phone. Still no word from Lumiana.

"Ready?" Adam clapped him on the back.

The four of them took the stage to thunderous applause and kicked off their show with a cover of Michael Jackson's "Man in the Mirror." They performed a few of Johnny's original songs, keeping his newest material for last. The energy from the audience was so contagious that they played two additional songs. And because his overly critical family was watching, Johnny gave it two hundred percent.

When the band played the first few notes of "Wonder," the crowd began cheering before Johnny even sang the first line. He looked at Adam, who pointed his chin toward the left side of the stage. Johnny nearly dropped his microphone.

Just like the first time he'd laid eyes on her, Lumiana was wearing her favorite white linen dress, locket in place, and a megawatt smile that lit up the night.

Milo, standing next to her, handed her a microphone. Lumiana walked out onto the stage and sang the first verse of the song with her gaze fixed on Johnny.

You show me with the light in your eyes
What everybody else can't see
Things aren't always so black and white
Your secret colors call to me

She gestured for him to sing the second verse.

You choose to be happy
Despite all the hardships life's put you through
You're still around
Life can't get you down
The scars from your past remind you to see

Lumiana joined him for the chorus.

The wonders of life
Big and small, try catching them all
When you open your eyes
Take off that grown-up disguise
Then maybe you will see
The wonders of life
They're all within reach
In this wonderful life

When the audience burst into applause, Lumiana took Johnny's hand. He couldn't believe she'd just sung his song with him in front of a thousand people. No drug could get him higher.

Lumiana left the stage before his band took a

bow.

"That was amazing," Earl said as they walked off the platform. "We should play more gigs like this."

When they came down the steps, Johnny saw Lumiana leaning against a tree near the stage. He walked up to her and stuffed his hands in his pockets to keep himself from tossing her over his shoulder and carting her off to bed.

Lumiana closed a hand over her locket and said, "You talk too much, you are nosy, smug, and everything I never thought to look for in a partner. But there is no one who gets under my skin the way you do. You make me want to be better. You make me hope for a happy ending."

She trailed her finger along the scar on his arm. "I love you, Johnny, and I mean the 'I wish we could grow old together' kind of love." Then she let out a big breath and pressed a hand to her stomach.

Johnny's skin prickled as he held her gaze. Behind him, Adam said, "Must feel good to finally get that off your chest."

"Shut up, Adam," Lumiana said with a smile. They liked each other, not that either would ever admit it.

Johnny reached for Lumiana's hand. He didn't know what would happen to them. But whatever it was would happen to them together.

FULL PLAYLIST

Chapter 1: "Wrong Side of a Love Song" — Melanie Fiona (2012)
"American Woman" — Lenny Kravitz (1999)
"At Last" — Etta James (1960)
"Stand By Me" — Ben E. King (1961)

Chapter 2: "(Nice to Meet You) Anyway" — Gavin DeGraw (2003)
"Raindrops" — Martin Jondo (2005)
"Singin' In The Rain" — Gene Kelly (1952)

Chapter 3: "Black Horse & The Cherry Tree" — KT Tunstall (2005)
"Burning Love" — Elvis Presley (1972)
"La Vie en Rose" — Daniela Andrade (2014)

Chapter 4: "The Waters Of March" — Susannah McCorkle (1993)
"Everyday" — Toby Lightman (2004)
"It Ain't Over 'Til It's Over" — Lenny Kravitz (1991)
"Ain't No Mountain High Enough" — Marvin

Gaye & Tammi Terrell (1967)
"Baby Got Back" — Sir Mix-a-Lot (1992)

Chapter 5: "Curse Me Good" — The Heavy (2012)
"A Teenager In Love" — Dion & The Belmonts (1959)

Chapter 6: "Just Like A Pill" — Pink (2001)
"Again" — Lenny Kravitz (2000)

Chapter 7: "Jackie And Wilson" — Hozier (2014)
"The Lazy Song" — Bruno Mars (2010)

Chapter 8: "Stuck In The Middle With You" — Stealers Wheel (1972)
"Everytime" — The Flames (2002)

Chapter 9: "You're Nobody 'Til Somebody Loves You" — James Arthur (2013)

Chapter 10: "Fever" — Little Willie John (1956)

Chapter 11: "Next Generation" — Culcha Candela (2005)
"The Girl From Ipanema" — Amy Winehouse (2011)
"She Loves You" — The Beatles (1964)

Chapter 12: "I Have This Hope" — Tenth Avenue North (2016)
"La Llorona" — Chavela Vargas (1990s)

Chapter 13: "Make You Feel My Love" — Adele (2008)
"The Flight Of The Bumble Bee" — David Garrett

(2007)

Chapter 14: "Girl On Fire" — Alicia Keys (2012)

Chapter 15: "Johnny" — Melanie Fiona (2009)

Chapter 16: "Bad" — Michael Jackson (1987)
"No Diggity" — Blackstreet feat. Dr. Dre & Queen Pen (1996)

Chapter 17: "Last Request" — Paolo Nutini (2006)
"Hey Jude" — The Beatles (1968)

Chapter 18: "Somewhere Only We Know" — Keane (2004)

Chapter 19: "Never Let You Go" — B.O.B feat. Ryan Tedder (2012)
"Feeling Good" — Nina Simone (1965)
"Beautiful Life" — James Morrison (2011)
"What Makes A Good Man?" — The Heavy (2012)
"Seasons Of Love" — Rent Cast (1996)
"When Love Comes To Town" — Herbie Hancock (2005)

Chapter 20: "Truth" — Alex Ebert (2011)
"Thong Song" — Sisqó (1999)

Chapter 21: "Try" — Backstreet Boys (2013)
"Bubble Toes" — Jack Johnson (2001)

Chapter 22: "One Life" — James Morrison (2011)
"Bewitched, Bothered, And Bewildered" — Ella Fitzgerald (1956)
"Where Is The Love?" — The Black Eyed Peas

(2003)
"Man In The Mirror" — Michael Jackson (1987)

ABOUT THE AUTHOR

As a bit of a free spirit herself, Alex writes love stories that challenge the status quo.

After spending most of her life in Germany, Italy, Ireland, Colombia, and California, she currently lives in the foothills of the Wasatch Mountains with her two favorite guys.

Her love of music, cultures, personal development, and the many unconventional people she's met along the way, inspired her family saga *Rebels Like Us*.

www.alexbenkast.com

ACKNOWLEDGE- MENTS

A giant thank you to Luis—my partner in life and love—for your continuous support in making my dream come true.

To my editor Nancy Doherty for taking my manuscript to the next level. I learned so much from you, and this book truly wouldn't be what it is without you. I hope we'll get to work together again soon.

To Candela, for patiently listening to Lumina's story over breakfast once a week while I was writing it.

To Torben Johannsen, for reading the story while it was still in its shitty first (130,000-word!!!) draft and for asking to be the first to read the sequel despite of it.

An extra special thanks to my other beta readers Kaya Massey (your ideas and suggestions were invaluable—and hilarious), Sabrina, Marisa, Dario, Shane, Sherri, and Shradha, for your encouragement and feedback.

To my mentor and one of my all-time favorite people, Jerry, for believing in me and for giving me the advice that got me started: just sit down and write something—it's okay if it's bad, you can always go back and edit it later—just get into the habit of writing something every day.

To Judith, for being the inspiration behind the characters' lifelong friendships. I can't imagine my life without you.

To Anna, for all our (mis-)adventures and conversations. Words can't describe how much I love you.

To my parents for teaching me strong values and morals, for allowing me to go my own way, and for always loving and supporting me, despite our different worldviews.

To Nathalie and Natalia for patiently listening to me talk about my book for the past three years, and for answering hundreds of questions.

To my international family and friends for all the ingenious things you keep saying to me that make me laugh and hopefully will now amuse my readers.

To my newest friend, Lynn Turner, for her moral support, witty suggestions, and those hilarious emails that brighten my days. I'm so grateful our paths have crossed and I hope we'll get to champion each other through many more book releases.

And last but not least, to Lu and Lumi, the two

amazing women who inspired Lumiana's name, and to the many artists whose songs move me every day, especially those that made it into the book's playlist—Jack Johnson's "Bubble Toes" in particular feels like the book's perfect summary.